THE GREENBOOK®
GUIDE TO
DEPARTMENT 56®
VILLAGES

SEVENTH EDITION
1997/1998

Including

THE ORIGINAL SNOW VILLAGE®
THE ORIGINAL SNOW VILLAGE® ACCESSORIES

THE HERITAGE VILLAGE COLLECTION®
Dickens' Village Series®
New England Village® Series
Alpine Village Series™
Christmas In The City® Series
Little Town Of Bethlehem™ Series
North Pole Series™
Disney Parks Village™
THE HERITAGE VILLAGE COLLECTION® ACCESSORIES

ADDITIONAL VILLAGE ACCESSORIES

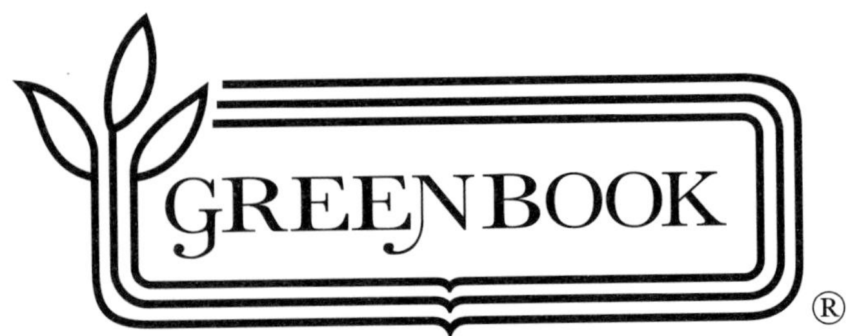

The Most Respected Guides To Popular Collectibles & Their After Market Values

Old Coach at Main, Box 515
East Setauket, NY 11733
516.689.8466
FAX 516.689.8177
http://www.greenbooks.com

Printed in Canada

ISBN 0-923628-41-X

The GREENBOOK would like to thank –

Department 56.

She loaded up her car with many prized pieces and drove from Akron, OH to Long Island. She gave of her time and expertise so that we might better present it to you. After a day in the photography studio and an evening of taking notes, I think we finally might even understand the three variations of the Snow Village *Stone Church*! GREENBOOK extends a heartfelt thanks to noted Department 56 authority, **Patsy Fryberger.**

The **collectors**, **retailers**, **secondary market dealers** and **newsletter publishers** across the country who take their valuable time to supply us with information including secondary market status and price.

Marilyn Bachman.

Harry & June McGowan.

Bob Dallow.

What is it they say? The older you get, the faster time flies, because every added day is a smaller percentage of your total life? I can't believe it's been a year since we published the first full-color GREENBOOK. We received many notes from collectors thanking us for giving them what they'd been asking for, full color photographs of all the buildings and accessories. In addition, we received some great ideas and suggestions for this, the 7th Edition GREENBOOK Guide to Department 56 Villages. In response to collector requests we have:

- increased the size of the photographs
- reorganized some of the detail information
- added photographs of variations that have a difference in Secondary Market Value

We're pleased with the changes and thank everyone who took the time to write.

And then, once in a while, we get an idea or two of our own! To help you evaluate secondary market trends, last year we added the percentage up or down as compared to the GBTru$ in the previous edition of the Guide. This year, we realized why not show you a piece's entire GBTru$ history. The GBTru$ History Line debuted earlier this year in the Snowbabies™ Guide to an overwhelmingly positive response. We're confident Village collectors will find it equally as useful.

One of the most commonly asked questions is how we determine GREENBOOK TruMarket Values. Since this is asked so often, I thought I'd answer it here.

Sometime around May, GREENBOOK sends out blank price sheets itemizing all the retired buildings and accessories to secondary market brokers and dealers throughout the country. This includes those people who deal in the secondary on a part time basis, those who do it as a full time business, and retailers who handle secondary market in their stores. This year we also sent price sheets to randomly selected collectors in order to incorporate classified ad sales, sales among friends and sales at club meetings. Participants are asked to list the prices of any pieces bought or sold over the last few months. When this information is returned to us, we review all the data. The erroneous highs and lows are removed and the rest of the information is tabulated. Results are reviewed by our Historian, Peter George, to see if the research data reflects what's truly happening in the marketplace. If a researched value is deemed to be inaccurate, a note is made and it is reviewed. Basically, that's it–the point being GREENBOOK TruMarket Values aren't from us, they're from you–the buyers and sellers–and reflect prices from actual sales that have taken place in every region of the country.

Don't forget GREENBOOK is not only for you to use as a reference for your collection, it's also a valued source for insuring it. We're very proud when collectors tell us their insurance company accepts GREENBOOK as documentation for insuring their collectibles.

GREENBOOK strives to publish the best, most accurate guide to your favorite collectibles. It's all we do and we do it better than anyone else. We realize the trust and respect we've earned in over 12 years of publishing guides to contemporary collectibles is put on the line with each new edition of every guide.

As always, your suggestions, comments and ideas are most welcome.

Thanks for buying the Guide–

Louise Patterson Langenfeld
Editor & Publisher

Note From The Publisher

Table of Contents

the Village Chronicle.

Throughout this edition of GREENBOOK are a variety of articles by Peter George, GREENBOOK's D56 Historian, that were previously printed in *the Village Chronicle* magazine. Though some of them appeared recently in the magazine and others are from issues dating back a year or more, the subject of each article is as valid now as when it was first published. These articles cover topics including particular buildings and accessories and collecting Department 56 in general. We think you will enjoy reading these articles for their historical, informational and entertaining values.

Peter George is the publisher of *the Village Chronicle* magazine which he founded in 1991. Along with his publishing responsibilities, he also writes some of the articles and features for the magazine. Considered a Department 56 authority, he is a frequent guest speaker at gatherings and other D56 related events throughout the United States. As you might expect, one of his favorite pastimes is collecting Department 56 villages. This is Peter's four year as GREENBOOK's Department 56 Historian.

If you enjoy the articles from *the Village Chronicle* subscribe to it today and continue the fun. Each issue entertains and informs you with page after page of:

- accurate, timely information
- articles about each of the villages
- varied points of view from nationally recognized D56 authorities
- display advice & tips
- product highlights
- secondary market updates
- a calendar of Department 56 events
- classified ads so you can buy, sell, and trade
- and always much more

$24 for one year - 6 issues	(Canadian res: $29 US funds)
$44 for two years - 12 issues	(Canadian res: $49 US funds)
	R.I. residents add 7% sales tax.

Visa, MasterCard, Discover, American Express, Checks accepted

Subscribe by phone, fax, mail, internet, or visit our web site.

Phone: 401-467-9343
Fax: 401-467-9359
Internet: d56er@aol.com
Web Site: http://www.villagechronicle.com
mail: the Village Chronicle
757 Park Ave.
Cranston, RI 02910

CONTINUING TO ENJOY YOUR COLLECTION

As I travel around the country I've realized many collectors wish collecting Department 56 villages was still as it used to be. They have noticed that with the passing of time and the rise in its popularity, collecting the villages has an entirely different feel to it. This is not to say it is a change for the worse ... it is just different.

Let's take a look at some of those differences, how they came to be, and how they may be viewed as a positive. The buildings and accessories are much more refined now than they were before. The older buildings are now considered by experienced collectors as "quaint" while they perceive the newer designs to be too polished. (Conversely, collectors who started collecting more recently see the older pieces as drab or plain. The newer ones are much more to their liking.)

What inspired Department 56 to "progress" to the cleaner more detailed designs? We did them by flocking to the more detailed designs when they were introduced. By purchasing these pieces in high numbers, we were sending signals to Department 56 that we wanted more detail, brighter colors, more attachments.

The buildings and accessories aren't the only things that have changed. The manner in which we purchase them has as well. Years ago, collectors would take the time to go to their local dealer and look at each piece, decide what they liked (or didn't like) about its design, and decide to buy it or not. Hours could be spent just looking at the new pieces. Remember?

Now, for too many of us, a call from the dealer is more likely to be "your pieces are in and already charged to your credit card ... please pick them up when you can" as opposed to "the new pieces are in ... come down and take a look!" Though neither way is right or wrong, if you're not having as much fun, think about this. Is having the pieces as soon as they hit the stores (usually to sit in a closet for months before being displayed) as much fun as buying a piece or two now and a couple more later on ... and so on?

"They're introducing too many pieces!" If this has become an often muttered phrase for you, think back to when you first started collecting. Could you get your hands on enough pieces? Probably not. That's how many newer collectors feel now. Besides ... with the introduction of a large number of pieces, you get to choose the ones you really like! No one has ever said that you have to buy every piece. Department 56 could introduce fewer pieces each year, but then again we would probably just collect more villages and end up with just as many buildings. It's much simpler to buy the ones you like and enjoy them.

If you have accumulated too many buildings already, sell some of them on the secondary market. Yes, I said it ... sell some! Look over your entire collection and you may see some pieces that make you wonder why you ever bought them in the first place. (Are you really fascinated with every piece Department 56 has produced?) Selling some is not a bad thing. How many times in life can you make a purchase, decide you don't really like it, and sell it for more than you paid for it? Not many. By selling those pieces you gain the two things that every collector needs–more money and, even more importantly, space for the pieces you truly like.

Yes, things have changed over the years, and they will continue to evolve. But this is a result of so many other people enjoying the various and fascinating aspects of collecting these buildings in much the same ways as you.

the Village Chronicle.

GREENBOOK
WHAT WE DO & HOW WE DO IT

ARTCHARTS & LISTINGS

The GREENBOOK ARTCHARTS developed for the Department 56 Villages feature colc photographs, factual information and TRUMARKET PRICES for each piece.

Factual information consists of:

- Name
- Item Number
- Year Of Introduction
- Market Status
- Description
- Variations
- Particulars

GREENBOOK TRUMARKET PRICE Listings include:

- Original Suggested Retail Price
- GREENBOOK TRUMARKET Secondary Market Price (**GBTru$**)
- The percentage up or down as compared to last year's 6th Ed. Guid (or "No Change" if the price is unchanged)
- The GBTru History Line–tracking the GREENBOOK Secondary Market Price for each piece over the years. If a piece is Current, the GBTru History Line tracks the suggested retail price.

GREENBOOK TRUMARKET PRICES

Secondary Market Prices are reported to us by retailers and collectors. The data is compile checked for accuracy, and a price established as a benchmark as a result of this researc There are many factors which determine the price a collector will pay for a piece; mo acquisitions are a matter of personal judgement. The price will fluctuate with the time year, section of the country and type of sale. GREENBOOK takes all of these factors in consideration when determining TRUMARKET Prices, and so **GREENBOOK TRUMARKET Price are never an absolute number**. Use them as a basis for comparison, as a point of informatio when considering an acquisition, and as a guide when insuring for replacement value.

The GREENBOOK does not trade on the Secondary Market. The GREENBOOK monito and reports prices, in the same way as the Wall Street Journal reports trades on the stoc markets in the United States and abroad.

HOW TO USE THIS GUIDE

This Guide is divided into three main sections: The Original Snow Village, The Heritag Village and Additional Village Accessories. Within The Snow Village and Heritage Villag sections, GREENBOOK Listings are in chronological date of introduction order. It's importa to remember "the year of introduction indicates the year in which the piece was designe sculpted and copyrighted" and the piece is generally available to collectors the followin calendar year.

Within each year, the Listings are in Department 56 Item Number order.

The Village Accessories Section is divided into categories such as Trees, Electrical, Fence etc. Within each of these sections, current items appear in D56 Item Number orde Discontinued accessories are referenced separately at the end, in D56 Item Number order

THE VILLAGES

Snow Village

NEW ENGLAND VILLAGE

CHRISTMAS IN THE CITY

Little Town of Bethlehem

North Pole

Disney Parks Village

Profiles

Ornaments

Bachman's

Meadowland

THE ACCESSORIES

Snow Village Accessories

Heritage Village Accessories

Add'l Village Accessories

The Original Snow Village

When Department 56 introduced Snow Village in 1976, no one could have realized what would happen during the next twenty years. What began as a line of giftware grew to be one of the most successful collectibles available today.

In 1977, the first six buildings arrived on dealers' shelves. Though not very detailed—many collectors consider them crude when contrasting them to today's designs—these ceramic buildings captured the hearts of consumers. Each year more designs were introduced, and the number of dealers selling the village continued to grow. In 1979, the first buildings—ten in all—retired, setting the stage for collectible status.

Representing the 1930's and '40's, Snow Village brought back memories to many collectors who saw in it places of their childhood, the church where they got married, or the stores where they shopped, perhaps stores like the Grocery. The 1950's and '60's were ushered in with buildings like Dinah's Drive-In that inspired images of dancing at hops and listening to Rock & Roll. Recently, the village entered the '90's with the introduction of Starbuck's Coffee, though designs that represent past decades are still being introduced.

Snow Village has hosted two "series within a series." The first, Meadowland, was introduced in 1979 and almost immediately retired in 1980. A summer-based series—the only pieces in Snow Village without snow, it consisted of a cottage, church, trees, and sheep. The other series—a continuing one—is the American Architecture Series. Beginning with the Prairie House and Queen Anne Victorian in 1990, it has grown to include eight designs.

An intriguing and important development took place in 1994 when the first building featuring a licensed brand name was introduced—Coca-Cola Bottling Plant. Since then, Department 56 has expanded this concept to include the Coca-Cola Corner Drugstore, Ryman Auditorium, Starbuck's Coffee, and the Harley-Davidson Motorcycle Shop, the latest addition.

Through twenty years, Snow Village has prospered while each year's designs have become more elaborate and more detailed. Likewise, it has become the second home for more and more collectors. It's evident that Snow Village's lights will continue to burn brightly for years to come.

THE BOTTOM LINE:

Cost of all pieces introduced to Snow Village through the 1997 midyear introductions, including accessories: (This does not include variations, special pieces, or "adopted" pieces such as John Deere Water Tower.) **$11,049.50.**

GREENBOOK TruMarket Value of all pieces through the 1997 midyear introductions including accessories: (This does not include variations, special pieces, or "adopted" pieces such as John Deere Water Tower.) **$52,000.00.**

The OSV Since We Last Met...

... NEW FOR SALE LISTINGS

Rockabilly Records - 1996

Featuring just about any type of music imaginable, Rockabilly Records gives your villagers a place to listen to and buy their records. The unique marquee lets all the villagers know that this is the place to find the latest hit, a sentimental oldie, or a proven classic.

Christmas Lake High School - 1996

At last, the teenagers in the village have a school of their own. This impressive structure is where they will prepare for their lives as adult villagers. We'll be needing a college in the village soon.

Birch Run Ski Chalet - 1996

There had to be a place where the village's skiers could stay while enjoying their favorite pastime, and now there is.

Rosita's Cantina - 1996

Tacos, burritos, fajitas, and other Mexican delights are on the menu at the village's newest restaurant. Villagers who are 21 and older can enjoy a refreshing, cold marguerita in the village's first bar, El Loco Lounge.

Shingle Victorian - 1996

This attractive Victorian is the eighth house to be included in Snow Village's American Architecture Series.

The Secret Garden Florist - 1996

This tall structure is home to the florist and wedding planner. Not only does it feature colorful flowers, but also the village's first cloth canopy.

Harley-Davidson Motorcycle Shop - 1996

This is the latest introduction based on a licensed brand name. Bringing its portion of Americana to Snow Village, it's one of the most popular buildings ever introduced to the village. Collectors of Harley-Davidson memorabilia have joined Department 56 collectors in praising this design.

Ronald McDonald House - 1997

This is a first for Department 56. Introduced as part of Snow Village, it was not produced for resale by D56 retailers. Available in limited numbers only at dealers participating in the November 1997 Homes For The Holidays Event to raise money for the Ronald McDonald House Charities.

Mainstreet Gift Shop - 1997

This building actually features two shops, the gift shop and a Christmas shop. Sold only by Gift Creations Concepts (GCC) dealers in November 1997 to celebrate their 20th anniversary. Gift Creations Concepts is a catalog syndicate/buying group that has supported Department 56 through the years.

The Original Snow Village Start-A-Tradition Set - 1997

This eight-piece set includes Kringle's Toy Shop (complete with revolving door), Nikki's Cocoa Shop featuring a "mug of hot chocolate," and a four-piece accessory set.

Old Chelsea Mansion - 1997

This is Department 56's rendition of the home of Clement C. Moore, author of the famous poem, *A Visit from St. Nicholas.* The building comes packed in a blue commemorative box and includes a 32 page book featuring information about Moore, his home, and the poem.

New Hope Church - 1997

This is the newest in the long line of churches in the village. Its most noticeable feature is the translucent stained glass windows.

... NO LONGER ON THE MARKET

5097-0	The Christmas Shop
5157-8	Queen Anne Victorian
5420-8	Grandma's Cottage
5424-0	Good Shepherd Chapel & Church School, Set/2
5439-9	Airport
5442-9	Mount Olivet Church
5444-5	Woodbury House
5445-3	Hunting Lodge
5447-0	Dinah's Drive-In
5448-8	Snowy Hills Hospital
5462-3	Snow Village Starter Set, Set/6
54856	Dutch Colonial

AMERICAN ARCHITECTURE SERIES

5156-0 Prairie House
5157-8 Queen Anne Victorian
5403-8 Southern Colonial
5404-6 Gothic Farmhouse
5437-2 Craftsman Cottage
5465-8 Federal House
54856 Dutch Colonial
54884 Shingle Victorian

SANTA COMES TO TOWN

54771 Santa Comes To Town, 1995
54862 Santa Comes To Town, 1996
54899 Santa Comes To Town, 1997

HOMES FOR THE HOLIDAYS

54623 The Original Snow Village Starter Set, 1994
- Shady Oak Church Building
- Sunday School Serenade Accessory

54902 The Original Snow Village Start A Tradition Set, 1997
- Kringles Toy Shop & The Hot Chocolate Stand Buildings
- Saturday Morning Downtown Accessory

Quikreference

RETIRED

5000-8	1984	Town Hall
5001-3	1979	Mountain Lodge
5001-6	1985	Grocery
5002-1	1979	Gabled Cottage
5002-4	1984	Victorian Cottage
5003-2	1985	Governor's Mansion
5003-9	1979	The Inn
5004-0	1986	Turn Of The Century
5004-7	1979	Country Church
5005-4	1979	Steepled Church
5005-9	1986	Main Street House
5006-2	1979	Small Chalet
5006-7	1989	St. Anthony Hotel & Post Office
5007-0	1979	Victorian House
5007-5	1986	Stratford House
5008-3	1987	Haversham House
5008-8	1979	Mansion
5009-1	1985	Galena House
5009-6	1979	Stone Church
5010-5	1987	River Road House
5011-2	1984	Homestead
5012-0	1980	General Store
5012-1	1986	Delta House
5013-0	1989	Snow Village Factory
5013-8	1980	Cape Cod
5014-6	1986	Nantucket
5015-3	1979	Skating Rink/Duck Pond Set
5015-6	1986	Bayport
5016-1	1989	Small Double Trees
5017-2	1984	Skating Pond
5019-9	1984	Street Car
5019-9	1990	Cathedral Church
5020-2	1984	Centennial House
5021-0	1984	Carriage House
5022-9	1984	Pioneer Church
5023-7	1984	Swiss Chalet
5024-5	1983	Bank
5024-5	1995	Cumberland House
5026-1	1984	Village Church
5027-0	1990	Springfield House
5028-8	1986	Gothic Church
5029-6	1985	Parsonage
5030-0	1988	Lighthouse
5031-8	1985	Wooden Church
5032-6	1984	Fire Station
5033-4	1985	English Tudor
5034-2	1985	Congregational Church
5035-0	1986	Trinity Church
5036-9	1985	Summit House
5037-7	1986	New School House
5039-3	1986	Parish Church
5041-5	1986	Waverly Place
5042-3	1986	Twin Peaks
5043-1	1986	2101 Maple
5044-0	1991	Village Market
5045-8	1986	Stucco Bungalow
5046-6	1988	Williamsburg House
5047-4	1987	Plantation House
5048-2	1988	Church Of The Open Door
5049-0	1987	Spruce Place
5050-4	1987	Duplex
5051-2	1988	Depot And Train With 2 Train Cars
5052-0	1987	Ridgewood
5054-2	1982	Victorian
5054-7	1990	Kenwood House
5055-9	1981	Knob Hill
5056-7	1981	Brownstone
5057-5	1981	Log Cabin
5058-3	1984	Countryside Church
5059-1	1980	Stone Church
5060-1	1988	Lincoln Park Duplex
5060-9	1982	School House
5061-7	1981	Tudor House
5062-5	1980	Mission Church
5062-8	1988	Sonoma House
5063-3	1980	Mobile Home
5063-6	1988	Highland Park House
5065-2	1988	Beacon Hill House
5065-8	1982	Giant Trees
5066-0	1988	Pacific Heights House
5066-6	1980	Adobe House
5067-4	1981	Cathedral Church
5067-9	1989	Ramsey Hill House
5068-2	1982	Stone Mill House
5068-7	1988	Saint James Church
5070-9	1982	Colonial Farm House
5071-7	1982	Town Church
5071-7	1988	Carriage House
5072-5	1984	Wooden Clapboard
5073-3	1982	English Cottage
5073-3	1990	Toy Shop

5074-1	1984	Barn
5076-8	1983	Corner Store
5076-8	1990	Apothecary
5077-6	1983	Bakery
5077-6	1991	Bakery
5078-4	1982	English Church
5078-4	1987	Diner
5080-6	1989	Large Single Tree
5081-4	1983	Gabled House
5081-4	1992	Red Barn
5082-2	1983	Flower Shop
5082-2	1991	Jefferson School
5083-0	1984	New Stone Church
5084-9	1984	Chateau
5085-6	1985	Train Station With 3 Train Cars
5089-0	1992	Farm House
5091-1	1989	Fire Station No. 2
5092-0	1989	Snow Village Resort Lodge
5097-0	1996	The Christmas Shop
5114-4	1991	Jingle Belle Houseboat
5119-5	1992	Colonial Church
5120-9	1992	North Creek Cottage
5121-7	1990	Maple Ridge Inn
5122-5	1992	Village Station And Train
5123-3	1992	Cobblestone Antique Shop
5124-1	1991	Corner Cafe
5125-0	1990	Single Car Garage
5126-8	1991	Home Sweet Home/ House & Windmill
5127-6	1992	Redeemer Church
5128-4	1991	Service Station
5140-3	1994	Stonehurst House
5141-1	1990	Palos Verdes
5142-0	1993	Paramount Theater
5143-8	1992	Doctor's House
5144-6	1993	Courthouse
5145-4	1992	Village Warming House
5149-7	1992	J. Young's Granary
5150-0	1995	Pinewood Log Cabin
5151-9	1992	56 Flavors Ice Cream Parlor
5152-7	1992	Morningside House
5153-5	1993	Mainstreet Hardware Store
5154-3	1993	Village Realty
5155-1	1992	Spanish Mission Church
5156-0	1993	Prairie House
5157-8	1996	Queen Anne Victorian
5400-3	1994	Oak Grove Tudor
5401-1	1993	The Honeymooner Motel
5402-0	1995	Village Greenhouse
5403-8	1994	Southern Colonial
5405-4	1993	Finklea's Finery Costume Shop
5406-2	1994	Jack's Corner Barber Shop
5407-0	1994	Double Bungalow
5420-8	1996	Grandma's Cottage
5421-6	1994	St. Luke's Church
5422-4	1995	Village Post Office
5423-2	1995	Al's TV Shop
5424-0	1996	Good Shepherd Chapel & Church School
5425-9	1994	Print Shop & Village News
5426-7	1995	Hartford House
5427-5	1995	Village Vet And Pet Shop
5437-2	1995	Craftsman Cottage
5439-9	1996	Airport
5442-9	1996	Mount Olivet Church
5444-5	1996	Woodbury House
5445-3	1996	Hunting Lodge
5447-0	1996	Dinah's Drive-In
5448-8	1996	Snowy Hills Hospital
5462-3	1996	Snow Village Starter Set
5462-3	1996	Shady Oak Church
54856	1996	Dutch Colonial

Mountain Lodge

Item #	Intro	Retired	OSRP	GBTru	↑
5001-3	1976	1979	$20	**$375**	15%

Particulars: One of the "Original 6." Color on roof is different from piece to piece. Bright colored skis lean against two-story lodge, upper windows painted to appear as lead panes, sunburst on end of building, snow laden tree at side.

DATE:_______	$:_______	'91	'92	'93	'94	'95	'96
❍ WISH	❍ HAVE	$525	550	405	370	375	32

Gabled Cottage

Item #	Intro	Retired	OSRP	GBTru	↑
5002-1	1976	1979	$20	**$365**	4%

Particulars: One of the "Original 6." Four-peaked roof with two chimneys, curtained windows, welcome mat. Ivy climbs walls to roof and door, several windows have wreath design. Attached snow laden tree with bluebird.

DATE:_______	$:_______	'91	'92	'93	'94	'95	'96
❍ WISH	❍ HAVE	$450	475	395	385	350	35

The Inn

Item #	Intro	Retired	OSRP	GBTru	↑
5003-9	1976	1979	$20	**$425**	16%

Particulars: One of the "Original 6." Colors on roof are no consistent. Two large brick chimneys, full length covere porch, welcome mat at timbered front doors, attached snow laden tree on side, bright yellow door on opposite side.

DATE:_______	$:_______	'91	'92	'93	'94	'95	'9
❍ WISH	❍ HAVE	$525	500	475	490	450	36

Country Church

Item #	Intro	Retired	OSRP	GBTru	↑
5004-7	1976	1979	$18	**$360**	4%

Particulars: One of the "Original 6." Also known as "Wayside Chapel." Vines and painted welcome on wal short-spired, door ajar, circular upper window, painted side windows, snow laden tree shades one wall. Authentic D56 pieces have hand-lettered signs. If they appear "rubber-stamped," they are not D56.

DATE:_______	$:_______	'91	'92	'93	'94	'95	'9
❍ WISH	❍ HAVE	$325	435	375	375	385	34

STEEPLED CHURCH

ITEM #	INTRO	RETIRED	OSRP	GBTRU	↑
5005-4	1976	1979	$25	**$550**	7%

Particulars: One of the "Original 6." Colors on roof are not consistent. One spire, large circular window over double wood front doors flanked by leaded lattice design windows, side chapel, snow covered tree, bluebird on steeple.

DATE:_______ $:_______

❍ WISH ❍ HAVE

'91	'92	'93	'94	'95	'96
$775	675	675	640	625	515

SMALL CHALET

ITEM #	INTRO	RETIRED	OSRP	GBTRU	↑
5006-2	1976	1979	$15	**$445**	19%

Particulars: One of the "Original 6." Also known as "Gingerbread Chalet." Variation in number of flowers in box (4, 5 or 6) and in color—tan to dark brown. Two-story small gingerbread look home, flower box with snow covered plants, attached tree.

DATE:_______ $:_______

❍ WISH ❍ HAVE

'91	'92	'93	'94	'95	'96
$360	415	415	365	400	375

VICTORIAN HOUSE

ITEM #	INTRO	RETIRED	OSRP	GBTRU	↑
5007-0	1977	1979	$30	**$430**	9%

Particulars: Variations in color—rust/white, salmon/white, pink/white & orange/yellow.Variations in birds—none to some. Orange/yellow color combination has no attached tree. Textured to portray shingles and clapboard. Steps lead up to front door. Stained glass inserts above windows.

DATE:_______ $:_______

❍ WISH ❍ HAVE

'91	'92	'93	'94	'95	'96
$400	485	375	435	455	395

MANSION

ITEM #	INTRO	RETIRED	OSRP	GBTRU	↑
5008-8	1977	1979	$30	**$515**	4%

Particulars: Variation in roof color—either forest green or turquoise. Forest green is considered to be the first shipped and is much harder to find. Amount and placement of snow varies with the roof colors. Building is white brick with porch supported by pillars, windows are shuttered, two chimneys plus cupola on roof. Attached snow laden evergreen tree.

DATE:_______ $:_______

❍ WISH ❍ HAVE

'91	'92	'93	'94	'95	'96
$600	600	500	550	495	495

Stone Church– "Original, Version 1"

Item #	Intro	Retired	OSRP	GBTru	No Change
5009-6	1977	1979	$35	**$555**	

Particulars: There are 2 Stone Churches: 1977, #5009-6 and 1979, #5059-1. There are 2 versions of #5009-6. Both versions of the original 1977 Church have 10 ½" steeples. The color on Version 1 is usually a pale mint green; the finish is very glossy. Version 1's top step on the tree side is flush with the edge of the bottom step. Both versions have a separate bell, attached by wire.

DATE:_______	$:_______	'91	'92	'93	'94	'95	'96
❍ WISH	❍ HAVE	$825	715	650	725	625	555

Stone Church– "Original, Version 2"

Item #	Intro	Retired	OSRP	GBTru	No Change
5009-6	1977	1979	$35	**$555**	

Particulars: The color on Version 2 of the original Church is usually a deeper greenish yellow. Version 2's top step is indented from the bottom step on the righthand side.

DATE:_______	$:_______	'91	'92	'93	'94	'95	'96
❍ WISH	❍ HAVE	$825	715	650	725	625	555

Homestead

Item #	Intro	Retired	OSRP	GBTru	↑
5011-2	1978	1984	$30	**$245**	26%

Particulars: Old-fashioned farmhouse, front porch full length of house. Second floor bay windows. Triple window in front gable. Attached tree.

DATE:_______	$:_______	'91	'92	'93	'94	'95	'96
❍ WISH	❍ HAVE	$250	310	285	240	250	195

General Store–"White"

Item #	Intro	Retired	OSRP	GBTru	↑
5012-0	1978	1980	$25	**$455**	5%

Particulars: Variations in color—White, Tan & Gold—affect GBTru Price. This "White" General Store w/gray roof is considered to be the first shipped, however the "Tan" and "Gold" are much harder to find. The sign on the "White" General Store most often is, "General Store, Y & L Brothers." All three colors have Christmas trees on the porch roof. General Stores supply food, postal service & gas.

DATE:_______	$:_______	'91	'92	'93	'94	'95	'96
❍ WISH	❍ HAVE	$440	500	450	450	450	435

General Store–"Tan"

Item #	Intro	Retired	OSRP	GBTru	↑
5012-0	1978	1980	$25	**$600**	12%

Particulars: This is the "Tan" General Store. The sign above the porch most often reads, "General Store, S & L Brothers."

DATE:_______ $:_______ ❍ WISH ❍ HAVE

'91	'92	'93	'94	'95	'96
$440	500	605	605	585	535

General Store–"Gold"

Item #	Intro	Retired	OSRP	GBTru	↓
5012-0	1978	1980	$25	**$525**	4%

Particulars: This is the "Gold" General Store. The sign above the porch most often reads simply, "General Store."

DATE:_______ $:_______ ❍ WISH ❍ HAVE

'91	'92	'93	'94	'95	'96
$440	500	560	560	550	545

Cape Cod

Item #	Intro	Retired	OSRP	GBTru	↓
5013-8	1978	1980	$20	**$375**	3%

Particulars: Steep gabled roof with chimney, small dormer and painted landscaping. Attached snow laden tree.

DATE:_______ $:_______ ❍ WISH ❍ HAVE

'91	'92	'93	'94	'95	'96
$385	385	375	360	375	385

Nantucket

Item #	Intro	Retired	OSRP	GBTru	↑
5014-6	1978	1986	$25	**$255**	9%

Particulars: Yellow cottage with green roof. Small front porch, attached greenhouse. Attached tree. Some have garland above two front windows, some don't. Also see the *Nantucket Renovation,* 1993, #5441-0, page 57.

DATE:_______ $:_______ ❍ WISH ❍ HAVE

'91	'92	'93	'94	'95	'96
$235	250	250	315	275	235

Skating Rink/Duck Pond Set

Item #	Intro	Retired	OSRP	GBTru	↑
5015-3	1978	1979	$16	**$1045**	8%

Particulars: Lighted. Set of 2. (The *Skating Rink* is the piece with the snowman, the *Duck Pond* is the piece with the bench and blue birds.) One of the first non-house pieces. In this set the trees were attached directly to the pond bases where their size and weight caused frequent breakage, therefore they were retired in 1979. The revised *Skating Pond* in 1982, #5017-2, page 27, was also a set of 2 with one piece being the pond and the other piece double lighted trees. Because the *Skating Rink* and *Duck Pond* are frequently sold separately on the Secondary Market there is confusion between the *Skating Rink* and *Skating Pond.* The Rink has one single lighted tree attached to the base, the Pond has separate double trees.

DATE:________ $:________ ❍ WISH ❍ HAVE

'91	'92	'93	'94	'95	'96
$1100	1200	950	1000	1000	970

Small Double Trees—"Blue Birds"

Item #	Intro	Retired	OSRP	GBTru	↑
5016-1	1978	1989	$13.50	**$180**	3%

Particulars: Lighted. One of the first non-house accessory pieces. Approximately 8 to 8 1/2" tall. Variations in color of birds—blue or red—affect GBTru Price. Blue are considered to be the first ones shipped; the change to red was made in late 1979. There were mold changes and a variation in the amount of snow over the years as well.

DATE:________ $:________ ❍ WISH ❍ HAVE

'91	'92	'93	'94	'95	'96
$150	150	225	175	175	175

Small Double Trees—"Red Birds"

Item #	Intro	Retired	OSRP	GBTru	↑
5016-1	1978	1989	$13.50	**$45**	13%

Particulars: This is the Small Double Trees—"Red Birds" and a photo illustrating changes in the mold and the variation in the amount of snow.

DATE:________ $:________ ❍ WISH ❍ HAVE

'91	'92	'93	'94	'95	'96
$40	48	48	52	50	40

VICTORIAN

ITEM #	INTRO	RETIRED	OSRP	GBTRU	⬆
5054-2	1979	1982	$30	**$350**	11%

Particulars: There are variations in color and in exterior finish. They are peach with smooth walls (1979), gold with smooth walls (1980) and gold clapboard (1981 on). The peach is the most difficult to find but the gold and gold clapboard look nicer and are preferred by collectors.

DATE:________ $:________
❍ WISH ❍ HAVE

'91	'92	'93	'94	'95	'96
$345	440	435	380	350	315

KNOB HILL–"GRAY"

ITEM #	INTRO	RETIRED	OSRP	GBTRU	⬆
5055-9	1979	1981	$30	**$350**	32%

Particulars: Variations in color in this three-story San Francisco-style Victorian row house—"Gray" or "Yellow"—affect GBTru Price. This is the "Gray" Knob Hill with a red roof and black trim. The "Gray" Knob Hill is considered to be the first shipped.

DATE:________ $:________
❍ WISH ❍ HAVE

'91	'92	'93	'94	'95	'96
$350	350	350	350	295	265

KNOB HILL–"YELLOW"

ITEM #	INTRO	RETIRED	OSRP	GBTRU	⬆
5055-9	1979	1981	$30	**$365**	6%

Particulars: This is the "Yellow" Knob Hill with a red roof and gray trim.

DATE:________ $:________
❍ WISH ❍ HAVE

'91	'92	'93	'94	'95	'96
$350	350	350	350	375	345

BROWNSTONE

ITEM #	INTRO	RETIRED	OSRP	GBTRU	⬆
5056-7	1979	1981	$36	**$565**	4%

Particulars: There are two roof colors—originally introduced with a gray roof, the following year the roof was red. Red is the most desired. Building is three stories with wreath trimmed bay windows on all floors, overall flat roof.

DATE:________ $:________
❍ WISH ❍ HAVE

'91	'92	'93	'94	'95	'96
$475	495	540	560	575	545

Log Cabin

Item #	Intro	Retired	OSRP	GBTru	↑
5057-5	1979	1981	$22	**$440**	10%

Particulars: Rustic log house with stone chimney, roof extends to cover porch, log pile at side, skis by door.

DATE:________ $:________ ❍ WISH ❍ HAVE

'91	'92	'93	'94	'95	'96
$450	475	475	475	475	400

Countryside Church

Item #	Intro	Retired	OSRP	GBTru	↑
5058-3	1979	1984	$27.50	**$275**	6%

Particulars: White clapboard church with central bell steeple, attached tree has all lower branches pruned. For a no-snow version, see 1979 MEADOWLAND *Countryside Church,* #5051-8, page 114.

DATE:________ $:________ ❍ WISH ❍ HAVE

'91	'92	'93	'94	'95	'96
$275	295	295	295	295	260

Stone Church

Item #	Intro	Retired	OSRP	GBTru	↑
5059-1	1979	1980	$32	**$955**	4%

Particulars: 8 ½" steeple. The color is yellow. It has a Department 56 sticker dated 1980 on the bottom. Also see the original *Stone Church,* 1977, #5009-6, page18.

DATE:________ $:________ ❍ WISH ❍ HAVE

'91	'92	'93	'94	'95	'96
$750	850	910	1000	1000	915

School House

Item #	Intro	Retired	OSRP	GBTru	↓
5060-9	1979	1982	$30	**$360**	1%

Particulars: Color varies from rust to dark brown. The first design to feature the American flag. It flies from the roof peak above the brick one-room school. The flag pole is metal and removable.

DATE:________ $:________ ❍ WISH ❍ HAVE

'91	'92	'93	'94	'95	'96
$400	360	405	340	345	365

Tudor House

Item #	Intro	Retired	OSRP	GBTru	↑
5061-7	1979	1981	$25	**$295**	4%

Particulars: Brick chimney and fireplace on simple L-shaped timber trimmed home, split-shingle roof.

DATE:_______ $:_______

❍ WISH ❍ HAVE

'91	'92	'93	'94	'95	'96
$415	385	330	330	325	285

Mission Church

Item #	Intro	Retired	OSRP	GBTru	↑
5062-5	1979	1980	$30	**$1275**	16%

Particulars: Sun dried clay with structural timbers visible at roof line. Small arched bell tower above entry. Ceramic bell is attached by wire.

DATE:_______ $:_______

❍ WISH ❍ HAVE

'91	'92	'93	'94	'95	'96
$785	950	950	1260	1250	1100

Mobile Home

Item #	Intro	Retired	OSRP	GBTru	↓
5063-3	1979	1980	$18	**$1725**	8%

Particulars: Similar to aluminum skinned Airstream mobile home. To be towed by car or truck for travel.

DATE:_______ $:_______

❍ WISH ❍ HAVE

'91	'92	'93	'94	'95	'96
$1350	1625	1700	1700	1750	1865

Giant Trees

Item #	Intro	Retired	OSRP	GBTru	↓
5065-8	1979	1982	$20	**$295**	12%

Particulars: Lighted snow covered large evergreen trees. Approximately 11" tall. Birds perch on branches.

DATE:_______ $:_______

❍ WISH ❍ HAVE

'91	'92	'93	'94	'95	'96
$310	295	295	360	360	335

Adobe House

Item #	Intro	Retired	OSRP	GBTru	↑
5066-6	1979	1980	$18	**$2400**	12%

Particulars: Small sun dried clay home. Outside oven on side, chili peppers hang from roof beams.

DATE:________ $:________

❍ WISH ❍ HAVE

'91	'92	'93	'94	'95	'96
$1000	2000	2400	2495	2500	2150

Cathedral Church

Item #	Intro	Retired	OSRP	GBTru	↑
5067-4	1980	1981	$36	**$2500**	19%

Particulars: First of two OSV Cathedral Churches. (See also 1987, #5019-9.) This church has a central dome with two shorter bell towers. The stained glass windows are acrylic. Production problems (fragile domes) forced retirement after one year. Inspired by St. Paul's Cathedral in St. Paul, MN.

DATE:________ $:________

❍ WISH ❍ HAVE

'91	'92	'93	'94	'95	'96
$725	825	2300	1895	2000	2100

Stone Mill House

Item #	Intro	Retired	OSRP	GBTru	↑
5068-2	1980	1982	$30	**$535**	26%

Particulars: Water wheel on dark weathered stone block mill, separate bag of oats hung with wire from block and tackle, another bag propped by door. Many pieces available on the Secondary Market are missing the separate bag of oats. The GBTru for a piece without the bag of oats is $425.

DATE:________ $:________

❍ WISH ❍ HAVE

'91	'92	'93	'94	'95	'96
$635	635	575	545	495	425

Colonial Farm House

Item #	Intro	Retired	OSRP	GBTru	↑
5070-9	1980	1982	$30	**$325**	3%

Particulars: House with wide front porch, two front dormers in attic, symmetrical layout of windows. The same Item # was used for the 1986 *All Saints Church.*

DATE:________ $:________

❍ WISH ❍ HAVE

'91	'92	'93	'94	'95	'96
$425	425	400	365	375	315

Town Church

Item #	Intro	Retired	OSRP	GBTru	↓
5071-7	1980	1982	$33	**$350**	1%

Particulars: A short bell tower rises from central nave area, an attached tree tucks in close to the side chapel. The same Item # was used for the 1986 *Carriage House*.

DATE:_______	$:_______	'91	'92	'93	'94	'95	'96
❍ WISH	❍ HAVE	$410	385	385	355	375	355

Train Station With 3 Train Cars

Item #	Intro	Retired	OSRP	GBTru	↓
5087-3 5086-5	1980	1985	$100	**$400**	6%

Particulars: First Snow Village train and station design. *Train Station With 3 Train Cars* was sold until 1981 under the Item #s 5087-3 and 5086-5, respectively. Though boxed separately, they were sold together. This Station has 6 window panes, a round window in the door, and brick on the front only. The three lighted train cars—an engine, passenger car and baggage/mail caboose—have "G & N RR" on the cars. All four pieces are lit and were made in Japan. After their introduction it was thought the train was too large for the station, so in 1981 a new larger station, now packaged with the train, #5085-6, was released.

DATE:_______	$:_______	'91	'92	'93	'94	'95	'96
❍ WISH	❍ HAVE	$350	375	375	375	395	425

Wooden Clapboard

Item #	Intro	Retired	OSRP	GBTru	↑
5072-5	1981	1984	$32	**$230**	10%

Particulars: White house with green roof and trim and wraparound porch. Red brick chimney.

DATE:_______	$:_______	'91	'92	'93	'94	'95	'96
❍ WISH	❍ HAVE	$300	320	300	260	260	210

English Cottage

Item #	Intro	Retired	OSRP	GBTru	⬆
5073-3	1981	1982	$25	**$295**	7%

Particulars: Cottage with thatched roof and timbered frame, two chimneys. 1 ½ stories. The roof comes down to meet the top of the first story. Available for only one year.

DATE:_______ $:_______

❍ WISH	❍ HAVE	'91	'92	'93	'94	'95	'96
		$300	350	325	285	295	275

Barn

Item #	Intro	Retired	OSRP	GBTru	⬆
5074-1	1981	1984	$32	**$430**	5%

Particulars: Red barn and silo. Gray roof, two vents on roof ridge, root cellar on side, hayloft over animals and equipment. Also known as the "Original Barn."

DATE:_______ $:_______

❍ WISH	❍ HAVE	'91	'92	'93	'94	'95	'96
		$450	425	425	460	460	410

Corner Store

Item #	Intro	Retired	OSRP	GBTru	⬆
5076-8	1981	1983	$30	**$245**	20%

Particulars: Red brick building with one large display window, entry door on corner, bay window in family living area, shutters on windows, shingled roof. The same Item # was used for the 1986 *Apothecary*.

DATE:_______ $:_______

❍ WISH	❍ HAVE	'91	'92	'93	'94	'95	'96
		$260	260	260	260	245	205

Bakery

Item #	Intro	Retired	OSRP	GBTru	⬆
5077-6	1981	1983	$30	**$265**	4%

Particulars: This is the original *Bakery*. The same Item # was used for the 1986 *Bakery*—a new and different design. This building with a bakery store beneath the family living area is white with a green roof. The 1986 *Bakery* is brown. There is a wide difference in Secondary Market Value between the two bakery designs. The original *Bakery* is modeled after The Scofield Building in Northfield, MN.

DATE:_______ $:_______

❍ WISH	❍ HAVE	'91	'92	'93	'94	'95	'96
		$275	275	275	275	250	255

English Church

Item #	Intro	Retired	OSRP	GBTru	↑
5078-4	1981	1982	$30	**$375**	3%

Particulars: Church with steep pitched roof, side chapel, a steeple topped by a gold cross, arched windows, and triangular window in gable above the entry double doors. The cross is separate and inserts into the steeple. The same Item # was used for the 1986 *Diner*. Only available for one year.

DATE:_______ $:_______ ❍ WISH ❍ HAVE

'91	'92	'93	'94	'95	'96
$250	375	375	390	395	365

Large Single Tree

Item #	Intro	Retired	OSRP	GBTru	↑
5080-6	1981	1989	$17	**$45**	29%

Particulars: One lighted, snow covered evergreen tree approximately 9" tall with birds perched on the branches. There were mold changes and variations in the amount of snow over the years.

DATE:_______ $:_______ ❍ WISH ❍ HAVE

'91	'92	'93	'94	'95	'96
$50	50	50	55	45	35

Train Station With 3 Train Cars

Item #	Intro	Retired	OSRP	GBTru	↑
5085-6	1981	1985	$100	**$360**	9%

Particulars: Set of 4. Revised Snow Village train and station design. (Original was 1980, #5087-3 and 5086-5.) All 4 pieces are lit. The larger station, w/8 window panes, 2 windows in the door, brick on the front & side wings & tudor style cross beams, is in better proportion to the train cars.

DATE:_______ $:_______ ❍ WISH ❍ HAVE

'91	'92	'93	'94	'95	'96
$350	375	325	325	325	330

Skating Pond

Item #	Intro	Retired	OSRP	GBTru	↓
5017-2	1982	1984	$25	**$355**	1%

Particulars: Set of 2. A small snow covered skating pond with a snowman on the edge and tree trunks piled together to provide seating is one piece. The second piece is two lighted evergreen trees. This set replaced and is sometimes confused with the *Skating Rink/Duck Pond Set*, 1978, #5015-3. In this piece, the trees are separate from the pond.

DATE:_______ $:_______ ❍ WISH ❍ HAVE

'91	'92	'93	'94	'95	'96
$350	350	350	390	380	360

Street Car

Item #	Intro	Retired	OSRP	GBTru	↑
5019-9	1982	1984	$16	**$375**	15%

Particulars: Lighted bright yellow with green "Main Street" sign on side. #2 car, hook-up on top for pole to connect to electric power. Same Item # was used for the 1987 *Cathedral Church.*

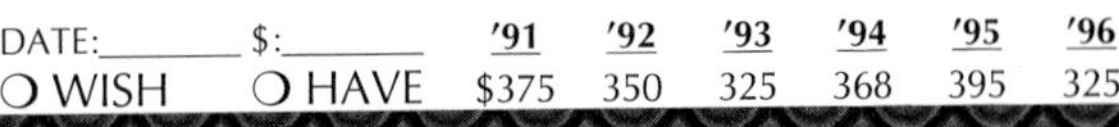

DATE:_______	$:_______	'91	'92	'93	'94	'95	'96
❍ WISH	❍ HAVE	$375	350	325	368	395	325

Centennial House

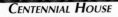

Item #	Intro	Retired	OSRP	GBTru	↑
5020-2	1982	1984	$32	**$325**	7%

Particulars: Two-story clapboard house, square tower, carved and curved window frames, wooden balcony and porch.

DATE:_______	$:_______	'91	'92	'93	'94	'95	'96
❍ WISH	❍ HAVE	$365	365	370	350	350	305

Carriage House

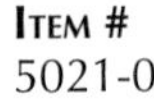

Item #	Intro	Retired	OSRP	GBTru	↑
5021-0	1982	1984	$28	**$315**	9%

Particulars: In this carriage house, bright lamps flank the entry to the storage area for the carriages. The driver has a small apartment above.

DATE:_______	$:_______	'91	'92	'93	'94	'95	'96
❍ WISH	❍ HAVE	$300	315	300	305	325	290

Pioneer Church

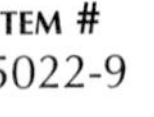

Item #	Intro	Retired	OSRP	GBTru	↑
5022-9	1982	1984	$30	**$320**	3%

Particulars: Simple cedar shake shingle church with front notice board sending joy to all who pass. Building has a short steeple on the front of the roof ridge.

DATE:_______	$:_______	'91	'92	'93	'94	'95	'96
❍ WISH	❍ HAVE	$285	355	305	310	300	310

Swiss Chalet

Item #	Intro	Retired	OSRP	GBTru	↑
5023-7	1982	1984	$28	**$430**	5%

Particulars: Stone base walls support the timber upper stories of the chalet. The upper floor has a front balcony with a railing and is enclosed by a roof overhang. This building has a very unusual roof.

DATE:_______	$:_______	'91	'92	'93	'94	'95	'96
❍ WISH	❍ HAVE	$335	450	435	415	450	410

Bank

Item #	Intro	Retired	OSRP	GBTru	↑
5024-5	1982	1983	$32	**$600**	3%

Particulars: Building is a corner bank with entry by revolving door. Outside there's a covered stairway leading to a second story. The "BANK" sign is part of the corner design. The same Item # was used for the 1987 *Cumberland House.* The Bank was available for only one year.

DATE:_______	$:_______	'91	'92	'93	'94	'95	'96
❍ WISH	❍ HAVE	$415	635	715	600	600	585

Gabled House

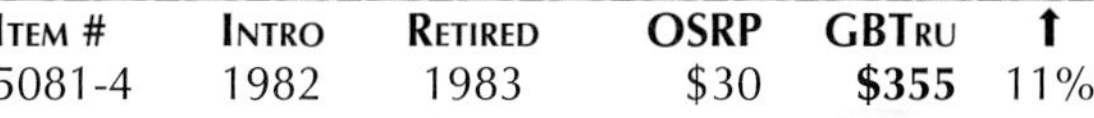

Item #	Intro	Retired	OSRP	GBTru	↑
5081-4	1982	1983	$30	**$355**	11%

Particulars: Production pieces of this design are quite different from the house pictured on the Snow Village poster. The house is white shingled with a very dark blue-green variegated four-gabled roof. In addition, the building has two small covered porches. The same Item # was used for the 1987 *Red Barn.* Piece was an Early Release to Gift Creations Concepts (GCC).

DATE:_______	$:_______	'91	'92	'93	'94	'95	'96
❍ WISH	❍ HAVE	$350	400	425	360	390	320

Flower Shop

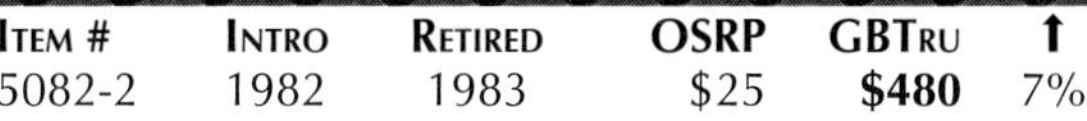

Item #	Intro	Retired	OSRP	GBTru	↑
5082-2	1982	1983	$25	**$480**	7%

Particulars: Flower boxes rest outside by the large display window. Shop has rolled up awnings above the front windows. There is a variation in the color of the window frames—they are either green or brown. The same Item # was used the the 1987 *Jefferson School.*

DATE:_______	$:_______	'91	'92	'93	'94	'95	'96
❍ WISH	❍ HAVE	$420	450	475	425	450	450

NEW STONE CHURCH

ITEM #	INTRO	RETIRED	OSRP	GBTRU	↑
5083-0	1982	1984	$32	**$370**	12%

Particulars: Church of stone block construction with long nave with side chapel, steeple rises on side opposite chapel. Front has arched windows and two lamps. Early release to Gift Creations Concepts (GCC).

DATE:_______	$:_______	'91	'92	'93	'94	'95	'96
❍ WISH	❍ HAVE	$245	325	325	370	395	330

TOWN HALL

ITEM #	INTRO	RETIRED	OSRP	GBTRU	↑
5000-8	1983	1984	$32	**$335**	6%

Particulars: Brick & stone Town Hall with 2 corner covered side entries. Building has symmetrical design (window over window) and a steeple above the front main wall. There's a ceramic bell in the tower. A separate, stamped metal weathervane came in an envelope inside the box. It's rare to find a piece that still has it. No doubt many were unknowingly discarded. Available for only one year.

DATE:_______	$:_______	'91	'92	'93	'94	'95	'96
❍ WISH	❍ HAVE	$225	300	330	330	345	315

GROCERY

ITEM #	INTRO	RETIRED	OSRP	GBTRU	↑
5001-6	1983	1985	$35	**$360**	11%

Particulars: Red brick grocery with full painted display windows and decorative cornice trim above and below front windows. The outside staircase leads to family quarters.

DATE:_______	$:_______	'91	'92	'93	'94	'95	'96
❍ WISH	❍ HAVE	$250	325	325	300	325	325

VICTORIAN COTTAGE

ITEM #	INTRO	RETIRED	OSRP	GBTRU	↑
5002-4	1983	1984	$35	**$360**	18%

Particulars: Cottage has ornate carved woodwork on front and an ornamental arched entry. First floor French windows are separated by pillars.

DATE:_______	$:_______	'91	'92	'93	'94	'95	'9
❍ WISH	❍ HAVE	$340	375	350	360	365	30

Governor's Mansion

Item #	Intro	Retired	OSRP	GBTru	↑
5003-2	1983	1985	$32	**$305**	9%

Particulars: Brick mansion with metal ironwork featured on the roof cupola (missing from photo). Building has wide entry steps, a repetitive design above the door, a second story and central attic windows.

DATE:_______ $:_______ ❍ WISH ❍ HAVE

'91	'92	'93	'94	'95	'96
$285	285	290	300	275	280

Turn Of The Century

Item #	Intro	Retired	OSRP	GBTru	↑
5004-0	1983	1986	$36	**$250**	2%

Particulars: Steps lead to the covered entry and a front triangular ornate design crowns the front gable of this building. A squared turret rises from the left front corner and ends in the highest roof peak. The pictured piece is missing a chimney—the center peak should have a chimney. The bottom of the piece reads, "Turn The Time Of Century."

DATE:_______ $:_______ ❍ WISH ❍ HAVE

'91	'92	'93	'94	'95	'96
$250	265	265	235	235	245

Gingerbread House

Item #	Intro	Retired	OSRP	GBTru	↑
5025-3	1983	1984	$24	**$335**	20%

Particulars: Two versions: Lighted house and coin bank. The coin bank version is extremely difficult to find. Designed like a Christmas edible treat. Cookies trim sides while candy canes and sugar hearts decorate the roof.

DATE:_______ $:_______ ❍ WISH ❍ HAVE

'91	'92	'93	'94	'95	'96
$310	370	395	270	270	280

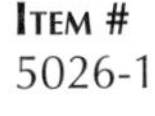

Village Church

Item #	Intro	Retired	OSRP	GBTru	↑
5026-1	1983	1984	$30	**$395**	3%

Particulars: Stone steps of the church lead to double carved doors. The design over the door repeats on the roof trim. The steeple has long narrow openings and pointed arch windows are featured. Collectors often confuse this piece with the *Parish Church*, #5039-3, page 36. Early release to Gift Creations Concepts (GCC).

DATE:_______ $:_______ ❍ WISH ❍ HAVE

'91	'92	'93	'94	'95	'96
$290	330	335	375	375	385

Gothic Church

Item #	Intro	Retired	OSRP	GBTru	↑
5028-8	1983	1986	$36	**$255**	9%

Particulars: Stone block church with the steeple rising straight from large double doors ending in a cross. The bell chamber has ornate grillwork. Smaller entry doors flank the central area repeating the design.

DATE:_______ $:_______ ❍ WISH ❍ HAVE

'91	'92	'93	'94	'95	'96
$225	250	245	275	275	235

Parsonage

Item #	Intro	Retired	OSRP	GBTru	↑
5029-6	1983	1985	$35	**$375**	25%

Particulars: A tower rises above the entry of the parsonage. The front gable has ornate coping topped by a cross. Th coping details are repeated around the windows, doors and small balcony. There are community rooms on first floor and the family lives upstairs.

DATE:_______ $:_______ ❍ WISH ❍ HAVE

'91	'92	'93	'94	'95	'96
$225	375	380	380	350	30

Wooden Church

Item #	Intro	Retired	OSRP	GBTru	↑
5031-8	1983	1985	$30	**$350**	23%

Particulars: White clapboard church with crossed timber design that repeats over the door, roof peak and steeple The side chapel has a separate entry door.

DATE:_______ $:_______ ❍ WISH ❍ HAVE

'91	'92	'93	'94	'95	'9
$400	400	375	375	350	28

Fire Station

Item #	Intro	Retired	OSRP	GBTru	↑
5032-6	1983	1984	$32	**$575**	5%

Particulars: The central door of the fire station opens to reveal a red fire truck. Brick columns from the base to the roof add to the sturdy look. A Dalmatian sits by the entry, ready when necessary. Some pieces are without the dog.

DATE:_______ $:_______ ❍ WISH ❍ HAVE

'91	'92	'93	'94	'95	'9
$675	675	650	650	625	55

English Tudor

Item #	Intro	Retired	OSRP	GBTru	↑
5033-4	1983	1985	$30	**$275**	22%

Particulars: Stucco finish building with brick chimneys. The three front roof peaks create the front gable design.

DATE:________ $:________

❍ WISH ❍ HAVE

'91	'92	'93	'94	'95	'96
$275	300	300	260	295	225

Chateau

Item #	Intro	Retired	OSRP	GBTru	↑
5084-9	1983	1984	$35	**$475**	7%

Particulars: First story large windows which include front and side bow windows are a feature of this building. There's a diamond design on the roof shingles, stone for walls and a cylindrical chimney with a domed flue cap. The front dormers and side peaks exhibit an ornate carved design. Early release to Gift Creations Concepts (GCC).

DATE:________ $:________

❍ WISH ❍ HAVE

'91	'92	'93	'94	'95	'96
$290	375	420	470	475	445

Main Street House

Item #	Intro	Retired	OSRP	GBTru	↑
5005-9	1984	1986	$27	**$240**	7%

Particulars: White and green 1 ½-story house with clapboard lower story and timbered upper story. There are two lamps on either side of the front door. Early release to Gift Creations Concepts (GCC).

DATE:________ $:________

❍ WISH ❍ HAVE

'91	'92	'93	'94	'95	'96
$165	250	250	250	275	225

Stratford House

Item #	Intro	Retired	OSRP	GBTru	↑
5007-5	1984	1986	$28	**$175**	6%

Particulars: English Tudor style house featuring vertical ornamental timbers. All gables rise to the same height.

DATE:________ $:________

❍ WISH ❍ HAVE

'91	'92	'93	'94	'95	'96
$110	225	225	215	195	165

Haversham House

Item #	Intro	Retired	OSRP	GBTru	↑
5008-3	1984	1987	$37	**$280**	17%

Particulars: All gables, balconies and porch are decorated with ornately carved woodwork. Early release to Gift Creations Concepts (GCC). Early release pieces are larger than subsequent ones.

DATE:________ $:________

		'91	'92	'93	'94	'95	'96
❍ WISH	❍ HAVE	$200	240	295	310	300	240

Galena House

Item #	Intro	Retired	OSRP	GBTru	↑
5009-1	1984	1985	$32	**$320**	12%

Particulars: Steps lead to double entry doors of this brick home. A bay window fills one side. The second floor is incorporated into the roof construction. Available for one year only.

DATE:________ $:________

		'91	'92	'93	'94	'95	'96
❍ WISH	❍ HAVE	$285	330	330	330	345	285

River Road House

Item #	Intro	Retired	OSRP	GBTru	↑
5010-5	1984	1987	$36	**$200**	8%

Particulars: A large and grand white house with many windows. There are 3 Versions. The First Version has cut out transoms above the two front windows, and a cut out middle arch above the front door. The Second Version repeats the cut out transoms with a solid middle arch. The Third Version has a cut out middle arch and solid transoms. Early release to Gift Creations Concepts (GCC).

DATE:________ $:________

		'91	'92	'93	'94	'95	'96
❍ WISH	❍ HAVE	$150	150	220	220	215	185

Delta House

Item #	Intro	Retired	OSRP	GBTru	↑
5012-1	1984	1986	$32	**$300**	15%

Particulars: A large brick house with a balcony above the wraparound porch which is separate from the entry. The decorative porch trim design is repeated where the roof and brick meet and on turret. The photograph is without the ornamental "iron works" atop the tower. Many collectors are unaware of the trim, in fact it's rare to find a piece that still has it. It came in an envelope inside the box.

DATE:________ $:________

		'91	'92	'93	'94	'95	'96
❍ WISH	❍ HAVE	$350	325	335	345	310	260

Bayport

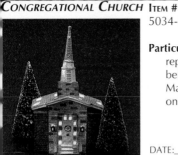

Item #	Intro	Retired	OSRP	GBTru	↑
5015-6	1984	1986	$30	**$235**	12%

Particulars: Gray clapboard corner entry home with a turret addition positioned between the two main wings of the two-story house.

DATE:________ $:________ ❍ WISH ❍ HAVE

'91	'92	'93	'94	'95	'96
$215	230	230	230	235	210

Congregational Church

Item #	Intro	Retired	OSRP	GBTru	↑
5034-2	1984	1985	$28	**$645**	5%

Particulars: Brick church with fieldstone front. The stone is repeated on the steeple. There are louver vents on the belfry. This is a difficult piece to locate on the Secondary Market due in part to the fact that it was available for only one year.

DATE:________ $:________ ❍ WISH ❍ HAVE

'91	'92	'93	'94	'95	'96
$250	360	415	540	595	615

Trinity Church

Item #	Intro	Retired	OSRP	GBTru	↑
5035-0	1984	1986	$32	**$285**	16%

Particulars: Church has steeples of different heights, clerestory windows to bring additional light to the nave and two large wreaths by the front doors.

DATE:________ $:________ ❍ WISH ❍ HAVE

'91	'92	'93	'94	'95	'96
$220	265	305	305	305	245

Summit House

Item #	Intro	Retired	OSRP	GBTru	↑
5036-9	1984	1985	$28	**$340**	10%

Particulars: Pink corner house features a rounded turret and large entry door with side lights. Cornices appear to support the roof edge. Each second story window is capped by a molded projection. Available for one year only.

DATE:________ $:________ ❍ WISH ❍ HAVE

'91	'92	'93	'94	'95	'96
$375	375	395	385	385	310

New School House

Item #	Intro	Retired	OSRP	GBTru	↑
5037-7	1984	1986	$35	**$235**	9%

Particulars: Two-story schoolhouse with bell tower and clock. There is a separate cloth flag on a wooden pole that can be inserted into a hole in the base.

DATE:_______ $:_______

❍ WISH ❍ HAVE

'91	'92	'93	'94	'95	'96
$240	270	275	275	275	215

Parish Church

Item #	Intro	Retired	OSRP	GBTru	↑
5039-3	1984	1986	$32	**$315**	11%

Particulars: White country church with unique three level steeple has arched windows, a red door and a circular window over the entry. Collectors often confuse this piece with the *Village Church,* #5026-1, page 31.

DATE:_______ $:_______

❍ WISH ❍ HAVE

'91	'92	'93	'94	'95	'96
$310	345	370	370	370	285

Stucco Bungalow

Item #	Intro	Retired	OSRP	GBTru	↑
5045-8	1985	1986	$30	**$365**	7%

Particulars: Two-story small house with one roof dormer as a mini tower has a second dormer featuring a timbered design. The entry door is built into the archway under a low roof peak. A wreath and garland decorate the door. This is a difficult piece to locate on the Secondary Market as it was available for only one year.

DATE:_______ $:_______

❍ WISH ❍ HAVE

'91	'92	'93	'94	'95	'96
$105	375	360	385	395	340

Williamsburg House

Item #	Intro	Retired	OSRP	GBTru	No Change
5046-6	1985	1988	$37	**$165**	

Particulars: A traditional two-story colonial with all windows shuttered, three dormers, two chimneys and a covered entry topped by a second floor balcony.

DATE:_______ $:_______

❍ WISH ❍ HAVE

'91	'92	'93	'94	'95	'96
$95	110	135	145	135	165

Plantation House

Item #	Intro	Retired	OSRP	GBTru	⬇
5047-4	1985	1987	$37	**$115**	4%

Particulars: The house features an entry with two-story wood columns, three dormers, two chimneys and four first floor windows with canopies.

DATE:_______ $:_______ ❍ WISH ❍ HAVE

'91	'92	'93	'94	'95	'96
$80	95	118	118	115	120

Church Of The Open Door

Item #	Intro	Retired	OSRP	GBTru	⬆
5048-2	1985	1988	$34	**$145**	12%

Particulars: Church with a steeple on the side chapel has design over front entry above circular window that is repeated in motif on eaves.

DATE:_______ $:_______ ❍ WISH ❍ HAVE

'91	'92	'93	'94	'95	'96
$110	105	135	135	125	130

Spruce Place

Item #	Intro	Retired	OSRP	GBTru	⬆
5049-0	1985	1987	$33	**$270**	6%

Particulars: Victorian house has a windowed turret rising above a covered porch. There's decorative molding above the porch, windows and dormer. A circular window over the porch is decorated with a wreath.

DATE:_______ $:_______ ❍ WISH ❍ HAVE

'91	'92	'93	'94	'95	'96
$275	315	320	270	275	255

Duplex

Item #	Intro	Retired	OSRP	GBTru	⬆
5050-4	1985	1987	$35	**$165**	6%

Particulars: The duplex is a two-family house with a shared entry. Each family has up and down rooms and a bay window. The building has a small second story balcony and roof dormers.

DATE:_______ $:_______ ❍ WISH ❍ HAVE

'91	'92	'93	'94	'95	'96
$100	105	110	165	165	155

Depot And Train With 2 Train Cars

Item #	Intro	Retired	OSRP	GBTru	↑
5051-2	1985	1988	$65	**$160**	7%

Particulars: Set of 4. Second Original Snow Village train & station design. Train is non-lighting. Depot has 2 wings, each w/ chimney, connected by a central area. There are 3 Versions: 1st Version of the depot (pictured) was brown w/gray corner stones & yellow passenger car windows; 2nd Version was a variegated brick w/no corner stones & yellow passenger car windows; 3rd Version was the brick w/white passenger car windows.

DATE:_______	$:_______	'91	'92	'93	'94	'95	'96
❍ WISH	❍ HAVE	$110	125	135	135	145	150

Ridgewood

Item #	Intro	Retired	OSRP	GBTru	No Change
5052-0	1985	1987	$35	**$180**	

Particulars: Porches run the length of both the first and second story on this house. The first floor front windows are arched as are the window over the front door and in the attic.

DATE:_______	$:_______	'91	'92	'93	'94	'95	'96
❍ WISH	❍ HAVE	$125	130	150	165	170	180

Waverly Place

Item #	Intro	Retired	OSRP	GBTru	↑
5041-5	1986	1986	$35	**$300**	3%

Particulars: This ornate Victorian home has two different turret-like window designs. The second story features half moon window highlights and carved moldings. Designed after the Gingerbread Mansion in Ferndale, CA. Early release to Gift Creations Concepts (GCC), in the Fall of 1985.

DATE:_______	$:_______	'91	'92	'93	'94	'95	'96
❍ WISH	❍ HAVE	$265	300	300	300	325	290

Twin Peaks

Item #	Intro	Retired	OSRP	GBTru	↓
5042-3	1986	1986	$32	**$440**	1%

Particulars: Building has two matching three-story stone turrets with a multitude of windows on each story to soften the fortress look. Wide steps lead to the red entry doors. Early release to Gift Creations Concepts (GCC), Fall 1985.

DATE:_______	$:_______	'91	'92	'93	'94	'95	'96
❍ WISH	❍ HAVE	$275	285	325	510	525	445

2101 Maple

Item #	Intro	Retired	OSRP	GBTru	↑
5043-1	1986	1986	$32	**$345**	6%

Particulars: Brick two-story home with the side of the front porch built out from a stone turret. The second story windows are capped by a half circle window. Early release to Gift Creations Concepts (GCC), Fall 1985.

DATE:_______	$:_______	'91	'92	'93	'94	'95	'96
❍ WISH	❍ HAVE	$195	330	330	360	375	325

Lincoln Park Duplex

Item #	Intro	Retired	OSRP	GBTru	NO
5060-1	1986	1988	$33	**$135**	CHANGE

Particulars: Two-family attached home reminiscent of Chicago's Lincoln Park. Occupants share a front door. The floor plan's unique feature is the placement of chimneys—as if the floor plans are reversed—one is at the front, the other is at the rear.

DATE:_______	$:_______	'91	'92	'93	'94	'95	'96
❍ WISH	❍ HAVE	$90	115	100	125	125	135

Sonoma House

Item #	Intro	Retired	OSRP	GBTru	↑
5062-8	1986	1988	$33	**$145**	4%

Particulars: Building exhibits the flavor of the Southwest with stucco walls and red roof. The decorative curved front rises 2 ½ stories. A square turret adjacent to the front door is capped by the same decorative design which also repeats on the chimney. Early release to Gift Creations Concepts (GCC), Fall 1985.

DATE:_______	$:_______	'91	'92	'93	'94	'95	'96
❍ WISH	❍ HAVE	$85	110	115	118	120	140

Highland Park House

Item #	Intro	Retired	OSRP	GBTru	NO
5063-6	1986	1988	$35	**$160**	CHANGE

Particulars: Brick, timbered, and gabled house brings English Tudor design to cozy home. Rounded arch front door repeats theme in two windows in mid-roof gable. Brick chimney on side. Early release to Gift Creations Concepts (GCC), Fall 1986.

DATE:_______	$:_______	'91	'92	'93	'94	'95	'96
❍ WISH	❍ HAVE	$100	105	120	150	150	160

Beacon Hill House

Item #	Intro	Retired	OSRP	GBTru	↑
5065-2	1986	1988	$31	**$175**	6%

Particulars: A green with black roof row house, typical of urban Boston, MA neighborhoods. Home features bay windows on first and second story highlighted by paneled framing.

DATE:_______ $:_______

❍ WISH ❍ HAVE

'91	'92	'93	'94	'95	'96
$95	120	150	165	150	165

Pacific Heights House

Item #	Intro	Retired	OSRP	GBTru	↓
5066-0	1986	1988	$33	**$100**	5%

Particulars: A beige with tan roof West Coast row house that appears tall and narrow due to the vertical theme of the front porch balcony support columns.

DATE:_______ $:_______

❍ WISH ❍ HAVE

'91	'92	'93	'94	'95	'96
$115	90	95	100	100	105

Ramsey Hill House

Item #	Intro	Retired	OSRP	GBTru	↑
5067-9	1986	1989	$36	**$100**	5%

Particulars: Victorian home with double chimneys. There are steps to the front door and a porch adjacent to the entry. The side door also features a small porch. A low balustrade fronts the second story windows. Hand painting adds detailing to the design. Early release to Gift Creations Concepts (GCC), Fall 1986. The early release piece colors are more vibrant.

DATE:_______ $:_______

❍ WISH ❍ HAVE

'91	'92	'93	'94	'95	'96
$90	96	96	98	95	95

Saint James Church

Item #	Intro	Retired	OSRP	GBTru	↑
5068-7	1986	1988	$37	**$160**	3%

Particulars: Church with long central nave flanked by lower roofed side sections fronted by two towers. The main center cross is reinforced by smaller crosses on each section of the tower roof. Smaller round side windows repeat the central window shape.

DATE:_______ $:_______

❍ WISH ❍ HAVE

'91	'92	'93	'94	'95	'96
$105	140	170	160	175	155

ALL SAINTS CHURCH

ITEM #	INTRO	RETIRED	OSRP	GBTRU	NO CHANGE
5070-9	1986	CURRENT	$38	**$45**	

Particulars: A small country church with simple design of long nave and entry door in the base of the bell tower. The same Item # was used for the 1980 *Colonial Farm House.*

DATE:_______	$:_______	'91	'92	'93	'94	'95	'96
❍ WISH	❍ HAVE	$45	45	45	45	45	45

CARRIAGE HOUSE

ITEM #	INTRO	RETIRED	OSRP	GBTRU	↑
5071-7	1986	1988	$29	**$125**	9%

Particulars: A small converted home from a building originally used to house carriages. A second story is achieved with many dormer windows. The fieldstone foundation allowed great weight when it was used for carriages. The same Item # was used for the 1980 *Town Church.*

DATE:_______	$:_______	'91	'92	'93	'94	'95	'96
❍ WISH	❍ HAVE	$95	110	110	110	110	115

TOY SHOP

ITEM #	INTRO	RETIRED	OSRP	GBTRU	↑
5073-3	1986	1990	$36	**$95**	6%

Particulars: The shop's front windows display toys while the roof molding draws attention to the teddy bear under the pediment. This Main Street design is based on the Finch Building in Hastings, MN.

DATE:_______	$:_______	'91	'92	'93	'94	'95	'96
❍ WISH	❍ HAVE	$75	100	95	90	90	90

APOTHECARY

ITEM #	INTRO	RETIRED	OSRP	GBTRU	↑
5076-8	1986	1990	$34	**$105**	5%

Particulars: This Main Street design is based on the former City Hall in Hastings, MN. Two doors flank a central display bow window. A mortar and pestle, symbolizing the profession of the proprietor, is on the front panel above the second floor family quarters windows. Some sleeves read "Antique Shop." The same Item # was used for the 1981 *Corner Store.*

DATE:_______	$:_______	'91	'92	'93	'94	'95	'96
❍ WISH	❍ HAVE	$70	92	92	85	90	100

BAKERY

ITEM #	INTRO	RETIRED	OSRP	GBTRU	↑
5077-6	1986	1991	$35	**$90**	6%

Particulars: This Main Street design is based on the Scofield Building in Northfield, MN. The corner bakery has two large multi-paned display windows protected by a ribbed canopy. Greek key designs around the roof edging highlight the bas-relief cupcake topped by a cherry that is centrally placed over the entry. The same Item # was used for the first Snow Village *Bakery* in 1981.

DATE:_______	$:_______	'91	'92	'93	'94	'95	'96
❍ WISH	❍ HAVE	$37.50	80	70	80	85	85

DINER

ITEM #	INTRO	RETIRED	OSRP	GBTRU	↑
5078-4	1986	1987	$22	**$655**	1%

Particulars: Also known as "Mickey's." Designed after Mickey's Diner in St. Paul, MN. Diners are an eating place based on the railroads' famous dining cars with a reputation for good, wholesome food. The glass block entry protects diners from the weather. Available for only one year. The same Item # was used for the 1981 *English Church.*

DATE:_______	$:_______	'91	'92	'93	'94	'95	'96
❍ WISH	❍ HAVE	$270	420	425	530	550	650

ST. ANTHONY HOTEL & POST OFFICE

ITEM #	INTRO	RETIRED	OSRP	GBTRU	↓
5006-7	1987	1989	$40	**$105**	9%

Particulars: This Main Street design three-story red brick building with green trim is dated "1886" and has an address of "56 Main Street." An American flag flies outside the ground floor of the Post Office. Metal flag is separate.

DATE:_______	$:_______	'91	'92	'93	'94	'95	'96
❍ WISH	❍ HAVE	$85	100	110	115	110	115

SNOW VILLAGE FACTORY

ITEM #	INTRO	RETIRED	OSRP	GBTRU	↑
5013-0	1987	1989	$45	**$135**	4%

Particulars: Set of 2. Smokestack is separate. The wood building rises on a stone block base with a tall smokestack at the rear. Factory products are sold in the small shop in the front.

DATE:_______	$:_______	'91	'92	'93	'94	'95	'96
❍ WISH	❍ HAVE	$90	105	110	110	120	130

Cathedral Church

Item #	Intro	Retired	OSRP	GBTru	↑
5019-9	1987	1990	$50	**$110**	5%

Particulars: Second of two OSV Cathedral Churches. (See also 1980, #5067-4.) Cathedral has mosaic "stained glass" decorating the Gothic windows on all sides as well as the large turret. Same Item # was used for the 1982 *Street Car.*

DATE:________ $:________ ❍ WISH ❍ HAVE

'91	'92	'93	'94	'95	'96
$85	110	110	110	100	105

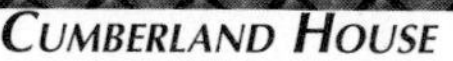

Cumberland House

Item #	Intro	Retired	OSRP	GBTru	↑
5024-5	1987	1995	$42	**$75**	15%

Particulars: Large garland decorated house has multi-colored roof supported by four columns, two chimneys and shuttered windows. The same Item # was used for the 1982 *Bank.*

DATE:________ $:________ ❍ WISH ❍ HAVE

'91	'92	'93	'94	'95	'96
$44	44	45	45	45	65

Springfield House

Item #	Intro	Retired	OSRP	GBTru	
5027-0	1987	1990	$40	**$80**	NO CHANGE

Particulars: Williamsburg blue clapboard home's lower level has two multi-paned bay windows—one is bowed. The upper level windows are shuttered. Roof dormers are half-circle sunbursts. A stone chimney completes this house.

DATE:________ $:________ ❍ WISH ❍ HAVE

'91	'92	'93	'94	'95	'96
$90	100	85	100	75	80

Lighthouse

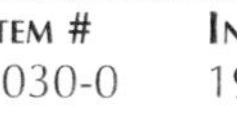

Item #	Intro	Retired	OSRP	GBTru	↓
5030-0	1987	1988	$36	**$595**	2%

Particulars: A favorite with collectors. Five-story lighthouse beacon rises from sturdy stone slab base and is connected to a caretaker's cottage. There are two versions of the piece. One has a white unglazed tower, the other has an off-white glazed tower.

DATE:________ $:________ ❍ WISH ❍ HAVE

'91	'92	'93	'94	'95	'96
$255	340	340	650	595	605

Red Barn

Item #	Intro	Retired	OSRP	GBTru	No Change
5081-4	1987	1992	$38	$85	

Particulars: Wooden barn has stone base, double cross-buck doors on the long side, and hayloft above the main doors. There are three ventilator cupolas on the roof ridge. A cat sleeps in the hayloft. The same Item # was used for the 1982 *Gabled House.* Early release to Gift Creations Concepts (GCC).

DATE:________ $:________ ❍ WISH ❍ HAVE

'91	'92	'93	'94	'95	'96
$42	42	75	75	75	85

Jefferson School

Item #	Intro	Retired	OSRP	GBTru	↑
5082-2	1987	1991	$36	$170	10%

Particulars: A two-room schoolhouse with large multi-paned windows with top transoms. There's a short bell tower incorporated into the roof. The same Item # was used for the 1982 *Flower Shop.* Early release to Gift Creations Concepts (GCC).

DATE:________ $:________ ❍ WISH ❍ HAVE

'91	'92	'93	'94	'95	'96
$40	90	108	115	145	155

Farm House

Item #	Intro	Retired	OSRP	GBTru	No Change
5089-0	1987	1992	$40	$75	

Particulars: A 2 ½-story wood frame home with front full-length porch. The roof interest is two low peaks, one high peak with attic window in highest peak.

DATE:________ $:________ ❍ WISH ❍ HAVE

'91	'92	'93	'94	'95	'96
$44	45	70	75	65	75

Fire Station No. 2

Item #	Intro	Retired	OSRP	GBTru	↓
5091-1	1987	1989	$40	$200	9%

Particulars: Fire Station has two large double doors housing two engines, the side stair leads to living quarters. It's a brick building with a stone arch design at engine doors and front windows. Early release to Gift Creations Concepts (GCC).

DATE:________ $:________ ❍ WISH ❍ HAVE

'91	'92	'93	'94	'95	'96
$70	120	140	140	185	220

Snow Village Resort Lodge

Item #	Intro	Retired	OSRP	GBTru	No Change
5092-0	1987	1989	$55	$145	

Particulars: Bright yellow and green lodge with scalloped roof, covered porch and side entry. There are bay windows on the front house section. The back section rises to dormered 3 ½ stories. Ventilator areas are directly under the roof cap.

DATE:_______ $:_______ ❍ WISH ❍ HAVE

'91	'92	'93	'94	'95	'96
$100	120	120	120	140	145

Village Market

Item #	Intro	Retired	OSRP	GBTru	No Change
5044-0	1988	1991	$39	$75	

Particulars: Silk-screened "glass" windows detail the merchandise available at the market. A red and white canopy protects shoppers using the in/out doors. There's a sign over the second story windows. The color varies from mint green to cream. Sisal tree on top is separate. Early release to Gift Creations Concepts (GCC).

DATE:_______ $:_______ ❍ WISH ❍ HAVE

'91	'92	'93	'94	'95	'96
$40	85	74	75	65	75

Kenwood House

Item #	Intro	Retired	OSRP	GBTru	No Change
5054-7	1988	1990	$50	$130	

Particulars: Three-story home has an old-fashioned wraparound veranda with arched openings. The front facade features scalloped shingles on third story. Early release to Gift Creations Concepts (GCC).

DATE:_______ $:_______ ❍ WISH ❍ HAVE

'91	'92	'93	'94	'95	'96
$100	105	105	100	125	130

Maple Ridge Inn

Item #	Intro	Retired	OSRP	GBTru	No Change
5121-7	1988	1990	$55	$75	

Particulars: Inn is a replica of a Victorian mansion. The ornamental roof piece concealed lightning rods. This piece is an interpretation of an American landmark in Cambridge, NY. 1991 Gift Creations Concepts (GCC) Catalog Exclusive at $75.00.

DATE:_______ $:_______ ❍ WISH ❍ HAVE

'91	'92	'93	'94	'95	'96
$100	98	92	75	65	75

Village Station And Train

Item #	Intro	Retired	OSRP	GBTru	↓
5122-5	1988	1992	$65	**$110**	4%

Particulars: Set of 4. The third Original Snow Village train and station design. Station features an outside ticket window, soft drink vending machine and outside benches. The three train cars do not light.

DATE:________ $:________ ❍ WISH ❍ HAVE

'91	'92	'93	'94	'95	'96
$70	70	105	105	100	115

Cobblestone Antique Shop

Item #	Intro	Retired	OSRP	GBTru	↑
5123-3	1988	1992	$36	**$75**	7%

Particulars: The silk-screened front windows display antiques for sale and a bay window fills the second story width. A building date of "1881" is on the arched cornice.

DATE:________ $:________ ❍ WISH ❍ HAVE

'91	'92	'93	'94	'95	'96
$37.50	37.50	65	70	65	70

Corner Cafe

Item #	Intro	Retired	OSRP	GBTru	↑
5124-1	1988	1991	$37	**$100**	11%

Particulars: There's "Pie" and "Coffee" silkscreened on the windows of this corner restaurant with red, white, and blue striped awnings. A building date of "1875" is inscribed on the turret.

DATE:________ $:________ ❍ WISH ❍ HAVE

'91	'92	'93	'94	'95	'96
$37.50	75	75	80	90	90

Single Car Garage

Item #	Intro	Retired	OSRP	GBTru	No Change
5125-0	1988	1990	$22	**$55**	

Particulars: Double doors open to house the car, there are two outside lights for safety and convenience. Designed to look like a house, the windows have shutters and the roof has dormers. The roof projects over a wood pile keeping it dry.

DATE:________ $:________ ❍ WISH ❍ HAVE

'91	'92	'93	'94	'95	'96
$50	50	50	65	50	55

Home Sweet Home/ House & Windmill

Item #	Intro	Retired	OSRP	GBTru	NO CHANGE
5126-8	1988	1991	$60	**$120**	

Particulars: Set of 2. Inspired by the East Hampton, NY landmark historic home of John Howard Payne, composer of "Home Sweet Home." The saltbox home has an asymmetrical arrangement of windows. Doors for root cellar are at the front corner and there's one central brick chimney. The four-bladed metal windmill is separate.

DATE:_______	$:_______	'91	'92	'93	'94	'95	'96
❍ WISH	❍ HAVE	$60	105	105	110	115	120

Redeemer Church

Item #	Intro	Retired	OSRP	GBTru	NO CHANGE
5127-6	1988	1992	$42	**$70**	

Particulars: The stone corners add strength and support to this church and bell tower. Arched windows and heavy wooden double doors complete the design.

DATE:_______	$:_______	'91	'92	'93	'94	'95	'96
❍ WISH	❍ HAVE	$45	45	74	75	60	70

Service Station

Item #	Intro	Retired	OSRP	GBTru	↓
5128-4	1988	1991	$37.50	**$265**	10%

Particulars: More commonly known as "Bill's Service Station." Set of 2 includes building and gas pumps. Pumps do not light. There's a big difference in the Secondary Market Price if the pumps are missing. Bill's has a candy machine, restroom, work area and office.

DATE:_______	$:_______	'91	'92	'93	'94	'95	'96
❍ WISH	❍ HAVE	$37.50	90	112	165	295	295

Stonehurst House

Item #	Intro	Retired	OSRP	GBTru	NO CHANGE
5140-3	1988	1994	$37.50	**$65**	

Particulars: Home of red brick punctuated with black and white painted bricks. The half circle sunburst design second story dormers restate the arch shape of the first floor windows.

DATE:_______	$:_______	'91	'92	'93	'94	'95	'96
❍ WISH	❍ HAVE	$37.50	37.50	37.50	37.50	60	65

Palos Verdes

Item #	Intro	Retired	OSRP	GBTru	NO CHANGE
5141-1	1988	1990	$37.50	**$85**	

Particulars: Spanish style stucco home with green tiled roof covered entry porch, and second floor shuttered windows. Coming forward from the main wing is a two-story round turret and ground floor window alcove. There's a separate potted miniature sisal tree on the porch.

DATE:_______ $:_______

❍ WISH ❍ HAVE

'91	'92	'93	'94	'95	'96
$60	85	75	75	80	85

Jingle Belle Houseboat

Item #	Intro	Retired	OSRP	GBTru	↑
5114-4	1989	1991	$42	**$150**	30%

Particulars: This floating house sports a Christmas tree on the wheelhouse roof and rear deck. The boat's name is stenciled on the bow and life preservers. The stamped metal bell that hangs on the side is separate and often lost.

DATE:_______ $:_______

❍ WISH ❍ HAVE

'91	'92	'93	'94	'95	'96
$42	90	80	80	100	11[illegible]

Colonial Church

Item #	Intro	Retired	OSRP	GBTru	↓
5119-5	1989	1992	$60	**$70**	13%

Particulars: Church has front entry with four floor-to-roof columns supporting the roof over the porch. The front facade repeats the design with four half columns set into the wall. A metal cross tops the three-tier steeple bell tower. Early release to Gift Creations Concepts (GCC).

DATE:_______ $:_______

❍ WISH ❍ HAVE

'91	'92	'93	'94	'95	'96
$60	60	85	75	75	80

North Creek Cottage

Item #	Intro	Retired	OSRP	GBTru	↓
5120-9	1989	1992	$45	**$65**	7%

Particulars: Cape cod style home with a colonial columned front porch. In addition, there's an attached garage with a deck on top, a front dormer and stone chimney. Early release to Gift Creations Concepts (GCC).

DATE:_______ $:_______

❍ WISH ❍ HAVE

'91	'92	'93	'94	'95	'96
$45	45	70	65	55	7[illegible]

Paramount Theater

Item #	Intro	Retired	OSRP	GBTru	↑
5142-0	1989	1993	$42	**$160**	28%

Particulars: The theater is a Spanish theme Art Deco building with double marques. A ticket booth in the center is flanked by two double doors. Corner billboards advertise "White Christmas" is *Now Showing* and "It's A Wonderful Life" is *Coming Soon*.

DATE:_______ $:_______

❍ WISH ❍ HAVE

'91	'92	'93	'94	'95	'96
$42	42	42	78	85	125

Doctor's House

Item #	Intro	Retired	OSRP	GBTru	↑
5143-8	1989	1992	$56	**$105**	5%

Particulars: The Doctor's home and office are within this house. A rounded turret completes the front. The three-story building has arched, porthole, and bay windows to add to its Victorian charm.

DATE:_______ $:_______

❍ WISH ❍ HAVE

'91	'92	'93	'94	'95	'96
$56	56	85	85	95	100

Courthouse

Item #	Intro	Retired	OSRP	GBTru	↑
5144-6	1989	1993	$65	**$180**	20%

Particulars: Courthouse has four corner roof turrets with a central clock tower, windows with half-circle sunbursts, decorative molding on the second story with two front windows being clear half-circles. The design is based on the Gibson County Courthouse in Princetown, IN.

DATE:_______ $:_______

❍ WISH ❍ HAVE

'91	'92	'93	'94	'95	'96
$65	65	65	110	125	150

Village Warming House

Item #	Intro	Retired	OSRP	GBTru	↓
5145-4	1989	1992	$42	**$65**	7%

Particulars: Used by skaters to warm up from the chill, this small red house has a steep front roof. The bench at the side is available for a brief rest. Sisal trees detach.

DATE:_______ $:_______

❍ WISH ❍ HAVE

'91	'92	'93	'94	'95	'96
$42	42	70	60	60	70

J. Young's Granary

Item #	Intro	Retired	OSRP	GBTru	↑
5149-7	1989	1992	$45	**$80**	7%

Particulars: Granary has a central water wheel for grinding grain, a stone silo on one side and a small store and storage area on other side. Named for Julia Young, a Department 56 retailer in New Jersey.

DATE:_______ $:_______ ❍ WISH ❍ HAVE

'91	'92	'93	'94	'95	'96
$45	45	65	75	65	75

Pinewood Log Cabin

Item #	Intro	Retired	OSRP	GBTru	No Change
5150-0	1989	1995	$37.50	**$60**	

Particulars: Cabin of log construction with two fireplaces for heating and cooking, tree trunk porch pillars, firewood stack and attached tree. The house name appears on the sign above the porch. Early release to Gift Creations Concepts (GCC), Fall 1990.

DATE:_______ $:_______ ❍ WISH ❍ HAVE

'91	'92	'93	'94	'95	'96
$37.50	37.50	37.50	37.50	37.50	60

56 Flavors Ice Cream Parlor

Item #	Intro	Retired	OSRP	GBTru	↑
5151-9	1990	1992	$42	**$145**	38%

Particulars: Ice cream parlor is decorated like a sundae. Peppermint pillars flank the door, there's a sugar cone roof with a cherry on its peak and window boxes hold ice cream cones. Cherry and stem on top are extremely fragile. Early release to Gift Creations Concepts (GCC).

DATE:_______ $:_______ ❍ WISH ❍ HAVE

'91	'92	'93	'94	'95	'96
$42	45	78	80	80	105

Morningside House

Item #	Intro	Retired	OSRP	GBTru	↓
5152-7	1990	1992	$45	**$60**	8%

Particulars: Home is a pink split level house with one car garage. It has a fieldstone chimney, curved front steps and terraced landscaping with removable sisal trees.

DATE:_______ $:_______ ❍ WISH ❍ HAVE

'91	'92	'93	'94	'95	'96
$45	45	55	50	50	65

Mainstreet Hardware Store

Item #	Intro	Retired	OSRP	GBTru	↑
5153-5	1990	1993	$42	**$80**	7%

Particulars: A three-story building with the store on the ground level. Access to the rental rooms on the second and third story is by the outside staircase. The store was originally photographed with blue awnings and window trim, however production pieces had green awnings and trim.

DATE:_______ $:_______ ❍ WISH ❍ HAVE

'91	'92	'93	'94	'95	'96
$42	42	42	55	65	75

Village Realty

Item #	Intro	Retired	OSRP	GBTru	↓
5154-3	1990	1993	$42	**$70**	7%

Particulars: The two-story main building houses a real estate office. A front bay display window showcases available properties. "J. Saraceno" over the door is a tribute to D56's late National Sales Manager. The small adjacent building is an intimate Italian dining place with colorful striped awning.

DATE:_______ $:_______ ❍ WISH ❍ HAVE

'91	'92	'93	'94	'95	'96
$42	42	42	60	70	75

Spanish Mission Church

Item #	Intro	Retired	OSRP	GBTru	↑
5155-1	1990	1992	$42	**$80**	7%

Particulars: Sun-dried clay creates this adobe Spanish style church. The arcade along one side gives protected access. Designed after the Enga Memorial Chapel In Minneapolis, MN.

DATE:_______ $:_______ ❍ WISH ❍ HAVE

'91	'92	'93	'94	'95	'96
$42	42	72	72	60	75

Prairie House

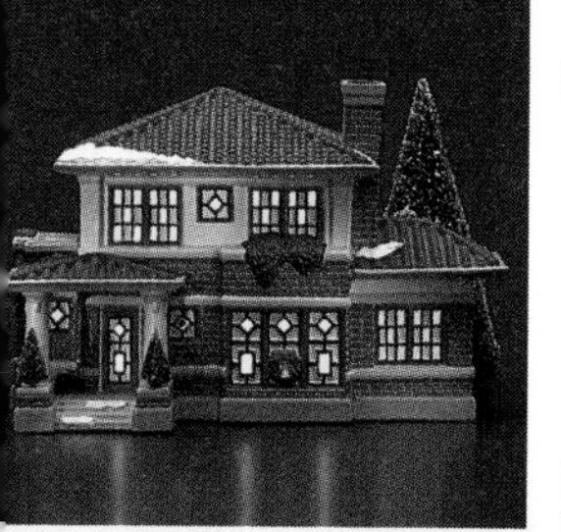

Item #	Intro	Retired	OSRP	GBTru	
5156-0	1990	1993	$42	**$70**	NO CHANGE

Particulars: Two-story home with upper floor set in and back atop the first story. A large chimney rises up through the first story. Two large pillars support the covered entry with separate, removable sisal trees on either side. Part of the American Architecture Series.

DATE:_______ $:_______ ❍ WISH ❍ HAVE

'91	'92	'93	'94	'95	'96
$42	42	44	50	60	70

Queen Anne Victorian

Item #	Intro	Retired	OSRP	GBTru	↑
5157-8	1990	1996	$48	**$65**	30%

Particulars: Broad steps lead up to a pillared porch with a unique corner gazebo style sitting area. An ornate turret on the corner of the second story is decorated with scalloped shingles. Part of the American Architecture Series.

DATE:_______	$:_______	'91	'92	'93	'94	'95	'96
❍ WISH	❍ HAVE	$48	48	50	50	50	50

The Christmas Shop

Item #	Intro	Retired	OSRP	GBTru	↑
5097-0	1991	1996	$37.50	**$60**	60%

Particulars: Pediment on the brick building advertises the holiday, the French "NOEL." There's a large teddy bear by the front window. Early release to Gift Creations Concepts (GCC) and Showcase Dealers.

DATE:_______	$:_______	'91	'92	'93	'94	'95	'96
❍ WISH	❍ HAVE	$37.50	37.50	37.50	37.50	37.50	37.50

Oak Grove Tudor

Item #	Intro	Retired	OSRP	GBTru	No Change
5400-3	1991	1994	$42	**$65**	

Particulars: Red brick base with stucco and timbered second-story home. There's a fireplace of brick and stone by the entry door. Rough stone frames the door and foundation. Early release to Showcase Dealers.

DATE:_______	$:_______	'91	'92	'93	'94	'95	'96
❍ WISH	❍ HAVE	$42	42	42	42	60	65

The Honeymooner Motel

Item #	Intro	Retired	OSRP	GBTru	↑
5401-1	1991	1993	$42	**$80**	14%

Particulars: A moon and stars sign above the office door is an advertisement for the motel. Motel is a white building with blue awnings and doors. There's a soda and ice machine by the office door. Middle class auto travelers were attracted to stay-over facilities that offered privacy and luxury offered by the Mom & Pop enterprises. By the 1940's there were motels coast to coast. Early release to Showcase Dealers.

DATE:_______	$:_______	'91	'92	'93	'94	'95	'96
❍ WISH	❍ HAVE	$42	42	44	75	70	70

Village Greenhouse

Item #	Intro	Retired	OSRP	GBTru	⬇
5402-0	1991	1995	$35	**$65**	13%

Particulars: Plant growing area has bricked bottom and "glass" roof to allow sunlight in. Attached small store sells accessories. It has brick chimney, shingled roof and covered entry.

DATE:_______ $:_______ ❍ WISH ❍ HAVE

'91	'92	'93	'94	'95	'96
$35	35	36	36	36	75

Southern Colonial

Item #	Intro	Retired	OSRP	GBTru	
5403-8	1991	1994	$48	**$75**	No Change

Particulars: Four columns rise from the ground to the roof with a second-story veranda across the front. Double chimneys are surrounded by a balustrade. Shutters by each window both decorate and shut out the heat of the sun. Two urns flank steps of entryway. Part of the American Architecture Series.

DATE:_______ $:_______ ❍ WISH ❍ HAVE

'91	'92	'93	'94	'95	'96
$48	48	50	50	65	75

Gothic Farmhouse

Item #	Intro	Retired	OSRP	GBTru	
5404-6	1991	Current	$48	**$48**	No Change

Particulars: Clapboard home with diamond patterned roof shingles has columned front porch and entry. The first floor has a large bay window. The second story rises to a gable with carved molding which is repeated on the two dormer windows over the porch. Part of the American Architecture Series.

DATE:_______ $:_______ ❍ WISH ❍ HAVE

'91	'92	'93	'94	'95	'96
$48	48	48	48	48	48

Finklea's Finery Costume Shop

Item #	Intro	Retired	OSRP	GBTru	
5405-4	1991	1993	$45	**$60**	No Change

Particulars: Dressed stone trims the facade of the three-story brick building. There are red awnings over the first floor display windows and a hood projects over the third-floor piano teacher's windows. The attached side setback is two stories with a decorated rental return door and an awning on upper window.

DATE:_______ $:_______ ❍ WISH ❍ HAVE

'91	'92	'93	'94	'95	'96
$45	45	45	70	55	60

Jack's Corner Barber Shop

Item #	Intro	Retired	OSRP	GBTru	⬆
5406-2	1991	1994	$42	**$70**	8%

Particulars: The barber shop also houses M. Schmitt Photography Studio and a second-floor tailor shop. A two-story turret separates two identical wings of the brick building. The fantail window design is repeated on the doors and on roof peaks. M. Schmitt is in honor of D56 photographer, Matthew Schmitt.

DATE:______	$:______	'91	'92	'93	'94	'95	'96
❍ WISH	❍ HAVE	$42	42	42	42	55	65

Double Bungalow

Item #	Intro	Retired	OSRP	GBTru	
5407-0	1991	1994	$45	**$65**	NO CHANGE

Particulars: An early two-family home—double entry doors, each side has bow window downstairs, a roof dormer, and own chimney. A brick facade dresses up the clapboard house.

DATE:______	$:______	'91	'92	'93	'94	'95	'96
❍ WISH	❍ HAVE	$45	45	45	45	55	65

Grandma's Cottage

Item #	Intro	Retired	OSRP	GBTru	⬆
5420-8	1992	1996	$42	**$65**	44%

Particulars: A small porch is nestled between two identical house sections. Each section has a hooded double window, flanked by evergreens. Chimneys rise off the main roof. Early release to Gift Creations Concepts (GCC).

DATE:______	$:______	'92	'93	'94	'95	'96
❍ WISH	❍ HAVE	$42	45	45	45	45

St. Luke's Church

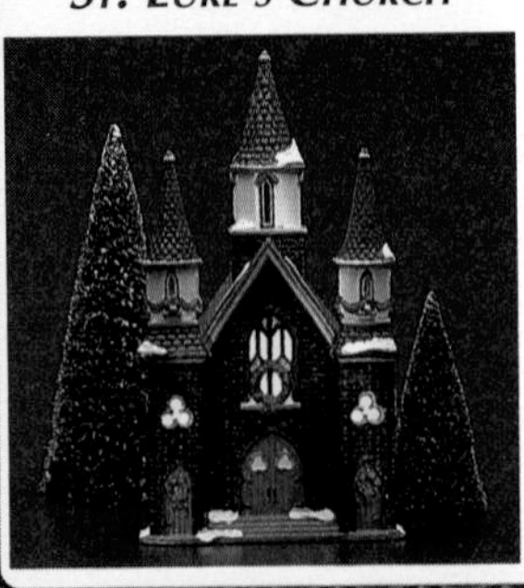

Item #	Intro	Retired	OSRP	GBTru	⬇
5421-6	1992	1994	$45	**$65**	7%

Particulars: Brick church features three square based steeples. The central steeple rises off the nave roof. The side steeples have doors at their base and are at the front corners of church. Trefoil designs on either side are repeated on the center main entry doors. Early release to Gift Creations Concepts (GCC).

DATE:______	$:______	'92	'93	'94	'95	'96
❍ WISH	❍ HAVE	$45	45	45	60	70

Village Post Office

Item #	Intro	Retired	OSRP	GBTru	NO CHANGE
5422-4	1992	1995	$35	**$70**	

Particulars: Doric columns support porch to the double entry doors. Building is a two-story brick with a two-story turret rising above the sign. A Greek key incised design separates the stories. Early release to Showcase Dealers.

DATE:_______ $:_______
❍ WISH ❍ HAVE

'92	'93	'94	'95	'96
$35	37.50	37.50	37.50	70

Al's TV Shop

Item #	Intro	Retired	OSRP	GBTru	NO CHANGE
5423-2	1992	1995	$40	**$65**	

Particulars: TV Shop has antenna on the roof. There are red awnings on the upper windows and a red canopy over the lower display window. The store entry is on the corner of the building.

DATE:_______ $:_______
❍ WISH ❍ HAVE

'92	'93	'94	'95	'96
$40	40	40	40	65

Good Shepherd Chapel & Church School

Item #	Intro	Retired	OSRP	GBTru	↑
5424-0	1992	1996	$72	**$95**	32%

Particulars: Set of 2. The white chapel with a red roof rises on a stone base and has a steeple at the front entry. The church school has double doors, tall windows, a small bell tower, and a stone chimney on the side. The church side door meets the school side door.

DATE:_______ $:_______
❍ WISH ❍ HAVE

'92	'93	'94	'95	'96
$72	72	72	72	72

Print Shop & Village News

Item #	Intro	Retired	OSRP	GBTru	↑
5425-9	1992	1994	$37.50	**$70**	17%

Particulars: The stone in the front pediment notes a "1893" construction date. A symmetrical building design is emphasized by double chimneys, matching windows and columns. The brick building also houses a Muffin Shop.

DATE:_______ $:_______
❍ WISH ❍ HAVE

'92	'93	'94	'95	'96
$37.50	37.50	37.50	55	60

Hartford House

Item #	Intro	Retired	OSRP	GBTru	
5426-7	1992	1995	$55	$80	No Change

Particulars: Home has a steeply pitched roof with an ornate front covered entry pediment design which is repeated in the steep front gable. Molding surrounds windows and is on the side porch columns.

DATE:_______ $:_______

❍ WISH ❍ HAVE

'92	'93	'94	'95	'96
$55	55	55	55	80

Village Vet And Pet Shop

Item #	Intro	Retired	OSRP	GBTru	
5427-5	1992	1995	$32	$65	No Change

Particulars: Building has arched crescents over picture windows that are screened designs depicting dogs, kittens, fish and birds. An ornamental molding outlines the roof edge. A dog sits on the entry steps to the Vet's Office. In first shipments hand lettered sign was misspelled "Vetrinary."

DATE:_______ $:_______

❍ WISH ❍ HAVE

'92	'93	'94	'95	'96
$32	32	32	32	65

Craftsman Cottage

Item #	Intro	Retired	OSRP	GBTru	
5437-2	1992	1995	$55	$75	No Change

Particulars: A stone based porch extends across the front of the house ending in a stone chimney. Large squared pillars are part of the support for the second story room above the entryway. There's a small dormer by chimney. Part of the American Architecture Series.

DATE:_______ $:_______

❍ WISH ❍ HAVE

'92	'93	'94	'95	'96
$55	55	55	55	75

Village Station

Item #	Intro	Retired	OSRP	GBTru	
5438-0	1992	Current	$65	$65	No Change

Particulars: A clock tower rises on one side of the two-story red brick station. The platform sign behind a stack of luggage announces arrivals and departures. The many-windowed waiting room for travelers extends the length of the station.

DATE:_______ $:_______

❍ WISH ❍ HAVE

'92	'93	'94	'95	'96
$65	65	65	65	65

Airport

Item #	Intro	Retired	OSRP	GBTru	↑
5439-9	1992	1996	$60	**$75**	25%

Particulars: The airport's semicircular vaulted roof extends the length of the plane hangar with the control tower rising off the central rear of the building. A one-engine prop plane sits in the hangar entrance. There's a fuel tank pump at the corner, plus thermometer, and a crop dusting schedule. The door at the opposite front corner is for passengers and freight business.

DATE:_______ $:_______
❍ WISH ❍ HAVE

'92	'93	'94	'95	'96
$60	60	60	60	60

Nantucket Renovation

Item #	Intro	Retired	OSRP	GBTru	No Change
5441-0	1993	1993 Annual	$55	**$75**	

Particulars: Available for one year only through retailers who carried Snow Village in 1986, Showcase Dealers and select buying groups. For the original *Nantucket* see 1978, Item #5014-6, page 19. Special box and hang tag. Blueprints of the renovation included.

DATE:_______ $:_______
❍ WISH ❍ HAVE

'93	'94	'95	'96
$55	105	70	75

Mount Olivet Church

Item #	Intro	Retired	OSRP	GBTru	↑
5442-9	1993	1996	$65	**$80**	23%

Particulars: Handsome brick church with large circular stained glass window above double door entry. Square bell tower with steeple roof. Smaller stained glass window design repeated on side chapel entry.

DATE:_______ $:_______
❍ WISH ❍ HAVE

'93	'94	'95	'96
$65	65	65	65

Village Public Library

Item #	Intro	Retired	OSRP	GBTru	No Change
5443-7	1993	Current	$55	**$55**	

Particulars: Sturdy brick and stone building with four Greek columns supporting the front portico. Entry is from the side steps through the double doors. A brick cupola rises from the center of the roof.

DATE:_______ $:_______
❍ WISH ❍ HAVE

'93	'94	'95	'96
$55	55	55	55

Woodbury House

Item #	Intro	Retired	OSRP	GBTru	↑
5444-5	1993	1996	$45	**$65**	44%

Particulars: Turned spindle posts support the front porch of this clapboard home. It has a double gable design with the lower gable featuring two story bow windows. A brick chimney extends through the roof.

DATE:_______ $:_______
❍ WISH ❍ HAVE

'93	'94	'95	'96
$45	45	45	45

Hunting Lodge

Item #	Intro	Retired	OSRP	GBTru	↑
5445-3	1993	1996	$50	**$80**	60%

Particulars: Lodge is a rustic log structure on a stone foundation with stone fireplace. Antlers decorate the front gable above the porch entry. Wreaths and garland add the final touch.

DATE:_______ $:_______
❍ WISH ❍ HAVE

'93	'94	'95	'96
$50	50	50	50

Dairy Barn

Item #	Intro	Retired	OSRP	GBTru	No Change
5446-1	1993	Current	$55	**$55**	

Particulars: Cow barn with attached silo, tin mansard roof and cow weathervane. Silo holds grain for winter feed. Wind-run ventilator fan keeps hay bales from collecting moisture.

DATE:_______ $:_______
❍ WISH ❍ HAVE

'93	'94	'95	'96
$55	55	55	55

Dinah's Drive-In

Item #	Intro	Retired	OSRP	GBTru	↑
5447-0	1993	1996	$45	**$75**	67%

Particulars: A burger in a bun and a bubbly soda top the circular fast food drive-in. As car travel increased, so did a need for informal eating places. A favorite stop for teenagers, children, and parents on a limited budget.

DATE:_______ $:_______
❍ WISH ❍ HAVE

'93	'94	'95	'96
$45	45	45	45

Pack everyone in the car, sit back and relax 'cause we're going to ... DINAH'S DRIVE-IN

Hamburgers, French fries, shakes, ice cream–good ol' American fare. That's what you'll enjoy at Dinah's Drive-In restaurant, one of the very popular Snow Village pieces.

If you were around in the 30's, 40's or 50's, you may remember driving down the street and hoping that your parents would pull into the parking lot of your favorite drive-in. Maybe you sat in your car with some friends or went to have a burger after the hop. Many of us do not realize that the drive-in even dates back that far. Actually, the first one opened its doors in 1921 in Texas. A Dallas tobacco and candy wholesaler, J. G. Kirby, started the trend with The Pig Stand. Mr. Kirby envisioned that, with the proliferation of the automobile, people would want to use any reason to drive. And, as he put it, people with cars would become so lazy, they would not want to get out of their cars to eat.

Well, for whatever reason, he was right in believing that the drive-in would be a hit. Though its concept caught on across the country, nowhere was it more natural than in California. There, the climate favored year 'round service to the cars by carhops–so called because they would hop onto the running boards to take your order. Also, Californians relied heavily on the automobiles because of the long distance from town to town.

Dinah's design resembles that of the California drive-ins very closely; as a matter of fact, it is most similar to Simon's, the first such restaurant on Wilshire Boulevard in Los Angeles. Many drive-ins featured a round or octagon building which allowed the approaching motorist to see much of the building as opposed to just the side of a rectangular structure. Also, once parked at the drive-in, you felt as if you were parked in a prime spot, no matter where you were.

The exterior of the drive-ins was the key to their success. Many times, every flat surface had information designed to entice the motorist to stop in, and once there, eat, eat, eat. Take a look at Dinah's. The name is up high, the area under the extended overhang is ringed with a sampling of the fare, and a portion of the menu is listed in the windows.

The color of the restaurants was often white to show how clean it was, with red or orange accents to attract the attention of the motorist. Nothing was more of an attraction, though, than the drive-ins' most noted feature, the sign or object that topped the buildings. Referred to as "programmation" architecture because of their ability to demand attention, these giant ice cream cones, tea pots, enormous hot dogs and, in the case of Dinah's, a juicy hamburger and frothy shake, could be seen by speeding motorists from a distance, allowing them the time to slow down and turn in. Not the most imaginative, but certainly the most to-the-point eye-catcher was the roof that reached toward the sky like a giant pylon with the words "EAT HERE" blazing in neon.

Keeping in character with the "California-style" drive-in, Dinah's has two doors allowing the people of Snow Village to sit down and relax inside–perhaps listening to the day's popular songs on the jukebox.

So, if you have Dinah's Drive-In, park some cars around it, put on some music that makes you think of the songs that played while you munched on a hamburger or laughed with family and friends, then sit back and remember when ...

the **Village Chronicle.**

Snowy Hills Hospital

Item #	Intro	Retired	OSRP	GBTru	↑
5448-8	1993	1996	$48	$75	56%

Particulars: A brick hospital with steps leading to double main entry doors. The roof of the Emergency entrance drive-up on the side is topped by a Christmas tree. Wreaths decorate the second story windows.

DATE:_______ $:_______
❍ WISH ❍ HAVE

'93	'94	'95	'96
$48	48	48	48

Fisherman's Nook Resort

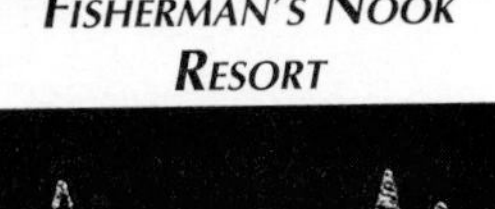

Item #	Intro	Retired	OSRP	GBTru	
5460-7	1994	Current	$75	$75	No Change

Particulars: Building is office for cabin rental, store for bait and gas for boats, plus places for boats to tie up.

DATE:_______ $:_______
❍ WISH ❍ HAVE

'94	'95	'96
$75	75	75

FISHERMAN'S NOOK CABINS

Item #	Intro	Retired	OSRP	GBTru	
5461-5	1994	Current	$50	$50	No Change

Particulars: Set of 2 includes *Fisherman's Nook Bass Cabin* and *Fisherman's Nook Trout Cabin.* Sold only as a set. Midyear release.

see below

DATE:_______ $:_______
❍ WISH ❍ HAVE

'94	'95	'96
$50	50	50

Fisherman's Nook Bass Cabin

Item #	Intro	Retired	OSRP	GBTru
5461-5	1994	Current	*	*

Particulars: 1 of a 2-piece set. *Sold only as a set. See FISHERMAN'S NOOK CABINS. Midyear release. Each cabin named for fish—rustic wood cabin with wood pile and fireplace for heat.

DATE:_______ $:_______
❍ WISH ❍ HAVE

Fisherman's Nook Trout Cabin

Item #	Intro	Retired	OSRP	GBTru
5461-5	1994	Current	*	*

Particulars: 1 of a 2-piece set. *Sold only as a set. See FISHERMAN'S NOOK CABINS. Midyear release. Each cabin named for fish—rustic wood cabin with wood pile and fireplace for heat.

DATE:_______ $:_______
❍ WISH ❍ HAVE

The Original Snow Village Starter Set

Item #	Intro	Retired	OSRP	GBTru	↑
5462-3	1994	1996	$49.99	**$70**	40%

Particulars: Set of 6. Featured at D56 National Open Houses hosted by participating Gift Creation Concepts (GCC) retailers the first weekend in November 1994. Set includes *Shady Oak Church* building, *Sunday School Serenade* accessory, three assorted "bottle-brush" sisal trees, and a bag of Real Plastic Snow.

DATE:_______ $:_______
❍ WISH ❍ HAVE

	'94	'95	'96
$	49.99	50	50

Wedding Chapel

Item #	Intro	Retired	OSRP	GBTru	
5464-0	1994	Current	$55	**$55**	No Change

Particulars: A white clapboard church with a brick tower supporting a wooden steeple. A bell hangs in the tower above the door. The arched windows have green shutters. Attached snow covered tree.

DATE:_______ $:_______
❍ WISH ❍ HAVE

'94	'95	'96
$55	55	55

Federal House

Item #	Intro	Retired	OSRP	GBTru	
5465-8	1994	Current	$50	**$50**	No Change

Particulars: Stately symmetrical brick structure has a white portico and columns at the front door. Roof dormers and four chimneys complete the mirrored effect. The lower windows are decorated with wreaths. Attached snow covered tree. Part of the American Architecture Series.

DATE:_______ $:_______
❍ WISH ❍ HAVE

'94	'95	'96
$50	50	50

Carmel Cottage

Item #	Intro	Retired	OSRP	GBTru	
5466-6	1994	Current	$48	$48	No Change

Particulars: Cottage with stucco walls, a steep pitched roof, dormer on side and chimney at rear. Stone trims the door, side passage and windows.

DATE:________ $:________
❍ WISH ❍ HAVE

'94	'95	'96
$48	48	48

Skate & Ski Shop

Item #	Intro	Retired	OSRP	GBTru	
5467-4	1994	Current	$50	$50	No Change

Particulars: Chalet style shop has stone chimney and slate roof. Timber trims the windows and base.

DATE:________ $:________
❍ WISH ❍ HAVE

'94	'95	'96
$50	50	50

Glenhaven House

Item #	Intro	Retired	OSRP	GBTru	
5468-2	1994	Current	$45	$45	No Change

Particulars: 2 ½-story home with bay windows on first floor. Small porch at entrance. House has formal look with an ornate pediment highlighting the attic windows on the front gable. Two trees attached at the right front corner.

DATE:________ $:________
❍ WISH ❍ HAVE

'94	'95	'96
$45	45	45

Coca-Cola® Brand Bottling Plant

Item #	Intro	Retired	OSRP	GBTru	
5469-0	1994	Current	$65	$65	No Change

Particulars: Large, red Coca-Cola logo sign set on roof above entry doors. Vending machine sits at back of loading dock, two cases sit at front. Two smoke stacks rise from roof near skylights. Prototypes did not have cases of soda on loading dock.

DATE:________ $:________
❍ WISH ❍ HAVE

'94	'95	'96
$65	65	65

Listen closely and you may hear the clinking of glass at the COCA-COLA BOTTLING PLANT

Dr. John Pemberton invented it, Asa Griggs Candler made it famous, Raymond Loewy designed the bottle that would contain it, Robert Woodruff made it an American institution, World War II soldiers longed for it, and it made a southern city world famous. It, of course, is Coca-Cola, one of the three most recognized brand names in the world. (No, Department 56 is not one of the other two.)

Invented in 1886 more as a remedy than as a beverage, Coca-Cola was first sold in Jacob's Pharmacy on Peachtree Street in Atlanta. Its popularity spread quickly throughout the South which had a great number of soda fountains. Dr. Pemberton, cutting out his partners, sold much of the company to Asa Candler. It was Mr. Candler, who after ultimately gaining control of the company, used his keen promotional skills to further develop the soft drink's popularity.

The advertising campaigns were considered to be ingenious for their time. Before the roaring 20's rolled around, "Coca-Cola Men" had painted more than 5 million square feet of billboards. Magazine ads even contained what many people considered risque double-entendres. In the 1930's, the Chicago bottler even used semi-naked women in its advertising that sent shock waves thoughout the country and directly back to Coca-Cola headquarters.

During the war, soldiers who were fortunate enough to receive Coca-Cola said that it was like having a little bit of America overseas.

Now, the country's number one soft drink is the world's number one soft drink. People in nations that a decade ago could only have bought Coca-Cola on the black market are enjoying it. Is it any surprise that D56 has a Coca-Cola Bottling Plant and various accessories?

The building was an instant hit. When it first began to be displayed on dealers' shelves, collectors were in the stores scooping them up. I don't really think that this surprised any one either. These pieces were a sure thing for two reasons. First, Department 56 married its design production capabilities with a highly recognized name that has its own collector base. Second, Snow Village has had a resurgence over the last few years due, in large part, to the broad appeal of the newer buildings.

When you have the opportunity to look at this building, you'll immediately notice a few things. The most obvious is the bright red "Coca-Cola disk" perched high above the double main entrances. The next things that may catch your eye are the twin chimneys and twin skylights that sit atop the roof. Look again and you will see that the building that, at first glance, appears to be symmetrical is not. At the front lower-right corner is a loading dock. Here, the Coca-Cola Delivery Truck is loaded by the Delivery Men and sent on its way to the stores.

If you purchase the Bottling Plant, you may have to think twice about how many trucks and men you will buy to go along with it. Can't you see a few trucks at the plant with men loading them up and a few more trucks scattered around the village delivering cases of soda to stores? It's a natural. I bet D56 sees it just about the same way, too.

Snow Village is definitely a village of Americana now. The next thing you'll know, they will introduce a flag factory and a bakery that specializes in apple pie. (That's meant to be a joke, not a hint.)

the **Village Chronicle.**

Marvel's Beauty Salon

Item #	Intro	Retired	OSRP	GBTru	NO
5470-4	1994	Current	$37.50	**$37.50**	CHANGE

Particulars: Brick first story houses the Beauty Salon where a picture window displays styles. The stucco second story houses a Wig Shop. Named for Marvel Foster who worked for Department 56.

DATE:_______ $:_______
❍ WISH ❍ HAVE

'94	'95	'96
$37.50	37.50	37.5

Christmas Cove Lighthouse

Item #	Intro	Retired	OSRP	GBTru	NO
5483-6	1995	Current	$60	**$60**	CHANGE

Particulars: Ship beacon atop white block tower. Steps leac to brick home of keeper. Attached trees. Midyear release 2-light socket cord. Lift-off top allows access to bulb in tower.

DATE:_______ $:_______
❍ WISH ❍ HAVE

'95	'96
$60	60

Coca–Cola® Brand Corner Drugstore

Item #	Intro	Retired	OSRP	GBTru	NO
5484-4	1995	Current	$55	**$55**	CHANG

Particulars: Oversize Coke bottle and logo sign is advertisement for soda shop in drugstore. Stone trims the corner shop with bow windows and roof cornices. Midyear release.

DATE:_______ $:_______
❍ WISH ❍ HAVE

'95	'96
$55	55

Snow Carnival Ice Palace

Item #	Intro	Retired	OSRP	GBTru	NO
54850	1995	Current	$95	**$95**	CHANC

Particulars: Set of 2. Turrets trim a fantasy frosty ice palace for festival King and Queen. Entry welcome gate with snowy trees leads to the magical creation built of block of ice. Northern American and Canadian cities often have Winter Holiday Festivals with grand ice buildings and sculptures.

DATE:_______ $:_______
❍ WISH ❍ HAVE

'95	'9
$95	9

Pisa Pizza

Item #	Intro	Retired	OSRP	GBTru	
54851	1995	Current	$35	**$35**	No Change

Particulars: A replica of the Leaning Tower of Pisa, a landmark building in Italy, is central design on restaurant. Flanking doors and window have striped canopies.

DATE:_______ $:_______
❍ WISH ❍ HAVE

'95	'96
$36	35

Peppermint Porch Day Care

Item #	Intro	Retired	OSRP	GBTru	
5485-2	1995	Current	$45	**$45**	No Change

Particulars: Day care center in white clapboard house. Mint candy theme on pillars and balcony. Boots, teddy bear on porch. Midyear release. Prototype had "Peppermint Place" as the name on the building.

DATE:_______ $:_______
❍ WISH ❍ HAVE

'95	'96
$45	45

Village Police Station

Item #	Intro	Retired	OSRP	GBTru	
54853	1995	Current	$48	**$48**	No Change

Particulars: The 56th Precinct is housed in a two-story brick building with stone coping capping off the roof edge. Arched windows accent the double entry design. There are awnings on the three upper windows with Department name above. Doughnut shop next door for a quick pick-me-up break.

DATE:_______ $:_______
❍ WISH ❍ HAVE

'95	'96
$48	48

Holly Brothers® Garage

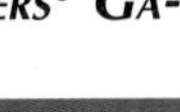

Item #	Intro	Retired	OSRP	GBTru	
54854	1995	Current	$48	**$48**	No Change

Particulars: Gas station with two pumps. Coke machine, wall phone, repair stalls, tires, free air, office and rest rooms are housed in a white building. Owner's name above gas pumps.

DATE:_______ $:_______
❍ WISH ❍ HAVE

'95	'96
$48	48

Ryman Auditorium

Item #	Intro	Retired	OSRP	GBTru	NO
54855	1995	Current	$75	**$75**	CHANGE

Particulars: Nashville's country music auditorium. Featured acts are country western artists.

DATE:_______ $:_______ '95 '96
❍ WISH ❍ HAVE $75 75

Dutch Colonial

Item #	Intro	Retired	OSRP	GBTru	↑
54856	1995	1996	$45	**$70**	56%

Particulars: Second story of colonial home is constructed as part of mansard roof that extends down to first floor level. Shuttered double windows frame front door two steps up from walk. One bedroom accesses an upper balustraded outdoor sitting area. Part of the American Architecture Series.

DATE:_______ $:_______ '95 '96
❍ WISH ❍ HAVE $45 45

Beacon Hill Victorian

Item #	Intro	Retired	OSRP	GBTru	NO
54857	1995	Current	$60	**$60**	CHANGE

Particulars: Covered porch encloses turret structure that rises up entire height of house and features shuttered windows. Brick home with transverse roof has ornate wood molding trim on gables. Snowy fir trees on front corner.

DATE:_______ $:_______ '95 '96
❍ WISH ❍ HAVE $60 60

Bowling Alley

Item #	Intro	Retired	OSRP	GBTru	NO
54858	1995	Current	$42	**$42**	CHANGE

Particulars: Bowling pins and ball atop brick building advertise sports activity within. Pins flank Village Lanes sign above archway of double entry doors. Snowy trees next to entrance.

DATE:_______ $:_______ '95 '96
❍ WISH ❍ HAVE $42 42

Starbucks Coffee

Item #	Intro	Retired	OSRP	GBTru	
54859	1995	Current	$48	**$48**	No Change

Particulars: Corner building features many varieties of coffee and baked treats. Stone structure with starred canopies over upper windows and larger awnings atop windows on street level. Store logo displayed on roof pediment.

DATE:_______ $:_______
❍ WISH ❍ HAVE

'95	'96
$48	48

Nick's Tree Farm

Item #	Intro	Retired	OSRP	GBTru	
54871	1996	Current	$40	**$40**	No Change

Particulars: Set of 10. Midyear release. Small wood hut provides office and warming area for Nick on a farm where he or you can select a live or cut tree. Nick pulls a cut tree on a sled.

DATE:_______ $:_______
❍ WISH ❍ HAVE

'96
$40

Smokey Mountain Retreat

Item #	Intro	Retired	OSRP	GBTru	
54872	1996	Current	$65	**$65**	No Change

Particulars: Midyear release. Log structure with two stone fireplaces has exposed log beams, covered entry and porch areas to hold sleds and outdoor gear. This building debuts a smoking chimney feature. A built-in Magic Smoking Element, powered by a separate transformer, heats a supplied non-toxic liquid causing it to smoke. See Trims, #52620 for refill *Village Magic Smoke*.

DATE:_______ $:_______
❍ WISH ❍ HAVE

'96
$65

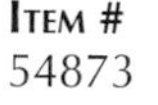

Boulder Springs House

Item #	Intro	Retired	OSRP	GBTru	
54873	1996	Current	$60	**$60**	No Change

Particulars: Midyear release. Clapboard house with 2 ½ stories has covered entry and front porch. Shutters frame front gable windows, attached tree behind side bow window.

DATE:_______ $:_______
❍ WISH ❍ HAVE

'96
$60

Reindeer Bus Depot

Item #	Intro	Retired	OSRP	GBTru	
54874	1996	Current	$42	$42	No Change

Particulars: Depot is two stories with restaurant and waiting room flanking central entry topped by depot name and vertical bus sign. Midyear release.

DATE:_______ $:_______
❍ WISH ❍ HAVE

'96
$42

Rockabilly Records

Item #	Intro	Retired	OSRP	GBTru
54880	1996	Current	$45	$45

Particulars: Art deco styled Rockabilly recording studio and business office. Roof sign created to look like vinyl record. Jukebox design on front building corners highlight coin operated record players found in soda fountains and entertainment areas. Light brick with barrel roll molding between the first and second floor.

DATE:_______ $:_______
❍ WISH ❍ HAVE

Christmas Lake High School

Item #	Intro	Retired	OSRP	GBTru
54881	1996	Current	$52	$52

Particulars: Variegated brick two-story school building has name above double entry doors with dedication date plaque in central roof gable.There are two chimneys where the side wings meet with the central portion of the building. Bell cupola above center gable. Basketball hoop by side entrance.

DATE:_______ $:_______
❍ WISH ❍ HAVE

Birch Run Ski Chalet

Item #	Intro	Retired	OSRP	GBTru
54882	1996	Current	$60	$60

Particulars: Peeled rough hewn logs used for ski lodge. Large fieldstone fireplace provides cozy lounge area after all day skiing. Chalet offers rooms, refreshments and even a first aid station for minor mishaps.

DATE:_______ $:_______
❍ WISH ❍ HAVE

ROSITA'S CANTINA

ITEM #	INTRO	RETIRED	OSRP	GBTRU
54883	1996	CURRENT	$50	**$50**

Particulars: Mexican restaurant in Southwest design to resemble smooth adobe with tile roof invites diners to taste the spicy food guaranteed to warm from the inside-out. El Loco Bar is tucked in at the side for those who want a beverage and a snack instead of dinner.

DATE:_______ $:_______
❍ WISH ❍ HAVE

SHINGLE VICTORIAN

ITEM #	INTRO	RETIRED	OSRP	GBTRU
54884	1996	CURRENT	$55	**$55**

Particulars: Bright blue and white 3-story home with wraparound porch. Top story features dormer windows. Formal living room has triple front window and a bow side window. Double entry doors with diamond shaped glass design. Sawtoothed roof ridge plus two chimneys. Part of the American Architecture Series.

DATE:_______ $:_______
❍ WISH ❍ HAVE

THE SECRET GARDEN FLORIST

ITEM #	INTRO	RETIRED	OSRP	GBTRU
54885	1996	CURRENT	$50	**$50**

Particulars: Canvas awning with silk screened lettering protects front of shop that features display boxes of flower arrangements and plants. Bridal planning is also available upstairs from the shop.

DATE:_______ $:_______
❍ WISH ❍ HAVE

HARLEY-DAVIDSON MOTORCYCLE SHOP

ITEM #	INTRO	RETIRED	OSRP	GBTRU
54886	1996	CURRENT	$65	**$65**

Particulars: Showroom and maintenance shop devoted to 'Hog' devotees. Cycle display on front entry reinforced canopy. Soda can and bottle ice chest and gas pump allow cyclist and cycle to fill-er-up. Repair area with roll up garage door and large disposal drums.

DATE:_______ $:_______
❍ WISH ❍ HAVE

Bachman's Flower Shop

Item #	Intro	Retired	OSRP	GBTru
8802	1997	1997 Annual	$50	**$50**

Particulars: Personalized for Bachman's Village Gathering with a purple canvas awning with silk screened lettering. Former company logo and year of establishment on front of shop. Display boxes with flower arrangements and plants. Bridal planning is also available upstairs.

DATE:________ $:________
❍ WISH ❍ HAVE

Ronald McDonald House (The House that ♥ Built)

Item #	Intro	Retired	OSRP	GBTru
8960	1997	Special	*	**NE**

Particulars: Two-story home with heart-trimmed tree and picket fence decorated with holly. These homes-away-from-home were created for the care and well-being of families of children undergoing treatment at nearby hospitals for very serious illnesses. This is a very limited piece available to1997 Homes For The Holidays participants. *The piece is not for retail sale. They will be raffled at the Homes For The Holidays Event, with proceeds going to the Ronald McDonald Houses.

DATE:________ $:________
❍ WISH ❍ HAVE

Mainstreet Gift Shop

Item #	Intro	Retired	OSRP	GBTru
54887	1997	Current	$50	**$50**

Particulars: An actual Original Snow Village house display is used as a focal point in the acrylic front window of the shop. Only available to Gift Creation Concepts (GCC) dealers to celebrate the 20th Anniversary of GCC. Two medallions come with the piece allowing display of the GCC Dealer logo or it can be personalized with the store name. A special GCC decal bottomstamp will be added to the usual D56 embossed stamp.

DATE:________ $:________
❍ WISH ❍ HAVE

The Original Snow Village Start A Tradition Set

Item #	Intro	Retired	OSRP	GBTru
54902	1997	Current	$100*	**$100**

Particulars: Set of 8. Two lighted buildings. *Kringles Toy Shop* has a revolving front door and acrylic windows. A jack-in-the-box decorates the front facade above the entry doors. *A Hot Chocolate Stand* is in the shape of a mug. Accessories include *Saturday Morning Downtown* where a little girl sips a mug of chocolate while a boy pulls a sled of presents and 2 *trimmed trees in drum bases*. A *Bag of Snow* and a *Cobblestone Road* complete the set which will be available at the Homes For The Holidays Event held 11/1/97 through 11/9/97. *Reduced to $75 during Event.

DATE:________ $:________
❍ WISH ❍ HAVE

OLD CHELSEA MANSION

ITEM #	INTRO	RETIRED	OSRP	GBTRU
54903	1997	CURRENT	$85	**$85**

Particulars: Represents the New York home of Clement Clarke Moore the author of *A Visit From St Nicholas.* Commemorates the 175th Anniversary of the poem. A 32-page hardcover, illustrated, full color book is included. The history of Moore, his home and the poem make this collector's book a Village "first." The brick three-story house has steps at the front entry and a door flanked by columns. Classical proportions produce a stately house.

DATE:________ $:________
❍ WISH ❍ HAVE

NEW HOPE CHURCH

ITEM #	INTRO	RETIRED	OSRP	GBTRU
54904	1997	CURRENT	$60	**$60**

Particulars: Brick church with turret-like tower features acrylic stained glass windows. Community Bingo enthusiasts attend and enjoy an evening out in the company of friends.

DATE:________ $:________
❍ WISH ❍ HAVE

MORE THAN JUST A COLLECTIBLE ... IT'S A HOBBY

Department 56 villages have accomplished something that most collectibles, limited edition type collectibles anyway, cannot. They have transcended the boundaries of their collectible status to be included in a much broader, more common field, a hobby. Its progression is very much the opposite of the model and toy trains, for instance. For the majority of collectors of such items, it was the hobby that drew them in. In time, the collectibility of the product grew from the popularity of the hobby.

Certainly, collecting in itself can be considered a hobby, but that is not the point of this article. The hobby referred to here is that of display making, be it a large, elaborate display, a series of small, independent vignettes or a wooden display built to house one or two favorite pieces.

Think for a moment how displays have evolved over the last few years. If you have been collecting the villages for a while, you have witnessed, or possibly even experienced firsthand, the evolution that has taken place. For many collectors, their first displays consisted of a layer of cotton batting as a base and the buildings placed on top. Other than accessories, plastic snow was the only probable addition to the scene.

But then, the awareness of more elaborate scenes and ideas spread. Collectors, seeing others' displays, took those ideas and expanded upon them, often using techniques that they never would have tried to implement previously. Having success with those, they tried others. Each new project was based upon the creativity and imagination of the

(cont. page 72)

one before. Like a snowball rolling downhill, this awareness brought collectors from displayers of their collectible to display makers with their collectibles used as the main attraction.

It could be argued that display making itself is not a hobby, but a means to enjoy a village-type product in a different light. This is absolutely true. Since a hobby is usually, though not necessarily, something that a person pursues regularly throughout the year, the creation of a display once in the fall would not lend itself to being considered in this category. However, no matter when their displays are built, collectors are making this a year long quest. They are constantly in search of an animal, fence, type of rock, snow, tree or any item that will bring to their display the image they had in mind.

Need proof of this theory? How many collectors carry pictures of their collection, D56 or otherwise? Very few. How many carry pictures of their displays? Just look and listen at the next D56 event you attend. These are the people who are not only collectors, they are hobbyists.

A strong proponent of the idea of display making as a hobby is D56 itself. This is for a number of reasons including the fact that it gives consumers yet one more reason to purchase villages. It also differentiates D56 products from other manufacturers' products and, it is more likely to involve a segment of the population that D56 sees as a growth opportunity ... men.

By promoting the idea of more elaborate and varied displays, D56 hopes to attract men who will see this as a creative hobby, not just collecting little ceramic and porcelain houses. Remember, many men became involved with these villages when they learned that they tend to appreciate in value. This will enlarge that group.

Further evidence that D56 marketing efforts include the idea of display making as a hobby to attract more men in the process can be found in many of the pieces produced in recent years. These products, for example, are targeted towards men: Hunting Lodge, Fisherman's Nook buildings, more lighthouses, and Coca-Cola related buildings (the majority of collectors of Coca-Cola memorabilia are men).

Looking back on the growth of the villages, a pattern can be seen. They evolved from giftware to a collectible to a hobby, making the collectible more collected and more collectible. Do you think this all happened by chance? Don't bet the farm, or castle or schoolhouse. The next thing you know, D56 will be encouraging us to keep our displays up longer. Hmmm... Fall Foliage Trees, do you think...?

the Village Chronicle.

018-0	1990	Snowman With Broom
038-5	1985	Scottie With Tree
040-7	1988	Monks-A-Caroling
053-9	1987	Singing Nuns
056-3	1987	Snow Kids Sled, Skis
057-1	1988	Family Mom/Kids, Goose/Girl
059-8	1988	Santa/Mailbox
064-1	1986	Carolers
069-0	1986	Ceramic Car
079-2	1986	Ceramic Sleigh
094-6	1990	Kids Around The Tree
095-4	1987	Girl/Snowman, Boy
096-2	1988	Shopping Girls With Packages
102-0	1988	3 Nuns With Songbooks
103-9	1988	Praying Monks
104-7	1989	Children In Band
105-5	1990	Caroling Family
107-1	1990	Christmas Children
108-0	1989	For Sale Sign
113-6	1990	Snow Kids
116-0	1992	Man On Ladder Hanging Garland
117-9	1990	Hayride
118-7	1990	School Children
129-2	1990	Apple Girl/Newspaper Boy
130-6	1991	Woodsman And Boy
131-4	1992	Doghouse/Cat In Garbage Can
133-0	1991	Water Tower
134-9	1993	Kids Decorating The Village Sign
136-5	1990	Woody Station Wagon
137-3	1991	School Bus, Snow Plow
146-2	1995	Village Gazebo
147-0	1992	Choir Kids
148-9	1990	Special Delivery
158-6	1993	Down The Chimney He Goes
5159-4	1993	Sno-Jet Snowmobile
5160-8	1992	Sleighride
5161-6	1992	Here We Come A Caroling
5162-4	1992	Home Delivery
5163-2	1993	Fresh Frozen Fish
5164-0	1995	A Tree For Me
5165-9	1996	A Home For The Holidays
5168-3	1991	Kids Tree House
5169-1	1992	Bringing Home The Tree
5170-5	1991	Skate Faster Mom
5171-3	1996	Crack The Whip
5172-1	1991	Through The Woods
5173-0	1991	Statue Of Mark Twain
5174-8	1991	Calling All Cars
5179-9	1990	Mailbox
5180-2	1994	Village Birds
5197-7	1992	Special Delivery
5408-9	1994	Wreaths For Sale
5409-7	1993	Winter Fountain
5410-0	1994	Cold Weather Sports
5411-9	1992	Come Join The Parade
5412-7	1992	Village Marching Band
5413-5	1994	Christmas Cadillac
5414-3	1993	Snowball Fort
5415-1	1993	Country Harvest
5418-6	1994	Village Greetings
5430-5	1994	Nanny And The Preschoolers
5431-3	1995	Early Morning Delivery
5432-1	1996	Christmas Puppies
5433-0	1995	Round & Round We Go!
5435-6	1994	We're Going To A Christmas Pageant
5436-4	1995	Winter Playground
5440-2	1996	Spirit Of Snow Village Airplane
5450-0	1996	Christmas At The Farm
5451-8	1995	Check It Out Bookmobile
5453-4	1996	Pint-Size Pony Rides
5458-5	1996	Spirit Of Snow Village Airplane
5459-3	1996	Village News Delivery
5462-3	1996	Sunday School Serenade
6459-9	1984	Monks-A-Caroling
8183-3	1991	Sisal Tree Lot

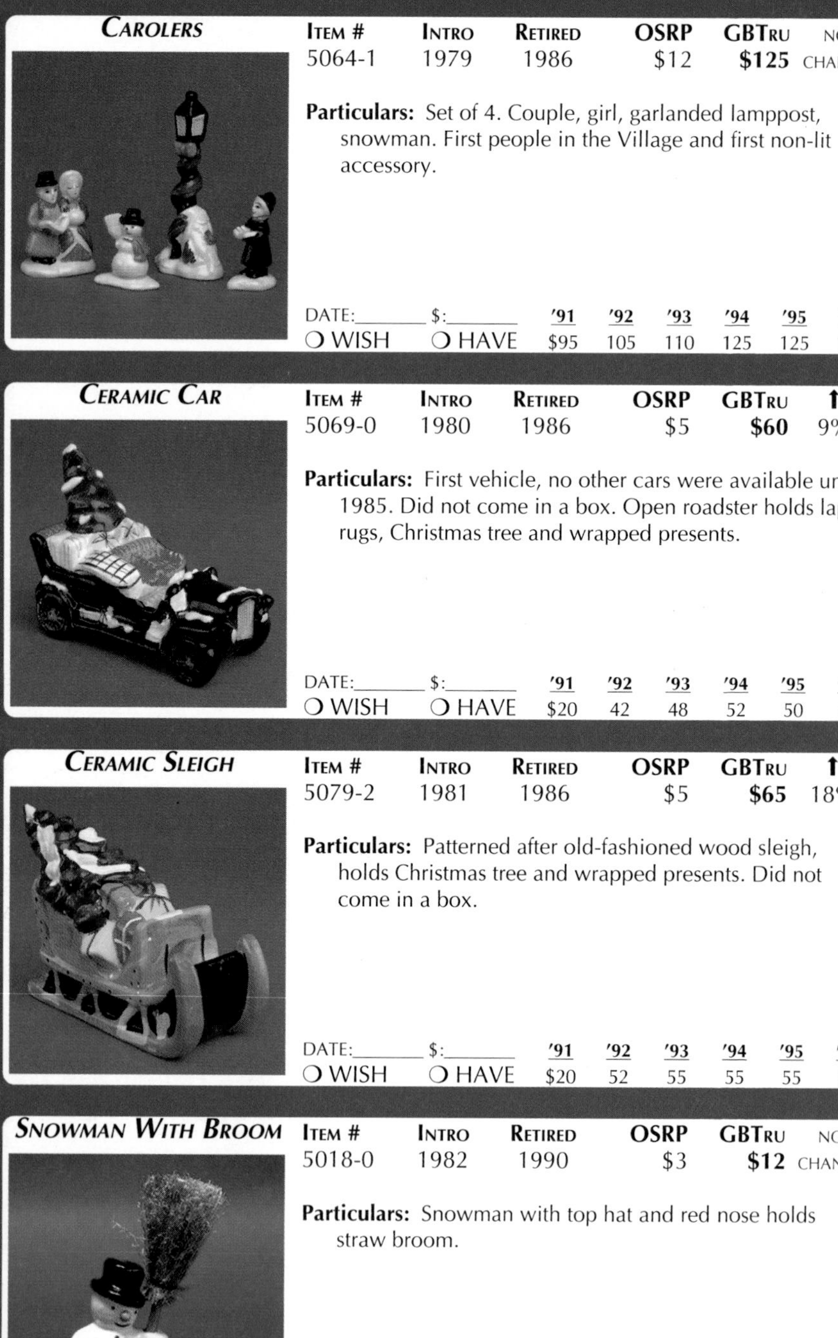

Carolers

Item #	Intro	Retired	OSRP	GBTru	NO
5064-1	1979	1986	$12	**$125**	CHANC

Particulars: Set of 4. Couple, girl, garlanded lamppost, snowman. First people in the Village and first non-lit accessory.

DATE:_______ $:_______
❍ WISH ❍ HAVE

'91	'92	'93	'94	'95	'9
$95	105	110	125	125	12

Ceramic Car

Item #	Intro	Retired	OSRP	GBTru	↑
5069-0	1980	1986	$5	**$60**	9%

Particulars: First vehicle, no other cars were available unti 1985. Did not come in a box. Open roadster holds lap rugs, Christmas tree and wrapped presents.

DATE:_______ $:_______
❍ WISH ❍ HAVE

'91	'92	'93	'94	'95	'96
$20	42	48	52	50	55

Ceramic Sleigh

Item #	Intro	Retired	OSRP	GBTru	↑
5079-2	1981	1986	$5	**$65**	18%

Particulars: Patterned after old-fashioned wood sleigh, holds Christmas tree and wrapped presents. Did not come in a box.

DATE:_______ $:_______
❍ WISH ❍ HAVE

'91	'92	'93	'94	'95	'96
$20	52	55	55	55	55

Snowman With Broom

Item #	Intro	Retired	OSRP	GBTru	NO
5018-0	1982	1990	$3	**$12**	CHANG

Particulars: Snowman with top hat and red nose holds straw broom.

DATE:_______ $:_______
❍ WISH ❍ HAVE

'91	'92	'93	'94	'95	'96
$10	15	15	15	10	12

Monks-A-Caroling

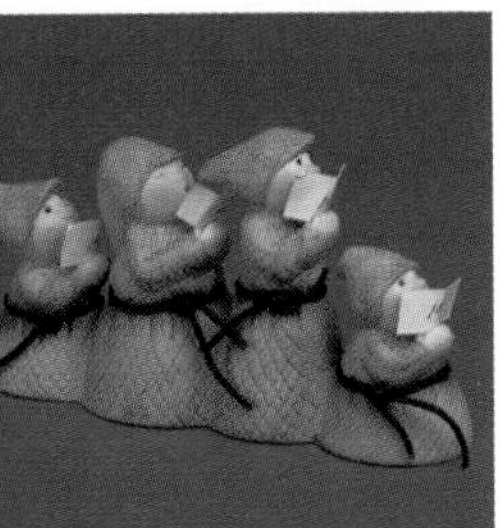

Item #	Intro	Retired	OSRP	GBTru
6460-2	1982	N/A	$6	**$200**

Particulars: These original four friars singing carols were giftware adopted as a Snow Village piece by collectors. The piece is unglazed, the Monks carry paper song books and have real cord for sashes.

DATE:_______ $:_______
❍ WISH ❍ HAVE

Monks-A-Caroling

Item #	Intro	Retired	OSRP	GBTru	
6459-9	1983	1984	$6	**$65**	NO CHANGE

Particulars: This is the 2nd *Monks-A-Caroling.* It was retired after one year due to the maker's inability to supply. This version is slightly smaller than the giftware piece, glazed, and the Monks carry ceramic songbooks and have painted-on ropes. The diffused rosy blush in the Monks' cheeks differentiate this piece from the 3rd version Monks (in 1984 as Item #5040-7 from another supplier).

DATE:_______ $:_______
❍ WISH ❍ HAVE

'91	'92	'93	'94	'95	'96
$70	70	75	75	70	65

Scottie With Tree

Item #	Intro	Retired	OSRP	GBTru	
5038-5	1984	1985	$3	**$165**	NO CHANGE

Particulars: A black dog waits by a snow covered tree. Some pieces have a white star on top of the tree.

DATE:_______ $:_______
❍ WISH ❍ HAVE

'91	'92	'93	'94	'95	'96
$95	115	132	140	150	165

Monks-A-Caroling

Item #	Intro	Retired	OSRP	GBTru	↑
5040-7	1984	1988	$6	**$50**	32%

Particulars: Replaced the 1983 *Monks-A-Caroling,* Item #6459-9. On this piece the Monks have a distinct pink circle to give the cheeks blush.

DATE:_______ $:_______
❍ WISH ❍ HAVE

'91	'92	'93	'94	'95	'96
$25	25	30	38	40	38

Singing Nuns

Item #	Intro	Retired	OSRP	GBTru	↑
5053-9	1985	1987	$6	**$135**	4%

Particulars: Four nuns in habits, sing carols.

DATE:_______ $:_______
❍ WISH ❍ HAVE

'91	'92	'93	'94	'95	'9
$65	75	85	105	125	13

Auto With Tree– "Squashed"

Item #	Intro	Retired	OSRP	GBTru
5055-5	1985	Variation	$5	**$75**

Particulars: First version of red VW Beetle with sisal tree strapped to roof looks as if the tree's weight crushed the car. Approximately 3 ³/₈" long. Did not come in a box.

DATE:_______ $:_______
❍ WISH ❍ HAVE

Auto With Tree

Item #	Intro	Retired	OSRP	GBTru	No
5055-5	1985	Current	$5	**$6.50**	Chang

Particulars: Second version of red VW Beetle with sisal tre strapped to roof. Approximately 3" long. Did not come a box.

DATE:_______ $:_______
❍ WISH ❍ HAVE

'91	'92	'93	'94	'95	'9
$6.50	6.50	6.50	6.50	6.50	6.5

Snow Kids Sled, Skis

Item #	Intro	Retired	OSRP	GBTru	↑
5056-3	1985	1987	$11	**$55**	10%

Particulars: Set of 2. Three children on a toboggan and one child on skis. See *Snow Kids,* 1987, #5113-6, page 81 for these kids as part of a set of 4 in a scaled down size.

DATE:_______ $:_______
❍ WISH ❍ HAVE

'91	'92	'93	'94	'95	'9
$20	48	48	50	50	5

Family Mom/Kids, Goose/Girl–"Large"

Item #	Intro	Retired	OSRP	GBTru	↓
5057-1	1985	1988	$11	**$42**	13%

Particulars: Set of 2. Mother holds hands of two children, one girl feeds corn to geese. First version. This is the original larger size. By 1987 the piece was downscaled. To date, there is no difference in Secondary Market Value.

DATE:_______	$:_______	'91	'92	'93	'94	'95	'96
❍ WISH	❍ HAVE	$30	35	35	45	45	48

Family Mom/Kids, Goose/Girl–"Small"

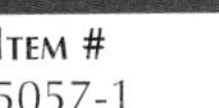

Item #	Intro	Retired	OSRP	GBTru	↓
5057-1	1985	1988	$11	**$42**	13%

Particulars: Set of 2. Second version. This is the downscaled version. In addition to being smaller, there is more detail in the pieces.

DATE:_______	$:_______	'91	'92	'93	'94	'95	'96
❍ WISH	❍ HAVE	$30	35	35	45	45	48

Santa/Mailbox–"Large"

Item #	Intro	Retired	OSRP	GBTru	↑
5059-8	1985	1988	$11	**$60**	13%

Particulars: Set of 2. Santa with toy bag and girl mails letter to Santa as dog watches. First version. This is the original larger size. Girl has brown hair. By 1987 the piece was downscaled. This is the first year we have tracked a difference in Secondary Market Value.

DATE:_______	$:_______	'91	'92	'93	'94	'95	'96
❍ WISH	❍ HAVE	$25	40	46	48	50	53

Santa/Mailbox–"Small"

Item #	Intro	Retired	OSRP	GBTru	↑
5059-8	1985	1988	$11	**$57**	8%

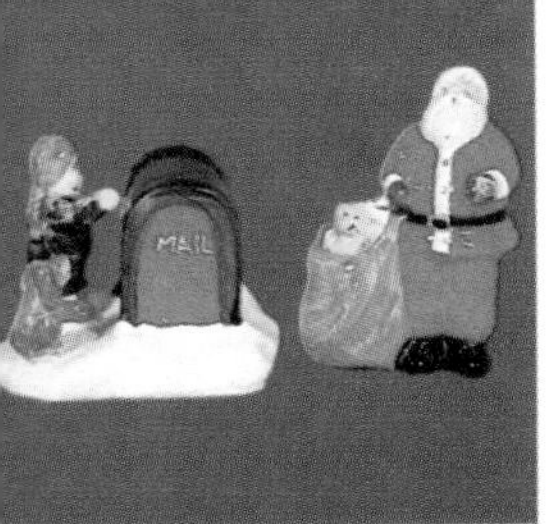

Particulars: Set of 2. Second version. This is the downscaled version. In addition to being shorter, Santa and the girl are also trimmer. In this version the girl has blonde hair. This is the first year we have tracked a difference in Secondary Market Value.

DATE:_______	$:_______	'91	'92	'93	'94	'95	'96
❍ WISH	❍ HAVE	$25	40	46	48	50	53

Kids Around The Tree–"Large"

Item #	Intro	Retired	OSRP	GBTru	↓
5094-6	1986	1990	$15	**$55**	8%

Particulars: First version of *Kids Around The Tree*. This is the original larger size, 5 3/4" in height. By 1987 the piece was dramatically downscaled. Children join hands to make a ring around the snow covered tree with a gold star.

DATE:_______	$:_______	'91	'92	'93	'94	'95	'96
❍ WISH	❍ HAVE	$60	60	60	70	60	60

Kids Around The Tree–"Small"

Item #	Intro	Retired	OSRP	GBTru	↑
5094-6	1986	1990	$15	**$40**	5%

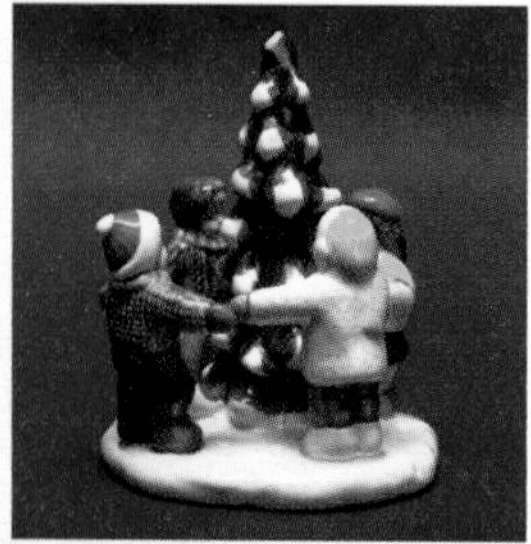

Particulars: Second version of *Kids Around The Tree*. This is the downscaled version, 4 1/2" in height.

DATE:_______	$:_______	'91	'92	'93	'94	'95	'96
❍ WISH	❍ HAVE	$30	32	32	40	35	38

Girl/Snowman, Boy

Item #	Intro	Retired	OSRP	GBTru	↑
5095-4	1986	1987	$11	**$65**	5%

Particulars: Set of 2. Girl puts finishing touches on snowman as boy reaches to place decorated hat atop head. See *Snow Kids,* 1987, #5113-6, page 81, for these kids as part of a set of 4 in a scaled down size.

DATE:_______	$:_______	'91	'92	'93	'94	'95	'96
❍ WISH	❍ HAVE	$35	50	55	70	70	62

Shopping Girls With Packages–"Large"

Item #	Intro	Retired	OSRP	GBTru	↑
5096-2	1986	1988	$11	**$50**	4%

Particulars: Set of 2. Girls dressed toasty for shopping with hats, mittens, coats, boots, stand by some of their wrapped packages. First version. This is the original larger size–3" in height. By 1987 the piece was downscaled. This is the first year we have tracked a difference in Secondary Market Value.

DATE:_______	$:_______	'91	'92	'93	'94	'95	'96
❍ WISH	❍ HAVE	$25	35	38	44	45	48

Shopping Girls With Packages–"Small"

Item #	Intro	Retired	OSRP	GBTru	↓
5096-2	1986	1988	$11	$47	2%

Particulars: Set of 2. Second version. This is the downscaled version–2 3/4" in height. This is the first year we have tracked a difference in Secondary Market Value.

DATE:_______	$:_______	'91	'92	'93	'94	'95	'96
❍ WISH	❍ HAVE	$25	35	38	44	45	48

3 Nuns With Songbooks

Item #	Intro	Retired	OSRP	GBTru	↑
5102-0	1987	1988	$6	$135	5%

Particulars: Three nuns in habits standing side-by-side carry songbooks to sing carols. Available for only one year.

DATE:_______	$:_______	'91	'92	'93	'94	'95	'96
❍ WISH	❍ HAVE	$50	75	95	115	125	128

Praying Monks

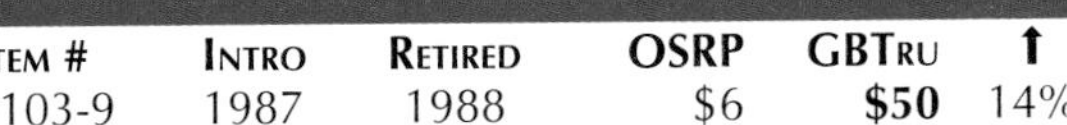

Item #	Intro	Retired	OSRP	GBTru	↑
5103-9	1987	1988	$6	$50	14%

Particulars: Three monks, standing side-by-side, praying. Available for only one year.

DATE:_______	$:_______	'91	'92	'93	'94	'95	'96
❍ WISH	❍ HAVE	$30	32	42	42	40	44

Children In Band

Item #	Intro	Retired	OSRP	GBTru	↓
5104-7	1987	1989	$15	$30	6%

Particulars: One child conducts three band players: horn, drum and tuba.

DATE:_______	$:_______	'91	'92	'93	'94	'95	'96
❍ WISH	❍ HAVE	$25	35	28	24	25	32

Caroling Family

Item #	Intro	Retired	OSRP	GBTru	↑
5105-5	1987	1990	$20	**$35**	25%

Particulars: Set of 3. Father holds baby, mother and son, and girl with pup.

DATE:_______	$:_______	'91	'92	'93	'94	'95	'9
❍ WISH	❍ HAVE	$25	35	30	32	30	2

Taxi Cab

Item #	Intro	Retired	OSRP	GBTru	
5106-3	1987	Current	$6	**$6.50**	NO CHAN

Particulars: Yellow Checker cab. Size is 3 ½" x 2".

DATE:_______	$:_______	'91	'92	'93	'94	'95	'9
❍ WISH	❍ HAVE	$6.50	6.50	6.50	6.50	6.50	6.

Christmas Children

Item #	Intro	Retired	OSRP	GBTru	
5107-1	1987	1990	$20	**$35**	NO CHAN

Particulars: Set of 4. Children at outdoor activities: girl an pup on sled, boy, girl holding wreath and girl feeding carrot to bunny.

DATE:_______	$:_______	'91	'92	'93	'94	'95	'9
❍ WISH	❍ HAVE	$25	35	35	30	30	3

For Sale Sign

Item #	Intro	Retired	OSRP	GBTru	
5108-0	1987	1989	$3.50	**$10**	NO CHAN

Particulars: First "For Sale Sign." This ceramic sign is trimmed with holly. This sign does not appear on the D56 Item History List.
See also *For Sale Sign,* 1989, #5166-7.

DATE:_______	$:_______	'91	'92	'93	'94	'95	'9
❍ WISH	❍ HAVE	$8	12	12	10	10	1

For Sale Sign– "GCC Blank"

Item #	Intro	Retired	OSRP	GBTru
581-9	1987	Promo	*	**$25**

Particulars: Gift Creations Concepts (GCC) 1989 Christmas Catalog Exclusive, *free with any $100 Department 56 purchase. Holly trims blank sign for personalization.

DATE:_______ $:_______
❍ WISH ❍ HAVE

Snow Kids

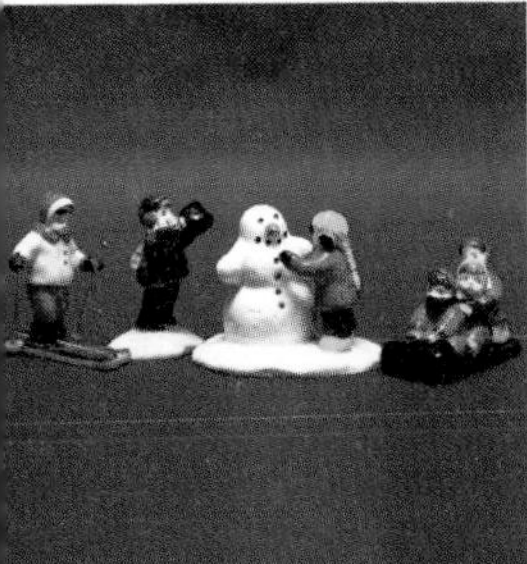

Item #	Intro	Retired	OSRP	GBTru	↑
5113-6	1987	1990	$20	**$55**	10%

Particulars: Set of 4 incorporates *Snow Kids Sled, Skis,* 1985, Item #5056-3, and *Girl/Snowman, Boy,* 1986, Item #5095-4, re-scaled to the smaller size. Three kids on toboggan, child on skis, boy and girl putting finishing touches on snowman.

DATE:_______ $:_______
❍ WISH ❍ HAVE

'91	'92	'93	'94	'95	'96
$30	52	52	48	45	50

Man On Ladder Hanging Garland

Item #	Intro	Retired	OSRP	GBTru	No Change
5116-0	1988	1992	$7.50	**$16**	

Particulars: Man carries garland up ladder to decorate eaves of house. Man is ceramic, ladder is wooden, garland is sisal.

DATE:_______ $:_______
❍ WISH ❍ HAVE

'91	'92	'93	'94	'95	'96
$8	8	18	16	18	16

Hayride

Item #	Intro	Retired	OSRP	GBTru	No Change
5117-9	1988	1990	$30	**$60**	

Particulars: Farmer guides horse-drawn hay-filled sleigh with children as riders.

DATE:_______ $:_______
❍ WISH ❍ HAVE

'91	'92	'93	'94	'95	'96
$45	65	70	65	60	60

School Children

Item #	Intro	Retired	OSRP	GBTru	↑
5118-7	1988	1990	$15	**$30**	20%

Particulars: Set of 3. Three children carrying school books.

DATE:_______ $:_______ ❍ WISH ❍ HAVE

'91	'92	'93	'94	'95	'96
$20	30	25	28	25	25

Apple Girl/ Newspaper Boy

Item #	Intro	Retired	OSRP	GBTru	
5129-2	1988	1990	$11	**$22**	NO CHANG

Particulars: Set of 2. Girl holds wood tray carrier selling apples for 5¢, newsboy sells the Village News.

DATE:_______ $:_______ ❍ WISH ❍ HAVE

'91	'92	'93	'94	'95	'96
$20	25	20	22	20	22

Woodsman And Boy

Item #	Intro	Retired	OSRP	GBTru	
5130-6	1988	1991	$13	**$30**	NO CHANGE

Particulars: Set of 2. Man chops and splits logs and boy prepares to carry supply to fireplace.

DATE:_______ $:_______ ❍ WISH ❍ HAVE

'91	'92	'93	'94	'95	'96
$13	26	22	25	30	30

Doghouse/Cat In Garbage Can

Item #	Intro	Retired	OSRP	GBTru	
5131-4	1988	1992	$15	**$27**	NO CHANGE

Particulars: Set of 2. Dog sits outside doghouse decorated with wreath; cat looks at empty boxes and wrappings in garbage can.

DATE:_______ $:_______ ❍ WISH ❍ HAVE

'91	'92	'93	'94	'95	'96
$15	15	30	30	25	27

Fire Hydrant & Mailbox

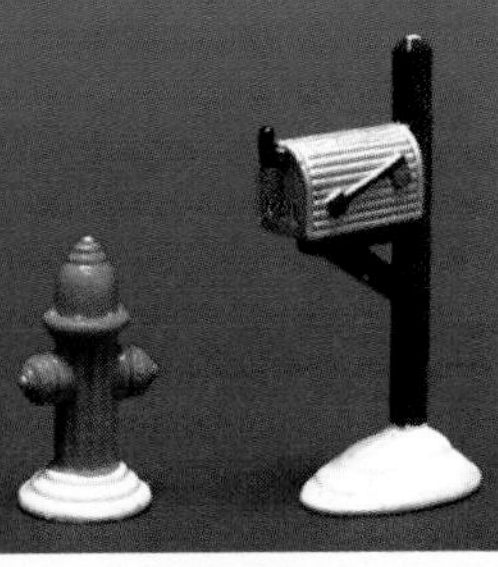

Item #	Intro	Retired	OSRP	GBTru	NO
5132-2	1988	Current	$6	**$6**	CHANGE

Particulars: Set of 2. Red fire hydrant and rural curbside mailbox on post. Sizes are 1 1/2" & 2 3/4", respectively.

DATE:_______	$:_______	'91	'92	'93	'94	'95	'96
❍ WISH	❍ HAVE	$6	6	6	6	6	6

Water Tower

Item #	Intro	Retired	OSRP	GBTru	↑
5133-0	1988	1991	$20	**$75**	7%

Particulars: 2 pieces. Metal scaffold base holds red ceramic Snow Village water container with green top, ladder leads to top.

DATE:_______	$:_______	'91	'92	'93	'94	'95	'96
❍ WISH	❍ HAVE	$22	48	48	52	65	70

Water Tower– "John Deere"

Item #	Intro	Retired	OSRP	GBTru	↑
2510-4	1988	Promo	$24	**$695**	3%

Particulars: Special piece, *John Deere Water Tower* is exactly the same as the *Snow Village Water Tower* with the exception that it reads, "Moline Home of John Deere." It was offered for sale through the John Deere catalog.

DATE:_______	$:_______	'91	'92	'93	'94	'95	'96
❍ WISH	❍ HAVE	$125	125	150	395	650	675

Nativity

Item #	Intro	Retired	OSRP	GBTru	NO
5135-7	1988	Current	$7.50	**$7.50**	CHANGE

Particulars: Holy Family, lamb, in creche scene. Size is 2 1/4".

DATE:_______	$:_______	'91	'92	'93	'94	'95	'96
❍ WISH	❍ HAVE	$7.50	7.50	7.50	7.50	7.50	7.50

Woody Station Wagon

Item #	Intro	Retired	OSRP	GBTru	↑
5136-5	1988	1990	$6.50	**$30**	20%

Particulars: "Wood" paneled sides on station wagon.

DATE:________ $:________ ❍ WISH ❍ HAVE

'91	'92	'93	'94	'95	'96
$12	20	22	30	25	25

School Bus, Snow Plow

Item #	Intro	Retired	OSRP	GBTru	↓
5137-3	1988	1991	$16	**$55**	4%

Particulars: Set of 2. Yellow school bus and red sand grave truck with snow plow.

DATE:________ $:________ ❍ WISH ❍ HAVE

'91	'92	'93	'94	'95	'96
$16	25	25	55	50	57

Tree Lot

Item #	Intro	Retired	OSRP	GBTru	No Change
5138-1	1988	Current	$33.50	**$37.50**	

Particulars: Christmas lights on tree lot's fence plus decorated shack and trees for sale. The shack is ceramic the fence is wood and the trees are sisal. Size is 9 ½" x 5" x 4 ½".

DATE:________ $:________ ❍ WISH ❍ HAVE

'91	'92	'93	'94	'95	'96
$37.50	37.50	37.50	37.50	37.50	37.5

"Up On A Roof Top"

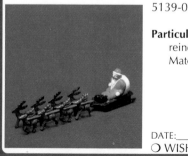

Item #	Intro	Retired	OSRP	GBTru	No Change
5139-0	1988	Current	$6.50	**$6.50**	

Particulars: 2 pieces–Santa and sleigh pulled by eight reindeer. Santa hitches onto the sleigh. Size is 4" long. Material is pewter. Can be used in all the villages.

DATE:________ $:________ ❍ WISH ❍ HAVE

'91	'92	'93	'94	'95	'96
$6.50	6.50	6.50	6.50	6.50	6.50

SISAL TREE LOT

ITEM #	INTRO	RETIRED	OSRP	GBTRU	↑
8183-3	1988	1991	$45	**$95**	12%

Particulars: A variety of cut trees for sale at a street lot. Signs identify the trees in each row.

DATE:_______	$:_______	'91	'92	'93	'94	'95	'96
❍ WISH	❍ HAVE	$45	80	85	85	75	85

VILLAGE GAZEBO

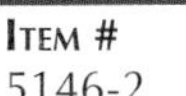

ITEM #	INTRO	RETIRED	OSRP	GBTRU	↓
5146-2	1989	1995	$27	**$40**	5%

Particulars: Small, open, red roofed garden structure that will protect folks from rain and snow, or be a private place to sit.

DATE:_______	$:_______	'91	'92	'93	'94	'95	'96
❍ WISH	❍ HAVE	$27.50	28	30	30	30	42

CHOIR KIDS

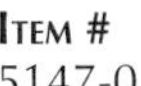

ITEM #	INTRO	RETIRED	OSRP	GBTRU	↑
5147-0	1989	1992	$15	**$28**	12%

Particulars: Four kids in white and red robes with green songbooks caroling.

DATE:_______	$:_______	'91	'92	'93	'94	'95	'96
❍ WISH	❍ HAVE	$15	15	20	28	25	25

SPECIAL DELIVERY

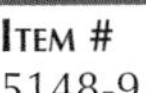

ITEM #	INTRO	RETIRED	OSRP	GBTRU	↑
5148-9	1989	1990	$16	**$50**	25%

Particulars: Set of 2. Mailman and mailbag with his mail truck in USPO colors of red, white and blue with the eagle logo. Discontinued due to licensing problems with the U.S. Postal Service. Replaced with 1990, *Special Delivery,* Item #5197-7, page 92.

DATE:_______	$:_______	'91	'92	'93	'94	'95	'96
❍ WISH	❍ HAVE	$45	42	42	42	45	40

For Sale Sign

Item #	Intro	Retired	OSRP	GBTru	No
5166-7	1989	Current	$4.50	**$4.50**	Change

Particulars: Enameled metal sign can advertise "For Sale" o "SOLD" depending which side is displayed. Birds decorate and add color. Size is 3".

DATE:________ $:________

❍ WISH ❍ HAVE

'91	'92	'93	'94	'95	'96
$4.50	4.50	4.50	4.50	4.50	4.50

For Sale Sign–"Bachman's"

Item #	Intro	Retired	OSRP	GBTru	No
539-8	1989	Promo	$4.50	**$25**	Change

Particulars: Bachman's Exclusive for their Village Gathering in 1990. Enameled metal sign reads "Bachman's Village Gathering 1990". Birds decorate and add color. Size is 3".

DATE:________ $:________

❍ WISH ❍ HAVE

'96
$25

Street Sign

Item #	Intro	Retired	OSRP	GBTru	↓
5167-5	1989	1992	$7.50	**$10**	17%

Particulars: 6 pieces per package. Green metal street signs. Use the street names provided (Lake St., Maple Dr., Park Ave., River Rd., Elm St., Ivy Lane ...) or personalize to give each village street a unique name. Size: 4 1/4" tall.

DATE:________ $:________

❍ WISH ❍ HAVE

'91	'92	'93	'94	'95	'96
$7.50	7.50	NE	8	8	12

Kids Tree House

Item #	Intro	Retired	OSRP	GBTru	↑
5168-3	1989	1991	$25	**$60**	9%

Particulars: Decorated club house built on an old dead tree Steps lead up to the hideaway. Material is resin.

DATE:________ $:________

❍ WISH ❍ HAVE

'91	'92	'93	'94	'95	'96
$25	48	45	45	50	55

Bringing Home The Tree

Item #	Intro	Retired	OSRP	GBTru	↓
5169-1	1989	1992	$15	**$25**	7%

Particulars: A man pulls a sled holding the tree as the girl watches to make sure it doesn't fall off. Tree is sisal.

DATE:_______	$:_______	'91	'92	'93	'94	'95	'96
❍ WISH	❍ HAVE	$15	15	20	22	25	27

Skate Faster Mom

Item #	Intro	Retired	OSRP	GBTru	↑
5170-5	1989	1991	$13	**$30**	7%

Particulars: Two children sit in the sleigh as their skating Mom pushes them across the ice.

DATE:_______	$:_______	'91	'92	'93	'94	'95	'96
❍ WISH	❍ HAVE	$13	30	28	24	20	28

Crack The Whip

Item #	Intro	Retired	OSRP	GBTru	↑
5171-3	1989	1996	$25	**$32**	28%

Particulars: Set of 3. A fast moving line of skaters hold tightly to the person in front of them. The first person does slow patterns but as the line snakes out, the last people are racing to keep up and they whip out.

DATE:_______	$:_______	'91	'92	'93	'94	'95	'96
❍ WISH	❍ HAVE	$25	25	25	25	25	25

Through The Woods

Item #	Intro	Retired	OSRP	GBTru	↑
5172-1	1989	1991	$18	**$28**	22%

Particulars: Set of 2. Children bring a tree and a basket of goodies to Grandma.

DATE:_______	$:_______	'91	'92	'93	'94	'95	'96
❍ WISH	❍ HAVE	$18	30	30	22	25	23

Statue Of Mark Twain

Item #	Intro	Retired	OSRP	GBTru	↑
5173-0	1989	1991	$15	**$40**	14%

Particulars: A tribute to the author who wrote about lives o American folk.

DATE:______	$:______	'91	'92	'93	'94	'95	'96
❍ WISH	❍ HAVE	$15	28	28	30	30	35

Calling All Cars

Item #	Intro	Retired	OSRP	GBTru	↑
5174-8	1989	1991	$15	**$65**	86%

Particulars: Set of 2. Police car and patrolman directing traffic.

DATE:______	$:______	'91	'92	'93	'94	'95	'96
❍ WISH	❍ HAVE	$15	32	30	30	35	35

Stop Sign

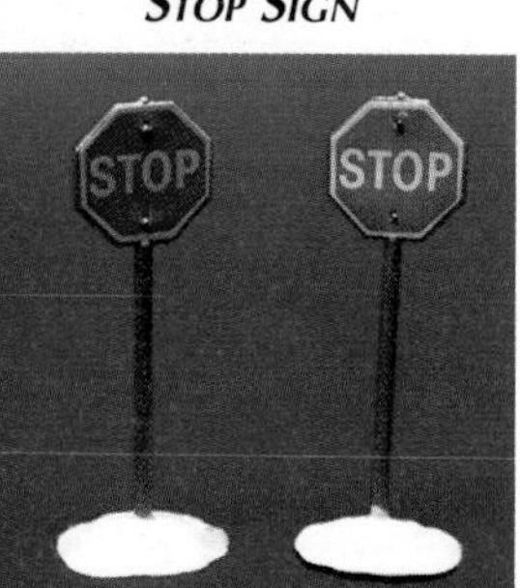

Item #	Intro	Retired	OSRP	GBTru	No Change
5176-4	1989	Current	$5	**$5**	

Particulars: 2 pieces per package. Octagonal sign, placed on a corner of dangerous entry/exit to cause vehicles to come to a complete stop. Size is 3" tall.

DATE:______	$:______	'91	'92	'93	'94	'95	'96
❍ WISH	❍ HAVE	$5	5	5	5	5	5

Flag Pole

Item #	Intro	Retired	OSRP	GBTru	No Change
5177-2	1989	Current	$8.50	**$8.50**	

Particulars: Pole with American Flag to display in public. Materials are a resin base, metal pole, cloth flag and thread rope. Size is 7" high.

DATE:______	$:______	'91	'92	'93	'94	'95	'96
❍ WISH	❍ HAVE	$8.50	8.50	8.50	8.50	8.50	8.50

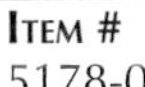

Parking Meter

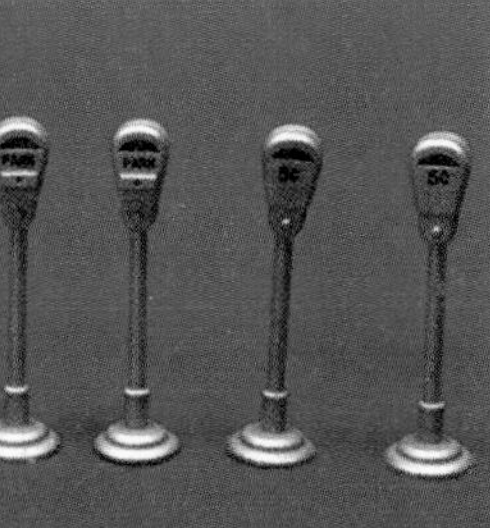

Item #	Intro	Retired	OSRP	GBTru	
5178-0	1989	Current	$6	$6	No Change

Particulars: 4 pieces per package. You can still park for 5¢ in the Snow Village. Size is 2" tall.

DATE:_______ $:_______ ❍ WISH ❍ HAVE

'91	'92	'93	'94	'95	'96
$6	6	6	6	6	6

Mailbox

Item #	Intro	Retired	OSRP	GBTru	
5179-9	1989	1990	$3.50	$20	No Change

Particulars: Freestanding public mailbox in USPO colors red, white and blue with logo. Discontinued due to licensing problems with the U.S. Postal Service. Replaced with *Mailbox,* 1990, Item #5198-5, page 92.

DATE:_______ $:_______ ❍ WISH ❍ HAVE

'91	'92	'93	'94	'95	'96
$20	20	15	20	20	20

Village Birds

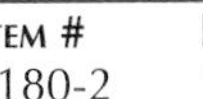

Item #	Intro	Retired	OSRP	GBTru	↑
5180-2	1989	1994	$3.50	$8	60%

Particulars: 6 pieces per package. Small red and blue sitting birds.

DATE:_______ $:_______ ❍ WISH ❍ HAVE

'91	'92	'93	'94	'95	'96
$3.50	3.50	3.50	3.50	4	5

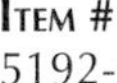

Village Potted Topiary Pair

Item #	Intro	Retired	OSRP	GBTru
5192-6	1989	1994	$5	$10

Particulars: Sisal trees in white resin planters. 2 pieces per package. Size is 4 $^{3}/_{4}$".

DATE:_______ $:_______ ❍ WISH ❍ HAVE

Snow Village Promotional Sign

Item #	Intro	Retired	OSRP	GBTru	↑
9948-1	1989	Disc. '90	Promo	$22	10%

Particulars: Earthenware sign intended to be used by D56 retailers as a promotional item. Sign displays the Snow Village logo. Brickwork at the base supports the sign.

DATE:_______ $:_______
❍ WISH ❍ HAVE

'95	'9
$15	2

Kids Decorating The Village Sign

Item #	Intro	Retired	OSRP	GBTru	No Change
5134-9	1990	1993	$12.50	$22	

Particulars: Two children place garland on a Snow Village sign.

DATE:_______ $:_______
❍ WISH ❍ HAVE

'91	'92	'93	'94	'95	'9
$12.50	12.50	12.50	21	20	2

Down The Chimney He Goes

Item #	Intro	Retired	OSRP	GBTru	No Change
5158-6	1990	1993	$6.50	$15	

Particulars: Santa with a big bag of toys enters chimney to make delivery on Christmas Eve. Chimney can be attached to a house rooftop.

DATE:_______ $:_______
❍ WISH ❍ HAVE

'91	'92	'93	'94	'95	'96
$6.50	6.50	6.50	14	14	15

Sno-Jet Snowmobile

Item #	Intro	Retired	OSRP	GBTru	No Change
5159-4	1990	1993	$15	$25	

Particulars: Red and silver trimmed snowmobile with front ski runners and rear caterpillar treads.

DATE:_______ $:_______
❍ WISH ❍ HAVE

'91	'92	'93	'94	'95	'96
$15	15	15	24	24	25

SLEIGHRIDE

ITEM #	INTRO	RETIRED	OSRP	GBTRU	↑
5160-8	1990	1992	$30	**$60**	20%

Particulars: Family rides in open old-fashioned green sleigh pulled by one horse.

DATE:_______ $:_______

❍ WISH ❍ HAVE

'91	'92	'93	'94	'95	'96
$30	30	52	54	55	50

HERE WE COME A CAROLING

ITEM #	INTRO	RETIRED	OSRP	GBTRU	↑
5161-6	1990	1992	$18	**$28**	17%

Particulars: Set of 3. Children and pet dog sing carols.

DATE:_______ $:_______

❍ WISH ❍ HAVE

'91	'92	'93	'94	'95	'96
$18	18	25	25	25	24

HOME DELIVERY

ITEM #	INTRO	RETIRED	OSRP	GBTRU	↑
5162-4	1990	1992	$16	**$35**	6%

Particulars: Set of 2. Milkman and milk truck.

DATE:_______ $:_______

❍ WISH ❍ HAVE

'91	'92	'93	'94	'95	'96
$16	16	30	30	30	33

FRESH FROZEN FISH

ITEM #	INTRO	RETIRED	OSRP	GBTRU	↑
5163-2	1990	1993	$20	**$42**	17%

Particulars: Set of 2. Ice fisherman and ice house.

DATE:_______ $:_______

❍ WISH ❍ HAVE

'91	'92	'93	'94	'95	'96
$20	20	20	35	35	36

A Tree For Me

Item #	Intro	Retired	OSRP	GBTru	⬇
5164-0	1990	1995	$7.50	**$12**	14%

Particulars: 2 pieces per package. Ceramic snowman with top hat, corn cob pipe, and red muffler carries his own small snow covered sisal tree.

DATE:______	$:______	'91	'92	'93	'94	'95	'9
❍ WISH	❍ HAVE	$7.50	7.50	8	8	8	1

A Home For The Holidays

Item #	Intro	Retired	OSRP	GBTru	⬆
5165-9	1990	1996	$6.50	**$10**	43%

Particulars: Birdhouse with blue bird sitting on roof. Pole decorated with garland and there's a small snow cover evergreen. Size is 4" tall.

DATE:______	$:______	'91	'92	'93	'94	'95	'9
❍ WISH	❍ HAVE	$6.50	6.50	7	7	7	

Special Delivery

Item #	Intro	Retired	OSRP	GBTru	
5197-7	1990	1992	$16	**$36**	NO CHANG

Particulars: Set of 2. Snow Village postman and truck in re and green Snow Village Mail Service colors. "S.V. Mail Service" replaced the discontinued 1985 *Special Delivery,* Item #5148-9, page 85. (Postman remained the same, only the truck changed.)

DATE:______	$:______	'91	'92	'93	'94	'95	'9
❍ WISH	❍ HAVE	$16	16	22	38	35	3

Village Mailbox

Item #	Intro	Retired	OSRP	GBTru	
5198-5	1990	Current	$3.50	**$3.50**	NO CHANG

Particulars: Snow Village mail receptacle in red and green S. V. Mail Service colors. Size is 2". S.V. Mail replaced the discontinued 1985 *Mailbox,* Item #5179-9, page 8

DATE:______	$:______	'91	'92	'93	'94	'95	'9
❍ WISH	❍ HAVE	$3.50	3.50	3.50	3.50	3.50	3.5

Christmas Trash Cans

Item #	Intro	Retired	OSRP	GBTru	No Change
5209-4	1990	Current	$6.50	**$7**	

Particulars: Set of 2. Two galvanized refuse cans filled with holiday wrappings and garbage. Tops come off. Size is 1 1/2".

DATE:_______ $:_______ ❍ WISH ❍ HAVE

'91	'92	'93	'94	'95	'96
$6.50	7	7	7	7	7

Wreaths For Sale

Item #	Intro	Retired	OSRP	GBTru	No Change
5408-9	1991	1994	$27.50	**$40**	

Particulars: Set of 4. Girl holds for sale sign, boy holds up wreaths, child pulls sled. Fence holds wreaths. Materials are ceramic, wood and sisal.

DATE:_______ $:_______ ❍ WISH ❍ HAVE

'91	'92	'93	'94	'95	'96
$27.50	27.50	27.50	27.50	45	40

Winter Fountain

Item #	Intro	Retired	OSRP	GBTru	↑
5409-7	1991	1993	$25	**$55**	10%

Particulars: Angel holds sea shell with water frozen as it flowed. Materials are ceramic and acrylic.

DATE:_______ $:_______ ❍ WISH ❍ HAVE

'91	'92	'93	'94	'95	'96
$25	25	25	45	50	50

Cold Weather Sports

Item #	Intro	Retired	OSRP	GBTru	No Change
5410-0	1991	1994	$27.50	**$45**	

Particulars: Set of 4. Three children play ice hockey.

DATE:_______ $:_______ ❍ WISH ❍ HAVE

'91	'92	'93	'94	'95	'96
$27.50	27.50	27.50	27.50	45	45

Come Join The Parade

Item #	Intro	Retired	OSRP	GBTru	↑
5411-9	1991	1992	$12.50	**$22**	10%

Particulars: Two children carry parade banner.

DATE:_______	$:_______	'91	'92	'93	'94	'95	'96
❍ WISH	❍ HAVE	$12.50	12.50	22	18	20	20

Village Marching Band

Item #	Intro	Retired	OSRP	GBTru	↑
5412-7	1991	1992	$30	**$60**	9%

Particulars: Set of 3. Drum Major, two horn players and tw drummers.

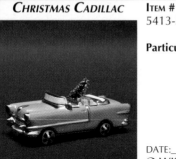

DATE:_______	$:_______	'91	'92	'93	'94	'95	'96
❍ WISH	❍ HAVE	$30	30	68	45	50	55

Christmas Cadillac

Item #	Intro	Retired	OSRP	GBTru	NO CHANG
5413-5	1991	1994	$9	**$15**	

Particulars: Pink car holds sisal tree and presents.

DATE:_______	$:_______	'91	'92	'93	'94	'95	'96
❍ WISH	❍ HAVE	$9	9	9	9	10	15

Snowball Fort

Item #	Intro	Retired	OSRP	GBTru	NO CHANG
5414-3	1991	1993	$27.50	**$40**	

Particulars: Set of 3. One boy behind wall, one hides behind tree, one in open clearing, all with snowballs to throw.

DATE:_______	$:_______	'91	'92	'93	'94	'95	'96
❍ WISH	❍ HAVE	$27.50	27.50	27.50	40	40	40

Country Harvest

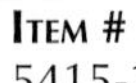

Item #	Intro	Retired	OSRP	GBTru	↑
5415-1	1991	1993	$13	**$27**	50%

Particulars: Farm folk with market basket and pitchfork. Reminiscent of Grant Wood's *American Gothic* painting.

DATE:_______ $:_______ ❍ WISH ❍ HAVE

'91	'92	'93	'94	'95	'96
$13	13	13	25	25	18

Village Greetings

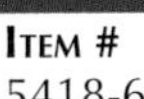

Item #	Intro	Retired	OSRP	GBTru	No Change
5418-6	1991	1994	$5	**$10**	

Particulars: Set of 3. Holiday banners to hang on side of buildings.

DATE:_______ $:_______ ❍ WISH ❍ HAVE

'91	'92	'93	'94	'95	'96
$5	5	5	5	10	10

Village Used Car Lot

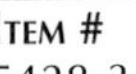

Item #	Intro	Retired	OSRP	GBTru	No Change
5428-3	1992	Current	$45	**$45**	

Particulars: Set of 5. Small office on a stone base with stone chimney. Attached tree. Free standing sign plus office sign advertises used cars and good terms. Three cars in the lot.

DATE:_______ $:_______ ❍ WISH ❍ HAVE

'92	'93	'94	'95	'96
$45	45	45	45	45

Village Phone Booth

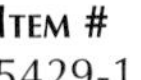

Item #	Intro	Retired	OSRP	GBTru	No Change
5429-1	1992	Current	$7.50	**$7.50**	

Particulars: Silver and red outdoor phone booth with accordion open/close doors. Size is 4" high.

DATE:_______ $:_______ ❍ WISH ❍ HAVE

'92	'93	'94	'95	'96
$7.50	7.50	7.50	7.50	7.50

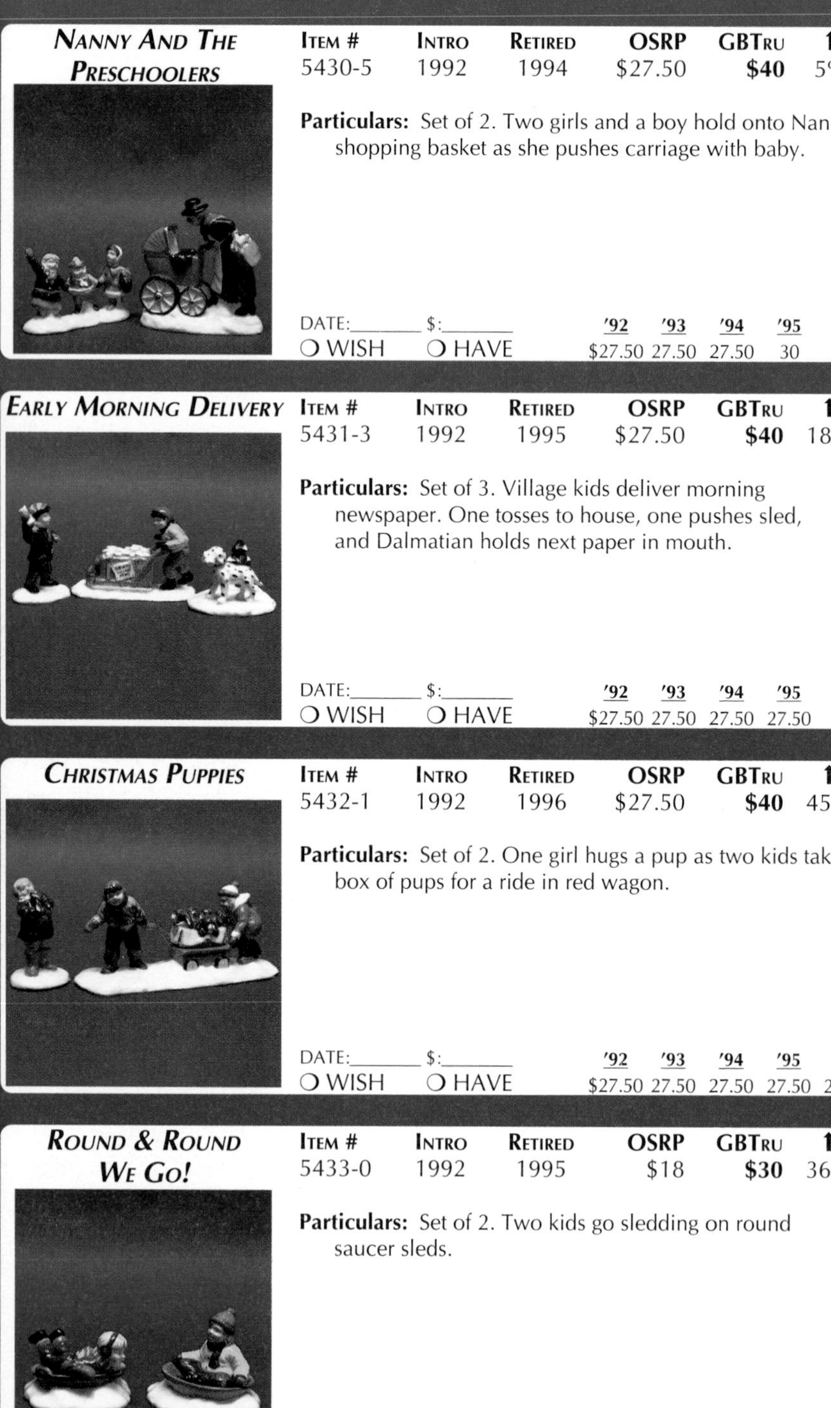

Nanny And The Preschoolers

Item #	Intro	Retired	OSRP	GBTru	↑
5430-5	1992	1994	$27.50	**$40**	5%

Particulars: Set of 2. Two girls and a boy hold onto Nann shopping basket as she pushes carriage with baby.

DATE:_______ $:_______
❍ WISH ❍ HAVE

'92	'93	'94	'95	'9
$27.50	27.50	27.50	30	3

Early Morning Delivery

Item #	Intro	Retired	OSRP	GBTru	↑
5431-3	1992	1995	$27.50	**$40**	18%

Particulars: Set of 3. Village kids deliver morning newspaper. One tosses to house, one pushes sled, and Dalmatian holds next paper in mouth.

DATE:_______ $:_______
❍ WISH ❍ HAVE

'92	'93	'94	'95	'9
$27.50	27.50	27.50	27.50	3

Christmas Puppies

Item #	Intro	Retired	OSRP	GBTru	↑
5432-1	1992	1996	$27.50	**$40**	45%

Particulars: Set of 2. One girl hugs a pup as two kids take box of pups for a ride in red wagon.

DATE:_______ $:_______
❍ WISH ❍ HAVE

'92	'93	'94	'95	'9
$27.50	27.50	27.50	27.50	27

Round & Round We Go!

Item #	Intro	Retired	OSRP	GBTru	↑
5433-0	1992	1995	$18	**$30**	36%

Particulars: Set of 2. Two kids go sledding on round saucer sleds.

DATE:_______ $:_______
❍ WISH ❍ HAVE

'92	'93	'94	'95	'9
$18	18	18	18	2

A Heavy Snowfall

Item #	Intro	Retired	OSRP	GBTru	NO CHANGE
5434-8	1992	Current	$16	**$16**	

Particulars: Set of 2. Girl stops to look at bird perched on handle of her shovel as boy shovels snow off the walkway.

DATE:_______ $:_______
❍ WISH ❍ HAVE

'92	'93	'94	'95	'96
$16	16	16	16	16

We're Going To A Christmas Pageant

Item #	Intro	Retired	OSRP	GBTru	NO CHANGE
5435-6	1992	1994	$15	**$20**	

Particulars: Children wear costumes of Santa, a decorated tree and a golden star.

DATE:_______ $:_______
❍ WISH ❍ HAVE

'92	'93	'94	'95	'96
$15	15	15	18	20

Winter Playground

Item #	Intro	Retired	OSRP	GBTru	⬇
5436-4	1992	1995	$20	**$30**	14%

Particulars: Two swings and a playground slide. Two trees and two birds complete the piece.

DATE:_______ $:_______
❍ WISH ❍ HAVE

'92	'93	'94	'95	'96
$20	20	20	20	35

Spirit Of Snow Village Airplane

Item #	Intro	Retired	OSRP	GBTru	⬆
5440-2	1992	1996	$32.50	**$45**	38%

Particulars: Red prop biplane. Metal strap spring on three-tree base allows positioning. Size is 7" x 6 1/2" x 5 1/4".

DATE:_______ $:_______
❍ WISH ❍ HAVE

'92	'93	'94	'95	'96
$32.50	32.50	32.50	32.50	32.50

Village Animated Skating Pond

Item #	Intro	Retired	OSRP	GBTru	NC
5229-9	1993	Current	$60	$60	CHAN

Particulars: Set of 15. Skaters move alone or in a pair in s patterns on the ice pond surface. UL Approved. Size is 17 1/2" x 14".

DATE:________ $:________
❍ WISH ❍ HAVE

'93	'94	'95	'
$60	60	60	

Safety Patrol

Item #	Intro	Retired	OSRP	GBTru	NO
5449-6	1993	Current	$27.50	$27.50	CHAN

Particulars: Set of 4. Older children are safety guards at street crossing for two younger children.

DATE:________ $:________
❍ WISH ❍ HAVE

'93	'94	'95	'
$27.50	27.50	27.50	27

Christmas At The Farm

Item #	Intro	Retired	OSRP	GBTru	↑
5450-0	1993	1996	$16	$28	75%

Particulars: Set of 2. Calf and lamb greet girl carrying a pa of feed.

DATE:________ $:________
❍ WISH ❍ HAVE

'93	'94	'95	'
$16	16	16	1

Check It Out Bookmobile

Item #	Intro	Retired	OSRP	GBTru	↑
5451-8	1993	1995	$25	$35	25%

Particulars: Set of 3. Bookmobile van carries stories to children in villages and farms. Boys and girls select books to borrow.

DATE:________ $:________
❍ WISH ❍ HAVE

'93	'94	'95	'9
$25	25	25	2

Tour The Village

Item #	Intro	Retired	OSRP	GBTru	NO
5452-6	1993	Current	$12.50	**$12.50**	CHANGE

Particulars: Tourist information booth with clerk to assist visitors new to the village. "Bayport" is misspelled. Has "q" instead of "p".

DATE:_______ $:_______
❍ WISH ❍ HAVE

'93	'94	'95	'96
$12.50	12.50	12.50	12.50

Pint-Size Pony Rides

Item #	Intro	Retired	OSRP	GBTru	↑
5453-4	1993	1996	$37.50	**$45**	20%

Particulars: Set of 3. One child waits to buy a pony ride as another rides and one offers a carrot to the pony. A stable building, bench and snow covered tree complete the scene.

DATE:_______ $:_______
❍ WISH ❍ HAVE

'93	'94	'95	'96
$37.50	37.50	37.50	37.50

Pick-up And Delivery

Item #	Intro	Retired	OSRP	GBTru	NO
5454-2	1993	Current	$10	**$10**	CHANGE

Particulars: Pick-up truck carries Christmas trees.

DATE:_______ $:_______
❍ WISH ❍ HAVE

'93	'94	'95	'96
$10	10	10	10

Notes: ________________________________

A Herd Of Holiday Heifers

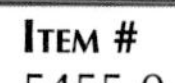

Item #	Intro	Retired	OSRP	GBTru	NC
5455-0	1993	Current	$18	**$18**	CHAN

Particulars: Set of 3 Holstein cows.

DATE:_______ $:_______
❍ WISH ❍ HAVE

'93	'94	'95
$18	18	18

Classic Cars

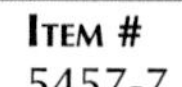

Item #	Intro	Retired	OSRP	GBTru	NC
5457-7	1993	Current	$22.50	**$22.50**	CHAN

Particulars: Set of 3. Station wagon with roof rack, two-to green sedan with tail fins, sedan with spare tire mount outside trunk.

DATE:_______ $:_______
❍ WISH ❍ HAVE

'93	'94	'95	'
$22.50	22.50	22.50	22

Spirit Of Snow Village Airplane

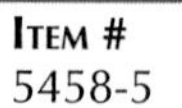

Item #	Intro	Retired	OSRP	GBTru	↑
5458-5	1993	1996	$12.50	**$22**	76%

Particulars: 2 Assorted—blue or yellow.
Size: 4 1/2" x 5 1/2" x 2 3/4".
Propeller double strut winged planes.

DATE:_______ $:_______
❍ WISH ❍ HAVE

'93	'94	'95	'
$12.50	12.50	12.50	12

Village News Delivery

Item #	Intro	Retired	OSRP	GBTru	↑
5459-3	1993	1996	$15	**$27**	80%

Particulars: Set of 2. Driver carries newspaper from van to stores and home delivery children carriers.

DATE:_______ $:_______
❍ WISH ❍ HAVE

'93	'94	'95	'
$15	15	15	1

Village Streetcar

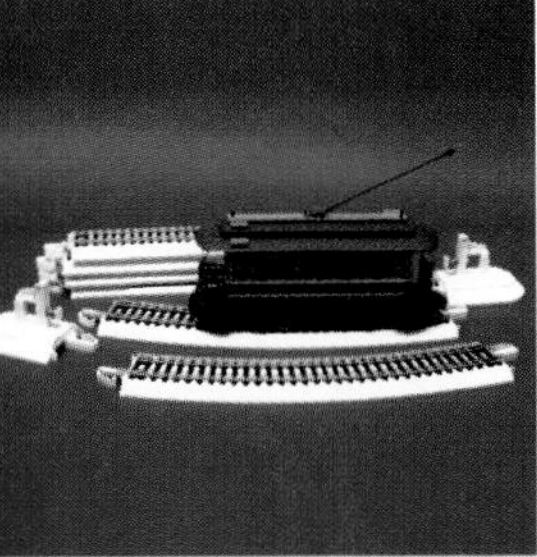

Item #	Intro	Retired	OSRP	GBTru	
5240-0	1994	Current	$65	**$65**	No change

Particulars: Set of 10. Midyear release. Track setup for inner city traveling. Car lights up. Passengers' silhouettes on windows. Appropriate for Heritage Village as well.

DATE:_______ $:_______
❍ WISH ❍ HAVE

'94	'95	'96
$65	65	65

Village Animated All Around The Park

Item #	Intro	Retired	OSRP	GBTru	
5247-7	1994	1996	$95	**$95**	No change

Particulars: Set of 18. People stroll through park on path that encircles tree. Stone wall edges park and archway marks entrance. UL Approved. Size is 19" x 15" x 16". Appropriate for Heritage Village as well.

DATE:_______ $:_______
❍ WISH ❍ HAVE

'94	'95	'96
$95	95	95

Caroling At The Farm

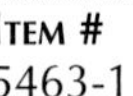

Item #	Intro	Retired	OSRP	GBTru	
5463-1	1994	Current	$35	**$35**	No change

Particulars: Farmer drives tractor pulling carolers on hay-covered wagon. One child pulls another onto the wagon. Midyear release. First ceramic accessory to be a midyear release.

DATE:_______ $:_______
❍ WISH ❍ HAVE

'94	'95	'96
$35	35	35

Stuck In The Snow

Item #	Intro	Retired	OSRP	GBTru	
5471-2	1994	Current	$30	**$30**	No change

Particulars: Set of 3. Dad pushes car, mom watches while son holds shovel and sand.

DATE:_______ $:_______
❍ WISH ❍ HAVE

'94	'95	'96
$30	30	30

Pets On Parade

Item #	Intro	Retired	OSRP	GBTru	NO
5472-0	1994	Current	$16.50	**$16.50**	CHANGE

Particulars: Set of 2. Two children walk dogs on cold wintry day.

DATE:_______ $:_______
❍ WISH ❍ HAVE

'94	'95	'96
$16.50	16.50	16.5

Feeding The Birds

Item #	Intro	Retired	OSRP	GBTru	NO
5473-9	1994	Current	$25	**$25**	CHANGE

Particulars: Set of 3. Woman and children are feeding birds as other birds sit on frozen birdbath.

DATE:_______ $:_______
❍ WISH ❍ HAVE

'94	'95	'96
$25	25	25

Mush!

Item #	Intro	Retired	OSRP	GBTru	NO
5474-7	1994	Current	$20	**$20**	CHANGE

Particulars: Set of 2. A small child sits on a sled that is harnessed to a St. Bernard. An older child shouts to them from behind the mailbox.

DATE:_______ $:_______
❍ WISH ❍ HAVE

'94	'95	'96
$20	20	20

Skaters & Skiers

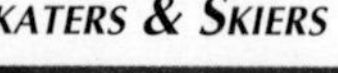

Item #	Intro	Retired	OSRP	GBTru	NO
5475-5	1994	Current	$27.50	**$27.50**	CHANGE

Particulars: Set of 3. One child laces up her skates while another is happy to be able to stand. As one skier looks on, another goes BOOM!

DATE:_______ $:_______
❍ WISH ❍ HAVE

'94	'95	'96
$27.50	27.50	27.5

Going To The Chapel

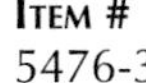

Item #	Intro	Retired	OSRP	GBTru	NO
5476-3	1994	Current	$20	**$20**	CHANGE

Particulars: Set of 2. Family walks to the chapel with gifts and a wreath as a clergyman waits to greet them.

DATE:_______ $:_______
❍ WISH ❍ HAVE

'94	'95	'96
$20	20	20

Santa Comes To Town, 1995

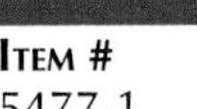

Item #	Intro	Retired	OSRP	GBTru	↑
5477-1	1994	1995 Annual	$30	**$42**	24%

Particulars: 1st in a Series of Dated Annual Santa pieces. Children circle Santa as he passes out presents. He is holding a sack of toys and a book dated "1995."

DATE:_______ $:_______
❍ WISH ❍ HAVE

'94	'95	'96
$30	30	34

Marshmallow Roast

Item #	Intro	Retired	OSRP	GBTru	NO
5478-0	1994	Current	$32.50	**$32.50**	CHANGE

Particulars: Set of 3. Lighted—fire glows. Children take skating rest roasting marshmallows over log fire. Battery operated or can be used with Adapter, Item #5225-6.

DATE:_______ $:_______
❍ WISH ❍ HAVE

'94	'95	'96
$32.50	32.50	32.50

Coca-Cola® brand Delivery Truck

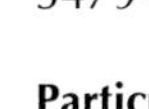

Item #	Intro	Retired	OSRP	GBTru	NO
5479-8	1994	Current	$15	**$15**	CHANGE

Particulars: Red and white Coca-Cola delivery truck with large wreath on the back.

DATE:_______ $:_______
❍ WISH ❍ HAVE

'94	'95	'96
$15	15	15

Coca–Cola® brand Delivery Men

Item #	Intro	Retired	OSRP	GBTru	
5480-1	1994	Current	$25	**$25**	NO CHANGE

Particulars: Set of 2. One man carries crates to truck as another stops to enjoy a Coke.

DATE:_______ $:_______
❍ WISH ❍ HAVE

'94	'95	'96
$25	25	25

Coca–Cola® brand Billboard

Item #	Intro	Retired	OSRP	GBTru	
5481-0	1994	Current	$18	**$18**	NO CHANGE

Particulars: Three lights shine on a billboard featuring Santa enjoying a Coke. Trees grow in the shade of the sign.

DATE:_______ $:_______
❍ WISH ❍ HAVE

'94	'95	'96
$18	18	18

A Visit With Santa

Item #	Intro	Retired	OSRP	GBTru
754-4	1995	1995 Annual	$25	**$60**

Particulars: Mother and children meet Santa on the street. Mother has shopping bag. Gifts are stacked on the snow Piece was crafted for specific stores. The store's logo is on the shopping bag. The retailers chose the colors for the gift packages.

The stores and individual Item Numbers are as follows:

Bachman's .... #754-4
Fortunoff .... #767-6
Pine Cone Christmas Shop .... #773-0
Stat's .... #765-0
The Lemon Tree .... #768-4
The Limited Edition .... #764-1
William Glen .... #766-8
Young's Ltd. .... #769-2

DATE:_______ $:_______
❍ WISH ❍ HAVE

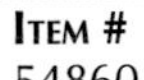

FROSTY PLAYTIME

ITEM #	INTRO	RETIRED	OSRP	GBTRU	NO CHANGE
54860	1995	CURRENT	$30	**$30**	

Particulars: Set of 3. Child rides on playground bouncing deer as another holds a hula hoop. Boys make snow and ice houses.

DATE:________ $:________
❍ WISH ❍ HAVE

'95	'96
$30	30

POINSETTIAS FOR SALE

ITEM #	INTRO	RETIRED	OSRP	GBTRU	NO CHANGE
54861	1995	CURRENT	$30	**$30**	

Particulars: Set of 3. Vendor offers choice of plants to shoppers.

DATE:________ $:________
❍ WISH ❍ HAVE

'95	'96
$30	30

ANTA COMES TO TOWN, 1996

ITEM #	INTRO	RETIRED	OSRP	GBTRU	⬆
54862	1995	1996 ANNUAL	$32.50	**$40**	23%

Particulars: 2nd in a Series of Annual Dated Santas. Santa pulls sleigh loaded with gifts as children catch a ride.

DATE:________ $:________
❍ WISH ❍ HAVE

'95	'96
$32.50	32.50

CHOPPING FIREWOOD

ITEM #	INTRO	RETIRED	OSRP	GBTRU	NO CHANGE
54863	1995	CURRENT	$16.50	**$16.50**	

Particulars: Set of 2. Father chops wood as son stacks into ventilated cords. Materials are ceramic and wood.

DATE:________ $:________
❍ WISH ❍ HAVE

'95	'96
$16.50	16.50

Firewood Delivery Truck

Item #	Intro	Retired	OSRP	GBTru	NO
54864	1995	Current	$15	**$15**	CHAN

Particulars: Holiday Farms truck loaded with firewood he in place by slatted wood panels.

DATE:_______ $:_______
❍ WISH ❍ HAVE

'95	'9
$15	1

Service With A Smile

Item #	Intro	Retired	OSRP	GBTru	NO
54865	1995	Current	$25	**$25**	CHAN

Particulars: Set of 2. One attendant at car service station cleans windshield as other holds new tire.

DATE:_______ $:_______
❍ WISH ❍ HAVE

'95	'9
$25	2

Pizza Delivery

Item #	Intro	Retired	OSRP	GBTru	NO
54866	1995	Current	$20	**$20**	CHAN

Particulars: Set of 2. Pisa Pizza green VW bug auto used f home delivery of fresh pizzas. Delivery person carries stacked boxed pies plus additional take-out.

DATE:_______ $:_______
❍ WISH ❍ HAVE

'95	'9
$20	2

Grand Old Opry Carolers

Item #	Intro	Retired	OSRP	GBTru	NO
54867	1995	Current	$25	**$25**	CHAN

Particulars: Singer and musicians present carols country-style.

DATE:_______ $:_______
❍ WISH ❍ HAVE

'95	'9
$25	2

Snow Carnival Ice Sculptures

Item #	Intro	Retired	OSRP	GBTru	
54868	1995	Current	$27.50	**$27.50**	No Change

Particulars: Set of 2. Mother and child get set to photograph an ice angel sculpture as the artist puts the final touches on penguins and snowflakes sculpture.

DATE:_______ $:_______
❍ WISH ❍ HAVE

'95	'96
$27.50	27.50

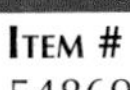

Snow Carnival King & Queen

Item #	Intro	Retired	OSRP	GBTru	
54869	1995	Current	$35	**$35**	No Change

Particulars: Ice carnival King and Queen arrive in sled-dog drawn sleigh.

DATE:_______ $:_______
❍ WISH ❍ HAVE

'95	'96
$35	35

Starbucks Coffee Cart

Item #	Intro	Retired	OSRP	GBTru	
54870	1995	Current	$27.50	**$27.50**	No Change

Particulars: Set of 2. Woman stops to purchase hot coffee from vendor with mobile cart.

DATE:_______ $:_______
❍ WISH ❍ HAVE

'95	'96
$27.50	27.50

Just Married

Item #	Intro	Retired	OSRP	GBTru	
54879	1995	Current	$25	**$25**	No Change

Particulars: Set of 2. Groom carries bride. Car is decorated in congratulatory balloons, tin cans and banner.

DATE:_______ $:_______
❍ WISH ❍ HAVE

'95	'96
$25	25

Here Comes Santa

Item #	Intro	Retired	OSRP	GBTru	↑
07750	1996	1996 Annual	$25	**$45**	80°

Particulars: Santa has banner with message "Joy To The World." Three children follow Santa and one carries a gift wrapped present.
The following retailers had this piece personalized for their store:

Bachman's	#07744
Bronner's Wonderland	#07745
Broughton Christmas Shoppe	#07748
Calabash Nautical Gifts	#07753
Carson Pirie Scott	#07763
Dickens' Gift Shoppe	#07750
European Imports	#07762
Fibber Magee's	#07747
Fortunoff	#07741
Gustaf's	#07759
Ingle's Nook	#07754
North Pole City	#07742
Pine Cone Christmas Shop	#07740
Royal Dutch Collectibles	#07760
Russ Country Gardens	#07756
St. Nick's	#07757
Seventh Avenue	#07758
Stat's	#07749
The Cabbage Rose	#07752
The Calico Butterfly	#07751
The Christmas Loft	#07755
The Limited Edition	#07746
William Glen	#07743
Young's Ltd.	#07761

DATE:_______ $:_______
❍ WISH ❍ HAVE

A Ride On The Reindeer Lines

Item #	Intro	Retired	OSRP	GBTru	
54875	1996	Current	$35	**$35**	No Chan

Particulars: Midyear release. Set of 3. Family ready to depart for the holidays. Child and Bus Driver and Reindeer Line Bus with racing deer on front and sides complete with large chrome bumper, wipers, and windows all around.

DATE:_______ $:_______
❍ WISH ❍ HAVE

On The Road Again

Item #	Intro	Retired	OSRP	GBTru
54891	1996	Current	$20	**$20**

Particulars: Set of 2. Station wagon carrying a canoe on roof rack hauls a trailer.

DATE:_______ $:_______
❍ WISH ❍ HAVE

Moving Day

Item #	Intro	Retired	OSRP	GBTru
54892	1996	Current	$32.50	**$32.50**

Particulars: Set of 3. New owners help moving men carry household goods from the moving van into their new home in the village.

DATE:_______ $:_______
❍ WISH ❍ HAVE

Holiday Hoops

Item #	Intro	Retired	OSRP	GBTru
54893	1996	Current	$20	**$20**

Particulars: Set of 3. Two students play one-on-one basketball.

DATE:_______ $:_______
❍ WISH ❍ HAVE

Men At Work

Item #	Intro	Retired	OSRP	GBTru
54894	1996	Current	$27.50	**$27.50**

Particulars: Set of 5. Village street and road repairs are handled by work crew and road vehicle.

DATE:_______ $:_______
❍ WISH ❍ HAVE

Terry's Towing

Item #	Intro	Retired	OSRP	GBTru
54895	1996	Current	$20	**$20**

Particulars: Set of 2. Track Compatible. Yellow tow truck hauls non-working cars to a service center.

DATE:________ $:________
❍ WISH ❍ HAVE

Caroling Through The Snow

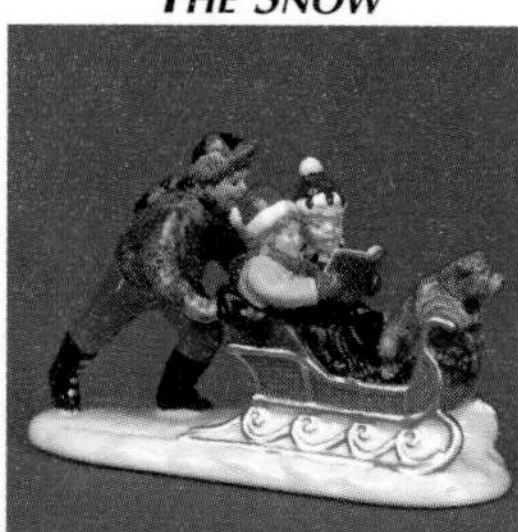

Item #	Intro	Retired	OSRP	GBTru
54896	1996	Current	$15	**$15**

Particulars: Track compatible. Boy pushes carolers in sleigh

DATE:________ $:________
❍ WISH ❍ HAVE

Heading For The Hills

Item #	Intro	Retired	OSRP	GBTru
54897	1996	Current	$8.50	**$8.50**

Particulars: Set of 2. Track compatible. Car with ski carriers mounted to the car roof.

DATE:________ $:________
❍ WISH ❍ HAVE

A Harley-Davidson Holiday

Item #	Intro	Retired	OSRP	GBTru
54898	1996	Current	$22.50	**$22.50**

Particulars: Set of 2. Father and child carry family presents to Harley-Davidson motorcycle and sidecar for trip home.

DATE:________ $:________
❍ WISH ❍ HAVE

Santa Comes To Town, 1997

Item #	Intro	Retired	OSRP	GBTru
54899	1996	Current	$35	**$35**

Particulars: Third in a Series of Dated Annual Santas. Mayor presents Santa with a key to the Village as a children's band strikes up a tune.

DATE:________ $:________
❍ WISH ❍ HAVE

Harley-Davidson Fat Boy & Softail

Item #	Intro	Retired	OSRP	GBTru
54900	1996	Current	$16.50	**$16.50**

Particulars: Set of 2. Two different popular motorcycle designs.

DATE:________ $:________
❍ WISH ❍ HAVE

Harley-Davidson Sign

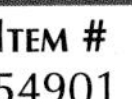

Item #	Intro	Retired	OSRP	GBTru
54901	1996	Current	$18	**$18**

Particulars: Motorcycle mounted on a sign advertises the location of Harley-Davidson Motor Sales, Parts and Service business.

DATE:________ $:________
❍ WISH ❍ HAVE

Ronald McDonald House Ornament (The House that ♥ Built)

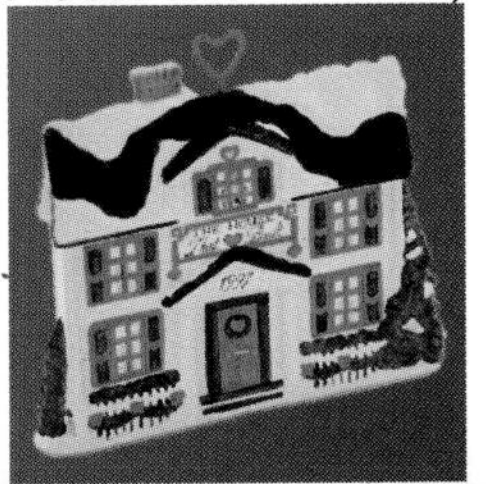

Item #	Intro	Retired	OSRP	GBTru
8961	1997	Current	$7.50	**$7.50**

Particulars: A miniature version of the two-story home piece, # 8960. A portion of the proceeds from the sale of this ornament will be donated to the Ronald McDonald Houses across the country.

DATE:________ $:________
❍ WISH ❍ HAVE

Treetop Tree House

Item #	Intro	Retired	OSRP	GBTru
54890	1997	Current	$35	**$35**

Particulars: Children's tree playhouse nestles in branches of a Jack Pine tree. A wooden ladder allows entry/exit and mailbox is attached to the base of the tree. A tire swing hangs from a bare branch. Material is resin.

DATE:_______ $:_______
❍ WISH ❍ HAVE

The Whole Family Goes Shopping

Item #	Intro	Retired	OSRP	GBTru
54905	1997	Current	$25	**$25**

Particulars: Set of 3. Mid-year release. Dad, Mom and children on a busy holiday shopping spree. Family Dalmatian joins in, hoping for a trip to the feed store for biscuits. (Girl carrying doll is missing from photo.)

DATE:_______ $:_______
❍ WISH ❍ HAVE

Sign

Intro
1987

Particulars: This sign was given to dealers who attended trade shows and showrooms around the country. It was never intended for resale and is one of the rarest Snow Village accessories. It came packed in a blister pack.

DATE:________ $:________
❍ WISH ❍ HAVE

Wooden Ornaments

Item #	Intro	Retired	OSRP	GBTru
5099-7	1982	Disc. 1983	$30	**$450**

Particulars: These six wooden ornaments are replicas of six Snow Village buildings from 1982. They include *Carriage House, Centennial House, Countryside Church, Gabled House, Pioneer Church* and *Swiss Chalet*. They have monofilament lines attached to the tops and/or clips attached to the bottoms.

DATE:________ $:________
❍ WISH ❍ HAVE

THATCHED COTTAGE

ITEM #	INTRO	RETIRED	OSRP	GBTRU	⬇
5050-0	1979	1980	$30	**$690**	5%

Particulars: Small thatched cottage with attached tree. Chimney at rear of stucco and timber trim.

'96
$725

COUNTRYSIDE CHURCH

ITEM #	INTRO	RETIRED	OSRP	GBTRU	⬇
5051-8	1979	1980	$25	**$545**	20%

Particulars: *Countryside Church* in a springtime setting. There's a large green tree against a simple white wood church with a steeple rising from the entry to the nave. For a snow version see OSV 1979, *Countryside Church,* Item #5058-3.

'96
$685

ASPEN TREES

ITEM #	INTRO	RETIRED	OSRP	GBTRU
5052-6	1979	1980	$16	**$265**

Particulars: The trees that shiver and tremble in the wind. Small leaves on a hardwood tree.

SHEEP

ITEM #	INTRO	RETIRED	OSRP	GBTRU
5053-4	1979	1980	$12	**NE**

Particulars: Set of 12 includes 9 white and 3 black sheep. The photograph shows one white sheep only.

Dickens' Village

Dickens' Village was introduced in 1984, and it wasn't long before it reached ts position as Department 56's most popular village. Featuring buildings and .ccessories based on Victorian England, it depicts the places and people we 'isualize when reading one of Charles Dickens' works.

Department 56's first porcelain series, Dickens' Village has experienced a popularity equalled by few products in the collectible industry. The reasons for ts success are varied, but they include the quality of the designs and production, he appeal of limited editions (there have been seven), and the fact that many ollectors associate the entire village with *A Christmas Carol*, Dickens' most amous work and perhaps the most popular Christmas story ever.

Four of Dickens' stories have been the basis for the village's designs. *A Christmas Carol, Nicholas Nickleby, David Copperfield,* and *Oliver Twist* have ll been featured in porcelain. Though *The Old Curiosity Shop* is both a Dickens' tory and a building in the village, they are not the same.

The Charles Dickens' Signature Series, introduced in 1992, features buildings where Charles Dickens may have stayed while traveling. The latest building, *Gad's Hill Place*, depicts his last home and was introduced in 1996. The buildings in the series are each limited to one year of production.

More than a decade since its introduction, and more than a century after the eath of its namesake, Dickens' Village is more popular than ever.

THE BOTTOM LINE:

Cost of all pieces introduced to Dickens' Village through the 1997 midyear ntroductions, including accessories: (This does not include variations or special ieces.) **$4,993**

GREENBOOK TruMarket Value of all pieces through the 1997 midyear ntroductions, including accessories: (This does not include variations or special ieces.) **$22,500**

... NEW FOR SALE LISTINGS

Nettie Quinn Puppets & Marionettes - 1996

This is a wonderful addition to the village that represents the country that made famous the antics of Punch and Judy. The front window of the shop doubles as a puppet theater.

Mulberrie Court - 1996

These rowhouses, with their curved architecture and light coloring, depict city life in England. This is the first multifamily dwelling in the village.

The Olde Camden Town Church - 1996

An addition to the *Christmas Carol Revisited Series*, this church represents the one that Bob Cratchit and Tiny Tim visited on Christmas morning.

The Melancholy Tavern - 1996

This is the tavern that Scrooge visited on a regular basis to take his "melancholy dinner." It's an addition to the *Christmas Carol Revisited Series.*

Quilly's Antiques - 1996

The residents of Dickens' Village will be able to sell and buy valuable antiques in this quaint little shop.

Gad's Hill Place - 1997

This is Department 56's rendition of Charles Dickens' last home, though it was the only one he ever owned. It is the last building to be introduced into the Charles Dickens' Signature Series and is limited to year of production.

Dickens' Village Start-A-Tradition Set - 1997

Consisting of *Sudbury Church, Old East Rectory*, and a three-piece accessory set, this offers Dickens' collectors the newest church and the first home for the clergy of the village.

J. Lytes Coal Merchant - 1997

This is a very tall building housing a coal merchant. The coverings for the upper windows are depicted as iron plates instead of glass, a common practice in those days.

Barmby Moor Cottage - 1997

This adorable stone cottage is located in Barmby Moor, a little village just east of York.

Tower of London - 1997

This is the first design in the new series within Dickens' Village, the Historical Landmark Series. Based on the actual Tower of London, it only has four towers and includes a gated wall, sign, and raven master with ravens.

... NO LONGER ON THE MARKET

5562-0 Old Michaelchurch
5568-9 KING'S ROAD, Set/2
- 55690 Tutbury Printer
- 55691 C.H. Watt Physician

5808-4 PUMP LANE SHOPPES, Set/3
- 58085 Bumpstead Nye Cloaks & Canes
- 58086 Lomas Ltd. Molasses
- 58087 W.M. Wheat Cakes & Puddings

5811-4 Kingford's Brew House
5832-7 Start A Tradition Set, Set/13
- 5832-7 Faversham Lamps & Oil
- 5832-7 Morston Steak & Kidney Pie

What Goes Where?

Trying to decide which pieces to buy? Everyone has the same problem. But for newer collectors deciding can be even more trying than for the experienced collectors. Why? Well, new collectors who want to or can only purchase a certain amount of buildings and accessories each year often want to complete series or stories within villages. But, how do you know what goes with what?

Here's a listing of what buildings and accessories are related. We've also included a short synopsis of each story.

A CHRISTMAS CAROL

Undoubtedly Charles Dickens' most famous work, *A Christmas Carol* was published in 1843. This would become his most requested story to "read" in public. Like many of his works, it deals with a man shaped by arrogance, ignorance, and to some degree, society. Again keeping with his design, Dickens demonstrates that a person can change, good can prosper, and the world can be a better place.

On Christmas Eve, Ebenezer Scrooge is visited by four people who are celebrating Christmas in their own generous manner. He would have nothing to do with their joyous Christmas spirit, and sends each on his way. This is typical of Scrooge's manner as we often see him dealing this way with Bob Cratchit, his clerk, the father of Tiny Tim.

That night he is again visited by four—the ghost of Marley, his departed partner; and the Spirits of Christmas Past, Present, and Future. These spirits warn him to change his ill-tempered ways or pay the price by being burdened throughout eternity. Each of the three Christmas spirits takes Scrooge on a journey showing him how he once celebrated Christmas, how others celebrate it, and how future Christmases will be.

After these journeys Scrooge is convinced that he must change his ways and promising to do so, remains true to his word. This is witnessed by Scrooge giving Bob Cratchit a raise and becoming a second father to Tiny Tim.

Buildings:

CHRISTMAS CAROL COTTAGES s/3	6500-5	1986-1995
• Fezziwig's Warehouse		
• Scrooge & Marley Counting House		
• The Cottage of Bob Cratchit & Tiny Tim		
The Flat Of Ebenezer Scrooge	5587-5	1989-
Nephew Fred's Flat	5557-3	1991-1994
Boarding & Lodging School (#18)	5809-2	1993-1993
Boarding & Lodging School (#43)	5810-6	1994-
Christmas Carol Cottage Revisited	58339	1996-
The Olde Camden Town Church	58346	1996-
The Melancholy Tavern	58347	1996-

ACCESSORIES:

Christmas Carol Figures s/3	6501-3	1986-1990
Fezziwig & Friends s/3	5928-5	1988-1990
Christmas Morning Figures s/3	5588-3	1989-
Christmas Spirits Figures s/4	5589-1	1989-
Vision Of A Christmas Past s/3	5817-3	1993-1996
Christmas Carol Holiday Trimming Set s/21	5831-9	1994-
Caroling w/The Cratchit Family s/3	58396	1996-
The Fezziwig Delivery Wagon	58400	1996-

DAVID COPPERFIELD

David Copperfield, published in 1850, was popular from the start, and has remained so today. Different from his other classics, Dickens wrote this story in the first person. And why shouldn't he have? It was a sometimes thinly disguised autobiography combining his actual life experiences with the turns he wished his life had taken. Even the main character's name is a clue. The main character's initials are D. C., the reverse of Dickens' initials. Copperfield is sent away to school and works in a factory placing labels on bottles. Dickens had endured a similar fate. In the story, we find that Copperfield is infatuated with a woman whom he later marries but never really loves. The same was true for Dickens. The story ends with Copperfield's becoming a successful, highly praised writer...Dickens' own story, once more.

David is brought up by his mother, and their housekeeper, Peggotty. His father had died before David's birth, and his mother marries Mr. Murdstone, a truly disagreeable man. Murdstone sends David to a school in London where he is very unhappy.

After his mother dies, Murdstone removes David from school and sends him to work in a factory, but he runs away to Dover where his aunt, Betsy Trotwood, lives. While attending a better school, he lives with a lawyer, Mr. Wickfield, and his daughter, Agnes. He later meets and marries his wife Dora, but a few years later, she dies.

David leaves the country, but eventually returns, and confesses to Agnes that she is the one he has always loved. They marry, and he becomes a successful writer.

BUILDINGS:

DAVID COPPERFIELD s/3	5550-6	1989-1992
• Mr. Wickfield Solicitor		
• Betsy Trotwood's Cottage		
• Peggotty's Seaside Cottage		

ACCESSORIES:

David Copperfield Characters s/5	5551-4	1989-1992

OLIVER TWIST

Published in 1838, *Oliver Twist* is probably the second most recognized work by Charles Dickens. This is due, in part, to the musical film *Oliver,* produced in the late 1960's.

The story chronicles the young life of a boy as he manages to escape life in a workhouse. The Artful Dodger introduces him to a gang of young criminals headed by a life-long thief named Fagin. Fagin and a treacherous murderer, Bill Sikes, plan to corrupt Oliver Twist and lead him into a life of crime. During this time Oliver's life becomes entwined with that of Mr. Brownlow whom he lives with for a short time before being brought back to Fagin's gang.

After a series of chance events and devious plots including Oliver's being shot in Mrs. Maylie's home while being forced to burglarize it, Sikes accidently hangs himself, Fagin is tried and executed, and the rest of the gang is disbanded. Oliver is adopted by Mr. Brownlow who provides him a good home. It is then that he learns who his parents were, and he inherits a portion of his father's estate.

BUILDINGS:

Fagin's Hide-A-Way	5552-2	1991-1995
OLIVER TWIST s/2	5553-0	1991-1993
• Brownlow House		
• Maylie Cottage		

ACCESSORIES:

Oliver Twist Characters s/3	5554-9	1991-1993

NICHOLAS NICKLEBY

Published in 1839, *Nicholas Nickleby* was written by Charles Dickens to bring attention to the practice of placing small children in boarding schools where they were "employed" as farmhands. This practice was not unusual in England, especially in Yorkshire.

After the death of his father, Nicholas Nickleby, along with his mother and sister, moves to London to live with his uncle, Ralph. Not a pleasant arrangement in Ralph's eyes, he sends Nicholas off to school in Yorkshire where he becomes a student of a contemptuous schoolmaster, Wackford Squeers.

Nicholas runs away from the school, and after a brief stop in London, goes to Portsmouth where he acts in a traveling theater. He later returns to London and meets Madeline with whom he falls in love. His uncle plots to force Madeline to marry an acquaintance of his, but Nicholas thwarts the plan.

A family tragedy leads Ralph to kill himself. Squeers is jailed and his school is closed down. Nicholas finds happiness when he marries Madeline.

BUILDINGS:

NICHOLAS NICKLEBY s/2	5925-0	1988-1991
• Nicholas Nickleby Cottage		
• Wackford Squeers Boarding School		

ACCESSORIES:

Nicholas Nickleby Characters s/4	5929-3	1988-1991

5550-6	1992	DAVID COPPERFIELD
5550-6	1992	Mr. Wickfield Solicitor
5550-6	1992	Betsy Trotwood's Cottage
5550-6	1992	Peggotty's Seaside Cottage
5552-2	1995	Fagin's Hide-A-Way
5553-0	1993	OLIVER TWIST
5553-0	1993	Brownlow House
5553-0	1993	Maylie Cottage
5555-7	1995	Ashbury Inn
5557-3	1994	Nephew Fred's Flat
5562-0	1996	Old Michaelchurch
5567-0	1992	Bishops Oast House
5568-9	1996	KING'S ROAD
55690	1996	Tutbury Printer
55691	1996	C. H. Watt Physician
5582-4	1995	Knottinghill Church
5583-2	1991	Cobles Police Station
5584-0	1992	Theatre Royal
5800-9	1995	Hembleton Pewterer
5808-4	1996	PUMP LANE SHOPPES
58085	1996	Bumpstead Nye Cloaks & Canes
58086	1996	Lomas Ltd. Molasses
58087	1996	W. M. Wheat Cakes & Puddings
5811-4	1996	Kingsford's Brew House
5832-7	1996	Start A Tradition Set
5832-7	1996	Faversham Lamps & Oil
5832-7	1996	Morston Steak & Kidney Pie
5900-5	1989	BARLEY BREE
5900-5	1989	Farmhouse
5900-5	1989	Barn
5902-1	1990	Counting House & Silas Thimbleton Barrister
5916-1	1988	Kenilworth Castle
5924-2	1990	COBBLESTONE SHOPS
5924-2	1990	The Wool Shop
5924-2	1990	Booter And Cobbler
5924-2	1990	T. Wells Fruit & Spice Shop
5925-0	1991	NICHOLAS NICKLEBY
5925-0	1991	Nicholas Nickleby Cottage
5925-0	1991	Wackford Squeers Boarding School
5926-9	1993	MERCHANT SHOPS
5926-9	1993	Poulterer
5926-9	1993	Geo. Weeton Watch-maker
5926-9	1993	The Mermaid Fish Shoppe
5926-9	1993	White Horse Bakery
5926-9	1993	Walpole Tailors
5927-7	1991	Ivy Glen Church
6500-5	1995	CHRISTMAS CAROL COTTAGES
6500-5	1995	Fezziwig's Warehouse
6500-5	1995	Scrooge & Marley Counting House
6500-5	1995	The Cottage of Bob Cratchit & Tiny Tim
6507-2	1989	DICKENS' LANE SHOPS
6507-2	1989	Thomas Kersey Coffee House
6507-2	1989	Cottage Toy Shop
6507-2	1989	Tuttle's Pub
6508-0	1990	Blythe Pond Mill House
6515-3	1988	THE ORIGINAL SHOPS OF DICKENS' VILLAGE
6515-3	1988	Crowntree Inn
6515-3	1988	Candle Shop
6515-3	1988	Green Grocer
6515-3	1988	Golden Swan Baker
6515-3	1988	Bean And Son Smithy Shop
6515-3	1988	Abel Beesley Butcher
6515-3	1988	Jones & Co. Brush & Basket Shop
6516-1	1989	Dickens' Village Church
6518-8	1988	DICKENS' COTTAGES
6518-8	1988	Thatched Cottage
6518-8	1988	Stone Cottage
6518-8	1988	Tudor Cottage
6528-5	1989	Chadbury Station And Train
6549-8	1989	Brick Abbey

LIMITED EDITIONS

5585-9	Ruth Marion Scotch Woolens	17,500
5586-7	Green Gate Cottage	22,500
58336	Ramsford Palace	27,500
5904-8	C. Fletcher Public House	12,500
6502-1	Norman Church	3,500
6519-6	Dickens' Village Mill	2,500
6568-4	Chesterton Manor House	7,500

CHARLES DICKENS SIGNATURE SERIES

5750-9	Crown & Cricket Inn	1992
5751-7	The Pied Bull Inn	1993
5752-5	Dedlock Arms	1994
5753-3	Sir John Falstaff Inn	1995
57534	The Grapes Inn	1996
57535	Gad's Hill Place	1997
5809-2	Boarding & Lodging (#18)	1993

HISTORICAL LANDMARK SERIES

58500	Tower Of London	1997

HOMES FOR THE HOLIDAYS

5832-7	Dickens' Village Start A Tradition Set • Faversham Lamps & Oil • Morston Steak & Kidney Pie • Town Square Carolers	1995
58322	Dickens' Village Start A Tradition Set • Sudbury Church • Old East Rectory • The Spirit of Giving	1997

THE ORIGINAL SHOPS OF DICKENS' VILLAGE

ITEM #	INTRO	RETIRED	OSRP	GBTRU	↓
6515-3	1984	1988	$175	**$1310**	1%

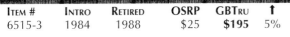

Particulars: Set of 7 includes *Crowntree Inn, Candle Shop, Green Grocer, Golden Swan Baker, Bean And Son Smithy Shop, Abel Beesley Butcher, Jones & Co. Brush & Basket Shop.*

see below

DATE:_______ $:_______ ❍ WISH ❍ HAVE

'91	'92	'93	'94	'95	'96
$1200	1375	1295	1325	1295	1325

CROWNTREE INN

ITEM #	INTRO	RETIRED	OSRP	GBTRU	↓
6515-3	1984	1988	$25	**$300**	2%

Particulars: 1 of the 7-piece set—THE ORIGINAL SHOPS OF DICKENS' VILLAGE. Large multi-paned windows run length of front of Inn with entry door decorated by wreath, second story stone, attic dormer.

DATE:_______ $:_______ ❍ WISH ❍ HAVE

'91	'92	'93	'94	'95	'96
$375	350	335	320	300	305

CANDLE SHOP

ITEM #	INTRO	RETIRED	OSRP	GBTRU	NO CHANGE
6515-3	1984	1988	$25	**$195**	

Particulars: 1 of the 7-piece set—THE ORIGINAL SHOPS OF DICKENS' VILLAGE. Timber framed windows, plaster on stone small house/store. Attic rental rooms, light over front entry.Variation in roof color—first ones shipped were gray followed by blue.

DATE:_______ $:_______ ❍ WISH ❍ HAVE

'91	'92	'93	'94	'95	'96
$235	210	210	190	190	195

GREEN GROCER

ITEM #	INTRO	RETIRED	OSRP	GBTRU	↑
6515-3	1984	1988	$25	**$195**	5%

Particulars: 1 of the 7-piece set—THE ORIGINAL SHOPS OF DICKENS' VILLAGE. Thatched roof over timber two-story grocery/provisions store. Bay window for display. Attached storage room on side of store.

DATE:_______ $:_______ ❍ WISH ❍ HAVE

'91	'92	'93	'94	'95	'96
$220	200	190	185	185	185

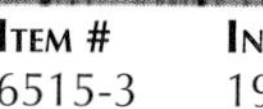

Golden Swan Baker

Item #	Intro	Retired	OSRP	GBTru	⬇
6515-3	1984	1988	$25	**$175**	3%

Particulars: 1 of the 7-piece set—THE ORIGINAL SHOPS OF DICKENS' VILLAGE. Painted sign with gold swan hangs above large bay window for display. Timbered building, brick chimney, light above entry door.

DATE:________ $:________

❍ WISH ❍ HAVE

'91	'92	'93	'94	'95	'96
$170	155	180	180	180	18(

Bean And Son Smithy Shop

Item #	Intro	Retired	OSRP	GBTru	⬆
6515-3	1984	1988	$25	**$195**	3%

Particulars: 1 of the 7-piece set—THE ORIGINAL SHOPS OF DICKENS' VILLAGE. Double wood door, stone first story, second story set on stone with overhang. Steep curved roof with brick chimney.

DATE:________ $:________

❍ WISH ❍ HAVE

'91	'92	'93	'94	'95	'9
$185	185	185	190	195	19

Abel Beesley Butcher

Item #	Intro	Retired	OSRP	GBTru	NO
6515-3	1984	1988	$25	**$130**	CHANC

Particulars: 1 of the 7-piece set—THE ORIGINAL SHOPS OF DICKENS' VILLAGE. Timbered bottom half, seconc story plaster over stone, two chimneys.

DATE:________ $:________

❍ WISH ❍ HAVE

'91	'92	'93	'94	'95	'9
$175	145	130	120	125	13

Jones & Co. Brush & Basket Shop

Item #	Intro	Retired	OSRP	GBTru	⬆
6515-3	1984	1988	$25	**$300**	3%

Particulars: 1 of the 7-piece set—THE ORIGINAL SHOPS OF DICKENS' VILLAGE. Cellar shop is a cobbler with small sign by his door to advertise, rest of building is fo basketry, mats, and brush. Narrow staircase leads to entry.

DATE:________ $:________

❍ WISH ❍ HAVE

'91	'92	'93	'94	'95	'9
$325	355	355	335	300	2

Dickens' Village Church—"White"

Item #	Intro	Retired	OSRP	GBTru	↑
6516-1	1985	1989	$35	**$400**	4%

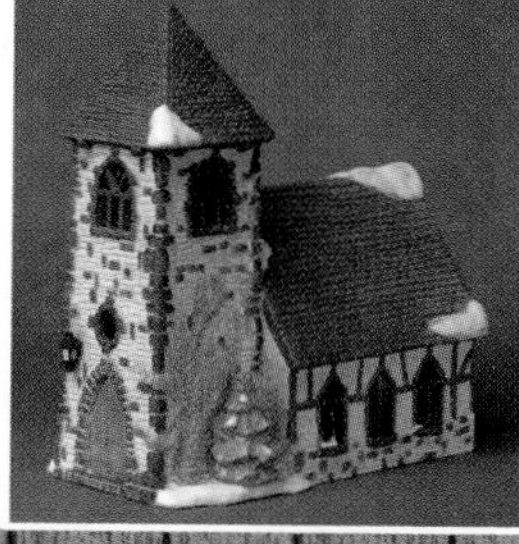

Particulars: There are five versions of the *Village Church:* "White," "Cream," "Green," "Tan" and "Dark." The variations in color affect GBTru$. "White" Church has off white to cream walls and brown roof matches brown cornerstones.

DATE:________ $:________
❍ WISH ❍ HAVE

'91	'92	'93	'94	'95	'96
$250	-	-	425	375	385

Dickens' Village Church—"Cream"

Item #	Intro	Retired	OSRP	GBTru	↑
6516-1	1985	1989	$35	**$285**	4%

Particulars: "Cream" Church has cream walls with light yellow coloring in mortar between stones and a butterscotch roof.

DATE:________ $:________
❍ WISH ❍ HAVE

'91	'92	'93	'94	'95	'96
$145	285	350	295	225	275

Dickens' Village Church—"Green"

Item #	Intro	Retired	OSRP	GBTru	↑
6516-1	1985	1989	$35	**$385**	18%

Particulars: "Green" Church has very light green tone on walls and a butterscotch roof.

DATE:________ $:________
❍ WISH ❍ HAVE

'91	'92	'93	'94	'95	'96
$225	350	415	350	330	325

Dickens' Village Church—"Tan"

Item #	Intro	Retired	OSRP	GBTru	↑
6516-1	1985	1989	$35	**$200**	14%

Particulars: "Tan" Church has tan walls and a butterscotch roof.

DATE:________ $:________
❍ WISH ❍ HAVE

'91	'92	'93	'94	'95	'96
$100	170	195	205	190	175

DICKENS' VILLAGE CHURCH—"DARK"

ITEM #	INTRO	RETIRED	OSRP	GBTRU	↑
6516-1	1985	1989	$35	**$160**	7%

Particulars: "Dark" Church or sometimes called "Butterscotch" has walls that are or nearly are the same color as the roof. This is the only sleeve to read "Village Church." All others read "Shops Of Dickens' Village."

DATE:_______ $:_______ ❍ WISH ❍ HAVE

'91	'92	'93	'94	'95	'96
$-	155	160	155	155	150

DICKENS' COTTAGES

ITEM #	INTRO	RETIRED	OSRP	GBTRU	↑
6518-8	1985	1988	$75	**$965**	5%

Particulars: Set of 3 includes *Thatched Cottage, Stone Cottage, Tudor Cottage.* Early release to Gift Creations Concepts (GCC).

see below

DATE:_______ $:_______ ❍ WISH ❍ HAVE

'91	'92	'93	'94	'95	'96
$875	1015	1015	1050	950	915

THATCHED COTTAGE

ITEM #	INTRO	RETIRED	OSRP	GBTRU	↑
6518-8	1985	1988	$25	**$195**	5%

Particulars: 1 of the 3-piece set—DICKENS' COTTAGES. Early release to Gift Creations Concepts (GCC). Double chimneys rise from thatched roof, second story plastered/timbered home with second story extending out on sides.

DATE:_______ $:_______ ❍ WISH ❍ HAVE

'91	'92	'93	'94	'95	'96
$210	210	200	200	200	185

STONE COTTAGE—"TAN"

ITEM #	INTRO	RETIRED	OSRP	GBTRU	↑
6518-8	1985	1988	$25	**$455**	14%

Particulars: 1 of the 3-piece set—DICKENS' COTTAGES. There are two versions of the *Stone Cottage:* "Tan" and "Green." Tan variation is considered the first color shipped. The color change affects GBTru$. Early release to Gift Creations Concepts (GCC).

DATE:_______ $:_______ ❍ WISH ❍ HAVE

'91	'92	'93	'94	'95	'96
$425	465	450	425	400	400

Stone Cottage—"Green"

Item #	Intro	Retired	OSRP	GBTru	↓
6518-8	1985	1988	$25	**$395**	1%

Particulars: The "Green" version of the *Stone Cottage* is considered to be later shipments. Cottage has variegated fieldstone walls and rough-hewn shingle roof.

DATE:________ $:________

❍ WISH ❍ HAVE

'91	'92	'93	'94	'95	'96
$425	380	375	425	400	400

Tudor Cottage

Item #	Intro	Retired	OSRP	GBTru	↑
6518-8	1985	1988	$25	**$385**	3%

Particulars: 1 of the 3-piece set—DICKENS' COTTAGES. Early release to Gift Creations Concepts (GCC). Stone foundation with timbered/plastered walls forming a small house. Two chimneys for heating/cooking.

DATE:________ $:________

❍ WISH ❍ HAVE

'91	'92	'93	'94	'95	'96
$400	455	450	450	400	375

Dickens' Village Mill

Item #	Intro	Retired	OSRP	GBTru	↑
6519-6	1985	Ltd Ed 2,500	$35	**$4995**	3%

Particulars: Rough-hewn stone makes up 3-section mill with large wooden mill wheel. Two sets double doors—one large set to allow carriage to be brought directly into building, smaller doors open into silo area. Early release to Gift Creations Concepts (GCC). Some sleeves read "Dickens' Village Cottage."

DATE:________ $:________

❍ WISH ❍ HAVE

'91	'92	'93	'94	'95	'96
$5550	5550	5550	5150	5000	4850

Christmas Carol Cottages

Item #	Intro	Retired	OSRP	GBTru	↑
6500-5	1986	1995	$75	**$125**	9%

Particulars: Set of 3 includes *Fezziwig's Warehouse, Scrooge & Marley Counting House, The Cottage Of Bob Cratchit & Tiny Tim.*

see next page

DATE:________ $:________

❍ WISH ❍ HAVE

'91	'92	'93	'94	'95	'96
$90	90	90	90	90	115

Fezziwig's Warehouse

Item #	Intro	Retired	OSRP	GBTru	
6500-5	1986	1995	$25	**$40**	NO CHANGE

Particulars: 1 of the 3-piece set—CHRISTMAS CAROL COTTAGES. Early pieces have panes cut out of front door (photo). Later pieces have a solid front door. This does not affect Secondary Market Value. In *A Christmas Carol*, Fezziwig was young Scrooge's employer. On one day a year, Christmas Eve, Fezziwig held a high-spirited party for his staff and family in the warehouse.

DATE:_______	$:_______	'91	'92	'93	'94	'95	'96
❍ WISH	❍ HAVE	$30	30	30	30	30	40

Scrooge & Marley Counting House

Item #	Intro	Retired	OSRP	GBTru	↑
6500-5	1986	1995	$25	**$45**	13%

Particulars: 1 of the 3-piece set—CHRISTMAS CAROL COTTAGES. The office of Scrooge and his departed partner, Jacob Marley, in *A Christmas Carol*. A Counting House kept books and transacted business for different accounts. You would go to a Counting House to borrow money or repay a loan. Building is simple rectangular shape. Bottom brick, second story plastered with shuttered windows.

DATE:_______	$:_______	'91	'92	'93	'94	'95	'96
❍ WISH	❍ HAVE	$30	30	30	30	30	40

The Cottage of Bob Cratchit & Tiny Tim

Item #	Intro	Retired	OSRP	GBTru	↑
6500-5	1986	1995	$25	**$60**	20%

Particulars: 1 of the 3-piece set—CHRISTMAS CAROL COTTAGES. This is the tiny home in which Bob & Mary Cratchit raised their children—most notably Tiny Tim. Many scholars believe that Dickens fashioned the home after his own childhood home on Bayham Street in Camden Town.

DATE:_______	$:_______	'91	'92	'93	'94	'95	'96
❍ WISH	❍ HAVE	$30	30	30	30	30	50

Norman Church

Item #	Intro	Retired	OSRP	GBTru	↑
6502-1	1986	Ltd Ed 3,500	$40	**$3325**	2%

Particulars: Solid four-sided tower used as both watch and bell tower. Doors and windows reflect the Romanesque rounded arches. The first pieces are light gray, the later pieces are darker gray. This does not affect Secondary Market Value. Early release to Gift Creations Concepts (GCC).

DATE:_______	$:_______	'91	'92	'93	'94	'95	'96
❍ WISH	❍ HAVE	$3500	3500	3500	3600	3000	325

DICKENS' LANE SHOPS

ITEM #	INTRO	RETIRED	OSRP	GBTRU	↑
6507-2	1986	1989	$80	**$620**	1%

Particulars: Set of 3 includes *Thomas Kersey Coffee House, Cottage Toy Shop, Tuttle's Pub.*

see below

DATE:_______	$:_______	'91	'92	'93	'94	'95	'96
❍ WISH	❍ HAVE	$475	490	565	650	595	615

THOMAS KERSEY COFFEE HOUSE

ITEM #	INTRO	RETIRED	OSRP	GBTRU	↑
6507-2	1986	1989	$27	**$190**	12%

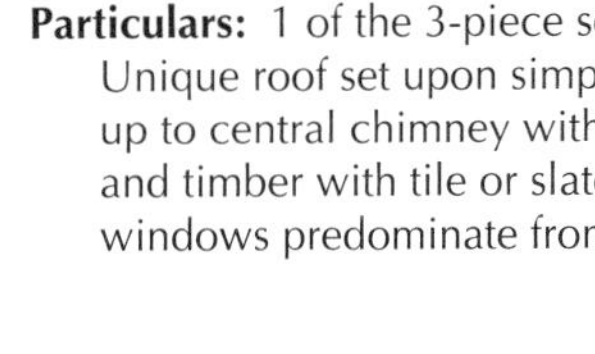

Particulars: 1 of the 3-piece set—DICKENS' LANE SHOPS. Unique roof set upon simple rectangular building rises up to central chimney with four flue pipes. Brick, plaster, and timber with tile or slate roof. Large multi-paned windows predominate front walls.

DATE:_______	$:_______	'91	'92	'93	'94	'95	'96
❍ WISH	❍ HAVE	$145	150	175	165	165	170

COTTAGE TOY SHOP

ITEM #	INTRO	RETIRED	OSRP	GBTRU	↓
6507-2	1986	1989	$27	**$225**	4%

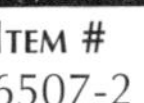

Particulars: 1 of the 3-piece set—DICKENS' LANE SHOPS. Small thatched roof cottage. Shop has large bay windows for light and display. Outside side stair/entry for family to living quarters.

DATE:_______	$:_______	'91	'92	'93	'94	'95	'96
❍ WISH	❍ HAVE	$175	215	265	250	225	235

TUTTLE'S PUB

ITEM #	INTRO	RETIRED	OSRP	GBTRU	↓
6507-2	1986	1989	$27	**$220**	2%

Particulars: 1 of the 3-piece set—DICKENS' LANE SHOPS. Building rises three stories, ground level has pub for refreshments plus stable area for horse and carriages, second and third story jut out in step fashion. Travelers could rent rooms.

DATE:_______	$:_______	'91	'92	'93	'94	'95	'96
❍ WISH	❍ HAVE	$185	220	240	245	225	225

Blythe Pond Mill House—"Correct"

Item #	Intro	Retired	OSRP	GBTru	↑
6508-0	1986	1990	$37	**$295**	5%

Particulars: Commonly referred to as the "correct" version, "Blythe Pond" is inscribed correctly on the bottom of the building. (The "Blythe Pond" sign above the door is correct in both versions.) Three-story timber house, fieldstone wing holds water wheel gears. Grinding stones rest next to house.

DATE:_______ $:_______

❍ WISH ❍ HAVE

'91	'92	'93	'94	'95	'96
$170	215	255	305	315	280

Blythe Pond Mill House—"By The Pond"

Item #	Intro	Retired	OSRP	GBTru	↓
6508-0	1986	1990	$37	**$130**	4%

Particulars: Commonly referred to as the "By The Pond" version because this is inscribed, in error, on the bottom of the building. (The "Blythe Pond" sign above the door is correct in both versions.) The error is more common than the correct piece.

DATE:_______ $:_______

❍ WISH ❍ HAVE

'91	'92	'93	'94	'95	'96
$95	105	125	135	135	135

Chadbury Station And Train

Item #	Intro	Retired	OSRP	GBTru	↓
6528-5	1986	1989	$65	**$380**	1%

Particulars: Set of 4. Three-car train. Station built of rough stone base and fieldstone. Columns support overhang to keep passengers dry. Indoor room warmed by fireplace. Wooden benches for waiting area. Early version of the station is 1/2" smaller than later version—no affect on Secondary Market Value.

DATE:_______ $:_______

❍ WISH ❍ HAVE

'91	'92	'93	'94	'95	'96
$315	385	385	385	375	385

BARLEY BREE

Item #	Intro	Retired	OSRP	GBTru	↑
5900-5	1987	1989	$60	**$380**	1%

Particulars: Set of 2 includes *Farmhouse* and *Barn*. Unlike many sets, it is very unusual for *Barley Bree* to be sold or sought-after as individual pieces. Early versions have dark roofs, later versions have lighter roofs.

see next page

DATE:_______ $:_______

❍ WISH ❍ HAVE

'91	'92	'93	'94	'95	'96
$285	370	380	395	395	375

Farmhouse

Item #	Intro	Retired	OSRP	GBTru
5900-5	1987	1989	$30	*NE

Particulars: 1 of the 2-piece set—BARLEY BREE. Thatched roof on small farmhouse with centralized chimney. Half-story tucked into steeply pitched roof. *Secondary Market Value not established for individual pieces in the set.

DATE:________ $:________

❍ WISH ❍ HAVE

'91	'92	'93	'94	'95	'96
NE	NE	NE	NE	NE	NE

Barn

Item #	Intro	Retired	OSRP	GBTru
5900-5	1987	1989	$30	*NE

Particulars: 1 of the 2-piece set—BARLEY BREE. Stone foundation, thatched roof, for livestock. *Secondary Market Value not established for individual pieces in the set.

DATE:________ $:________

❍ WISH ❍ HAVE

'91	'92	'93	'94	'95	'96
NE	NE	NE	NE	NE	NE

The Old Curiosity Shop

Item #	Intro	Retired	OSRP	GBTru	↑
5905-6	1987	Current	$32	$45	7%

Particulars: Generally thought to be designed after the Old Curiosity Shop on Portsmouth St. in London, as stated on the front of the actual building. However, many historians believe that this is not the building Dickens used as a model when writing *The Old Curiosity Shop.* Antiques corner shop is adjacent to rare book store. Curiosity shop has large display window and two chimneys. Book shop is taller and narrower.

DATE:________ $:________

❍ WISH ❍ HAVE

'91	'92	'93	'94	'95	'96
$37.50	37.50	40	40	42	42

Kenilworth Castle

Item #	Intro	Retired	OSRP	GBTru	↓
5916-1	1987	1988	$70	$675	3%

Particulars: Inspired by the remains of Kenilworth Castle, Warwickshire, England. A stronghold for Kings & Lords, it began in 1122 as a fortress, then passed to the Earl of Leicester in 1244. With living quarters it became a Medieval Palace, a favorite of Elizabeth I who visited as a guest of Robert Dudley. Early pieces are larger. It's not unusual for the Castle to have concave walls. Relatively straight walls can be found and are generally considered to be more valuable.

DATE:________ $:________

❍ WISH ❍ HAVE

'91	'92	'93	'94	'95	'96
$375	440	495	540	675	695

Brick Abbey

Item #	Intro	Retired	OSRP	GBTru	No Change
6549-8	1987	1989	$33	$375	

Particulars: Two spires flank front doors, rose window above entry oak doors. Example of a stage of Gothic architecture. Many pieces have spires that lean inward. Those with straight spires are considered to be premiere pieces and usually command a higher price.

DATE:_______ $:_______ ❍ WISH ❍ HAVE

'91	'92	'93	'94	'95	'96
$350	400	380	405	395	375

Chesterton Manor House

Item #	Intro	Retired	OSRP	GBTru	↓
6568-4	1987	Ltd Ed 7,500	$45	$1575	5%

Particulars: Known as a Great House, countryside home with many acres of land. Stone facade, slate roof, plaster and half timber, open pediment above wood entry door with double gable roof design. Early release to Gift Creations Concepts (GCC).

DATE:_______ $:_______ ❍ WISH ❍ HAVE

'91	'92	'93	'94	'95	'96
$1800	1875	1825	1725	1650	1665

Counting House & Silas Thimbleton Barrister

Item #	Intro	Retired	OSRP	GBTru	No Change
5902-1	1988	1990	$32	$90	

Particulars: Square, 3-story, 3-chimney, offices. Equal angle gables create 4-section roof. Attached plaster/timbered 3-story building is smaller and narrower. Initial shipments had natural porcelain panes. Later shipments had yellow panes.

DATE:_______ $:_______ ❍ WISH ❍ HAVE

'91	'92	'93	'94	'95	'96
$95	95	90	90	85	90

C. Fletcher Public House

Item #	Intro	Retired	OSRP	GBTru	↑
5904-8	1988	Ltd Ed 12,500*	$35	$580	6%

Particulars: *Plus Proof Editions. Market Price for Proofs is not established. Pub windows wrap around corner. Wood ribs support wider/longer 2nd story. Sweet Shop tucks in next to pub, is plaster/timber design. Early release to Gift Creations Concepts (GCC).

DATE:_______ $:_______ ❍ WISH ❍ HAVE

'91	'92	'93	'94	'95	'96
$725	700	645	590	575	54

COBBLESTONE SHOPS

ITEM #	INTRO	RETIRED	OSRP	GBTRU	⬇
5924-2	1988	1990	$95	**$375**	1%

Particulars: Set of 3 includes *The Wool Shop, Booter And Cobbler, T. Wells Fruit & Spice Shop.*

see below

DATE:________ $:________ ❍ WISH ❍ HAVE

'91	'92	'93	'94	'95	'96
$245	300	310	355	365	380

THE WOOL SHOP

ITEM #	INTRO	RETIRED	OSRP	GBTRU	NO CHANGE
5924-2	1988	1990	$32	**$175**	

Particulars: 1 of the 3-piece set—COBBLESTONE SHOPS. Low turret rounds out one front corner of shop. Wood framing of three front windows and lattice design. Light by front door.

DATE:________ $:________ ❍ WISH ❍ HAVE

'91	'92	'93	'94	'95	'96
$120	140	170	170	180	175

BOOTER AND COBBLER

ITEM #	INTRO	RETIRED	OSRP	GBTRU	NO CHANGE
5924-2	1988	1990	$32	**$125**	

Particulars: 1 of the 3-piece set—COBBLESTONE SHOPS. Some box sleeves picture the *T. Wells Fruit & Spice Shop*. Shoes made and repaired in this stone building with entry via Tannery where leather is cured and dyed.

DATE:________ $:________ ❍ WISH ❍ HAVE

'91	'92	'93	'94	'95	'96
$85	90	115	105	115	125

T. WELLS FRUIT & SPICE SHOP

ITEM #	INTRO	RETIRED	OSRP	GBTRU	⬇
5924-2	1988	1990	$32	**$95**	5%

Particulars: 1 of the 3-piece set—COBBLESTONE SHOPS. Some box sleeves picture *Booter And Cobbler*. White washed brick and timbered building. Front window has stone ledge. Outdoor covered produce bin for food.

DATE:________ $:________ ❍ WISH ❍ HAVE

'91	'92	'93	'94	'95	'96
$85	90	95	95	95	100

NICHOLAS NICKLEBY

ITEM #	INTRO	RETIRED	OSRP	GBTRU	↑
5925-0	1988	1991	$72	$175	9%
			W/ERROR	$200	NC

Particulars: Set of 2 includes *Nicholas Nickleby Cottage, Wackford Squeers Boarding School.*

see below

	'91	'92	'93	'94	'95	'96
Nic"k"olas error:	$90	210	195	195	185	200
	$82	170	155	155	155	160

DATE:_______ $:_______
❍ WISH ❍ HAVE

NICHOLAS NICKLEBY COTTAGE

ITEM #	INTRO	RETIRED	OSRP	GBTRU	NO CHANGE
5925-0	1988	1991	$36	$85	

Particulars: 1 of the 2-piece set—NICHOLAS NICKLEBY. This is the cottage where Nicholas Nickleby lived as the main character in Dickens' work by the same name. On this piece the name on the sign and bottom inscription are spelled correctly.

DATE:_______ $:_______
❍ WISH ❍ HAVE

'91	'92	'93	'94	'95	'96
$41	90	80	80	80	85

NIC"K"OLAS NICKLEBY COTTAGE

ITEM #	INTRO	RETIRED	OSRP	GBTRU	↑
5925-0	1988	1991	$36	$125	4%

Particulars: The error in spelling—Nic"k"olas rather than Nicholas—appears only on the bottom of the piece (see photo). The sign over the window is correct.

DATE:_______ $:_______
❍ WISH ❍ HAVE

'91	'92	'93	'94	'95	'96
$90	120	120	120	100	120

WACKFORD SQUEERS BOARDING SCHOOL

ITEM #	INTRO	RETIRED	OSRP	GBTRU	NO CHANGE
5925-0	1988	1991	$36	$85	

Particulars: 1 of the 2-piece set—NICHOLAS NICKLEBY. In *Nicholas Nickleby* headmaster Wackford Squeers "employs" students as farm hands. Due to its size, the building's roof sags in the middle. One with a flat roof commands a higher value. Dickens based his version of the school on the Bowes Academy that once stood in Yorkshire.

DATE:_______ $:_______
❍ WISH ❍ HAVE

'91	'92	'93	'94	'95	'96
$41	92	85	85	85	85

MERCHANT SHOPS

Item #	Intro	Retired	OSRP	GBTru	↑
5926-9	1988	1993	$150	**$260**	6%

Particulars: Set of 5 includes *Poulterer, Geo. Weeton Watchmaker, The Mermaid Fish Shoppe, White Horse Bakery, Walpole Tailors.*

see below

DATE:_______	$:_______	'91	'92	'93	'94	'95	'96
❍ WISH	❍ HAVE	$175	175	180	230	255	245

POULTERER

Item #	Intro	Retired	OSRP	GBTru	↑
5926-9	1988	1993	$32.50	**$60**	9%

Particulars: 1 of the 5-piece set—MERCHANT SHOPS. Three-story stone block and timber, fresh geese hang outside front door.

DATE:_______	$:_______	'91	'92	'93	'94	'95	'96
❍ WISH	❍ HAVE	$35	35	36	60	55	55

GEO. WEETON WATCHMAKER

Item #	Intro	Retired	OSRP	GBTru	NO CHANGE
5926-9	1988	1993	$32.50	**$55**	

Particulars: 1 of the 5-piece set—MERCHANT SHOPS. All brick, rounded bay window, slate roof, fan light window in oak front door.

DATE:_______	$:_______	'91	'92	'93	'94	'95	'96
❍ WISH	❍ HAVE	$35	35	36	60	55	55

THE MERMAID FISH SHOPPE

Item #	Intro	Retired	OSRP	GBTru	↑
5926-9	1988	1993	$32.50	**$75**	7%

Particulars: 1 of the 5-piece set—MERCHANT SHOPS. Roadside fish bins, bay windows, angled doors and walls, wooden trap door in roof.

DATE:_______	$:_______	'91	'92	'93	'94	'95	'96
❍ WISH	❍ HAVE	$35	35	36	70	65	70

White Horse Bakery

Item #	Intro	Retired	OSRP	GBTru	↑
5926-9	1988	1993	$32.50	**$70**	27%

Particulars: 1 of the 5-piece set—MERCHANT SHOPS. Two large windows to display baked goods, roof is hipped and gabled with scalloped shingles.

DATE:________ $:________ ❍ WISH ❍ HAVE

'91	'92	'93	'94	'95	'96
$35	35	36	55	55	55

Walpole Tailors

Item #	Intro	Retired	OSRP	GBTru	No Change
5926-9	1988	1993	$32.50	**$55**	

Particulars: 1 of the 5-piece set—MERCHANT SHOPS. Stone and brick covered by stucco. Large first floor windows have wood panels under sills. 2nd floor has bow window.

DATE:________ $:________ ❍ WISH ❍ HAVE

'91	'92	'93	'94	'95	'96
$35	35	36	55	55	55

Ivy Glen Church

Item #	Intro	Retired	OSRP	GBTru	↑
5927-7	1988	1991	$35	**$85**	6%

Particulars: Square-toothed parapet tops stone turret by front entry of a thatched roof church. Curved timber design above door is repeated on bell chamber of turret. Arched windows. This church has a chimney.

DATE:________ $:________ ❍ WISH ❍ HAVE

'91	'92	'93	'94	'95	'96
$37.50	80	85	80	85	80

DAVID COPPERFIELD

Item #	Intro	Retired	OSRP	GBTru	↑
5550-6	1989	1992	$125	**$180**	9%
			w/Tan Pegotty's	**$235**	↑2%

Particulars: Set of 3 includes *Mr. Wickfield Solicitor, Betsy Trotwood's Cottage, Peggotty's Seaside Cottage*. Early release to Showcase Dealers, 1989.

see next page

	'91	'92	'93	'94	'95	'96
Set w/original Tan Peggotty's:	$220	220	310	250	225	230
DATE:________ $:________ ❍ WISH ❍ HAVE	$125	125	230	190	175	165

R. WICKFIELD SOLICITOR

ITEM #	INTRO	RETIRED	OSRP	GBTRU	NO CHANGE
5550-6	1989	1992	$42.50	**$95**	

Particulars: 1 of the 3-piece set—DAVID COPPERFIELD. This is the home and office of Mr. Wickfield in *David Copperfield.* He resides in Canterbury and is a friend of Betsy Trotwood. It's thought that Dickens used the house at 71 St. Dunstan's Street in Canterbury as the model for Mr. Wickfield's residence. Early release to Showcase Dealers, 1989.

DATE:_______	$:_______	'91	'92	'93	'94	'95	'96
❍ WISH	❍ HAVE	$42.50	42.50	90	96	95	95

BETSY TROTWOOD'S COTTAGE

ITEM #	INTRO	RETIRED	OSRP	GBTRU	NO CHANGE
5550-6	1989	1992	$42.50	**$60**	

Particulars: 1 of the 3-piece set—DAVID COPPERFIELD. This cottage is the home of David Copperfield's aunt, Betsy Trotwood. Though the story places the cottage in Dover, historians believe that Dickens based the cottage on the one owned by Mary Strong in Broadstairs. It's now a Dickens museum. Early release to Showcase Dealers, 1989.

DATE:_______	$:_______	'91	'92	'93	'94	'95	'96
❍ WISH	❍ HAVE	$42.50	42.50	78	65	65	60

PEGGOTTY'S SEASIDE COTTAGE—"TAN"

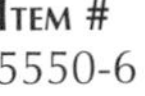

ITEM #	INTRO	RETIRED	OSRP	GBTRU	↑
5550-6	1989	1992	$42.50	**$135**	8%

Particulars: 1 of the 3-piece set—DAVID COPPERFIELD. The hull of the boat was actually unpainted. Department 56 stated that the particular green paint they intended to use would not adhere to the porcelain, so they shipped them unpainted until the problem could be corrected. Early release to Showcase Dealers, 1989.

DATE:_______	$:_______	'91	'92	'93	'94	'95	'96
❍ WISH	❍ HAVE	$155	155	175	150	150	125

PEGGOTTY'S SEASIDE COTTAGE—"GREEN"

ITEM #	INTRO	RETIRED	OSRP	GBTRU	NO CHANGE
5550-6	1989	1992	$42.50	**$55**	

Particulars: 1 of the 3-piece set—DAVID COPPERFIELD. This overturned boat converted into a cottage belongs to Daniel Peggotty in *David Copperfield.* Though a similar cottage was located in Yarmouth, it's strongly believed that Dickens based his Peggotty's Cottage on an actual boat-turned-dwelling on the bank of the Canal at Gravesend.

DATE:_______	$:_______	'91	'92	'93	'94	'95	'96
❍ WISH	❍ HAVE	$42.50	42.50	70	60	60	55

Victoria Station

Item #	Intro	Retired	OSRP	GBTru	No Change
5574-3	1989	Current	$100	**$112**	

Particulars: Designed after Victoria Station in London. Brownstone with granite pillars and facings—central section with domed red tile roof, two side wings, covered front drive-through, gold clock above entry. Early release to Showcase Dealers and National Association Of Limited Edition Dealers (NALED), 1990.

DATE:_______	$:_______	'91	'92	'93	'94	'95	'96
❍ WISH	❍ HAVE	$100	105	105	110	112	11

Knottinghill Church

Item #	Intro	Retired	OSRP	GBTru	↑
5582-4	1989	1995	$50	**$75**	15%

Particulars: Beige/honey stone with gray slate roof, arched windows. Turret bell chamber rises where church wings intersect.

DATE:_______	$:_______	'91	'92	'93	'94	'95	'9
❍ WISH	❍ HAVE	$50	50	52	52	55	65

Cobles Police Station

Item #	Intro	Retired	OSRP	GBTru	↑
5583-2	1989	1991	$37.50	**$150**	3%

Particulars: Two-story brick, stone outlines front entry and upper windows. Two watch turrets on second story corners.

DATE:_______	$:_______	'91	'92	'93	'94	'95	'9
❍ WISH	❍ HAVE	$37.50	85	85	90	125	14

Theatre Royal

Item #	Intro	Retired	OSRP	GBTru	↓
5584-0	1989	1992	$45	**$80**	6%

Particulars: Inspired by the Theatre Royal in Rochester, England where Charles Dickens saw his first Shakespearean play. Double set of doors fill theatre frontage. Garlands and gold bells add festive touch. Second floor rounded arch windows are separated by pilasters.

DATE:_______	$:_______	'91	'92	'93	'94	'95	'9
❍ WISH	❍ HAVE	$45	48	80	80	80	8

Ruth Marion Scotch Woolens

Item #	Intro	Retired	OSRP	GBTru	↑
5585-9	1989	Ltd Ed 17,500*	$65	**$395**	1%

Particulars: *Plus Proof Editions. Proofs have "Proof" stamped on the bottom of the piece instead of a number. **GBTru for Proof is $350.** Herringbone brick design between timbers decorates front of 1 1/2-story shops and home. Small flower shop tucked onto one side. Named for the wife of D56 artist, Neilan Lund. Early release to Gift Creations Concepts (GCC).

DATE:________ $:________ ❍ WISH ❍ HAVE

'91	'92	'93	'94	'95	'96
$350	405	380	405	385	390

Green Gate Cottage

Item #	Intro	Retired	OSRP	GBTru	↑
5586-7	1989	Ltd Ed 22,500*	$65	**$275**	2%

Particulars: *Plus Proof Editions. Proofs have "Proof" stamped on the bottom of the piece instead of a number. **GBTru for Proof is $245.** 3-story home. Repeated vault design on chimney, dormers, and third-story windows. Balcony above door. Fenced courtyard and 2 doors give impression of 2 homes. Small part has steep roof, crooked chimney, and ornamental molding.

DATE:________ $:________ ❍ WISH ❍ HAVE

'91	'92	'93	'94	'95	'96
$300	340	280	275	275	270

The Flat Of Ebenezer Scrooge—"Taiwan/ Panes"

Item #	Intro	Retired	OSRP	GBTru	↓
5587-5	1989	Variation	$37.50	**$85**	11%

Particulars: There are three variations of *The Flat Of Ebenezer Scrooge* that affect Secondary Market Value. The First Version was made in Taiwan, has yellow panes in the windows and the far left shutter on the 4th floor is slightly open allowing light to shine through. Early release to National Association Of Limited Edition Dealers (NALED), 1989. Addition to "Christmas Carol" grouping.

DATE:________ $:________ ❍ WISH ❍ HAVE

'91	'92	'93	'94	'95	'96
$-	-	-	135	100	95

The Flat Of Ebenezer Scrooge—"Taiwan/ No Panes"

Item #	Intro	Retired	OSRP	GBTru	↑
5587-5	1989	Variation	$37.50	**$75**	15%

Particulars: The Second Version was made in Taiwan but doesn't have panes in the windows.

DATE:________ $:________ ❍ WISH ❍ HAVE

'91	'92	'93	'94	'95	'96
$-	115	-	85	60	65

The Flat Of Ebenezer Scrooge

Item #	Intro	Retired	OSRP	GBTru	
5587-5	1989	Current	$37.50	**$37.50**	No Chang

Particulars: The latest version is back to panes in the windows and is made in the Philippines or China.

Date:_______	$:_______	'91	'92	'93	'94	'95	'96
❍ Wish	❍ Have	$-	-	-	37.50	37.50	37.5

Bishops Oast House

Item #	Intro	Retired	OSRP	GBTru	↓
5567-0	1990	1992	$45	**$75**	6%

Particulars: Large attached barn, round cobblestone oasts contain a kiln for drying malt or hops to produce ale. Exterior finished as a rough-cast surface over brick.

Date:_______	$:_______	'91	'92	'93	'94	'95	'9
❍ Wish	❍ Have	$45	48	85	85	75	8

KING'S ROAD

Item #	Intro	Retired	OSRP	GBTru	↑
5568-9	1990	1996	$72	**$100**	25%

Particulars: Set of 2 includes *Tutbury Printer*, #55690 and *C.H. Watt Physician*, #55691.

see below

Date:_______	$:_______	'91	'92	'93	'94	'95	'9
❍ Wish	❍ Have	$72	75	80	80	80	8

Tutbury Printer

Item #	Intro	Retired	OSRP	GBTru	↑
55690	1990	1996	$36	**$50**	25%

Particulars: 1 of the 2-piece set—KING'S ROAD. Timbere plaster design with decorative molding between first ar second story. Ground floor bay window with smaller bays on second floor. Steeply pitched roof with a dorm

Date:_______	$:_______	'91	'92	'93	'94	'95	'9
❍ Wish	❍ Have	$36	37.50	40	40	40	4

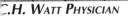

C.H. WATT PHYSICIAN

ITEM #	INTRO	RETIRED	OSRP	GBTRU	↑
55691	1990	1996	$36	**$50**	25%

Particulars: 1 of the 2-piece set—KING'S ROAD. Doctor's office on ground floor, outside staircase leads to family residence, bricks used above most windows as decorative arch, exposed stone edges on four corners of house walls.

DATE:_______ $:_______ ❍ WISH ❍ HAVE

'91	'92	'93	'94	'95	'96
$36	37.50	40	40	36	40

FAGIN'S HIDE-A-WAY

ITEM #	INTRO	RETIRED	OSRP	GBTRU	↑
5552-2	1991	1995	$68	**$85**	6%

Particulars: Two attached buildings in disrepair. Broken shutters, cracks in wall. Barrel warehouse with step roof, gate across doors. In *Oliver Twist,* this is the hide-out for Fagin and his gang of young criminals. Dickens based many of the characters on people who frequented a series of underground passages near the Strand in London. These passages are now used by automobiles.

DATE:_______ $:_______ ❍ WISH ❍ HAVE

'91	'92	'93	'94	'95	'96
$68	68	72	72	72	80

OLIVER TWIST

see below

ITEM #	INTRO	RETIRED	OSRP	GBTRU	
5553-0	1991	1993	$75	**$135**	NO CHANGE

Particulars: Set of 2 includes *Brownlow House* and *Maylie Cottage.*

DATE:_______ $:_______ ❍ WISH ❍ HAVE

'91	'92	'93	'94	'95	'96
$75	75	80	140	130	135

BROWNLOW HOUSE

ITEM #	INTRO	RETIRED	OSRP	GBTRU	
5553-0	1991	1993	$37.50	**$75**	NO CHANGE

Particulars: 1 of the 2-piece set—OLIVER TWIST. Two-story stone house with two brick chimneys and three front gables. Double doors. The gentleman living in this house befriends Oliver and later adopts him. The house at 39 Craven Street in London is thought to be Dickens' model for the house.

DATE:_______ $:_______ ❍ WISH ❍ HAVE

'91	'92	'93	'94	'95	'96
$37.50	37.50	40	75	70	75

Maylie Cottage

Item #	Intro	Retired	OSRP	GBTru	NO
5553-0	1991	1993	$37.50	**$65**	CHANGE

Particulars: 1 of the 2-piece set—OLIVER TWIST. Oliver was forced to burglarize Mrs. Maylie's London house and was wounded. He recuperated under her care at the cottage. This cottage has a pronounced roof ridge, curved cone roof shape repeated on dormers and front door. One chimney rises up the front facade, a second chimney on side of house.

DATE:_______	$:_______	'91	'92	'93	'94	'95	'96
❍ WISH	❍ HAVE	$37.50	37.50	40	75	65	65

Ashbury Inn

Item #	Intro	Retired	OSRP	GBTru	↑
5555-7	1991	1995	$55	**$75**	7%

Particulars: Tudor timbered Inn for coach travelers. Food, lodging, and drink. Double chimneys, two roof dormers and double peaks over multi-paned windows by entry.

DATE:_______	$:_______	'91	'92	'93	'94	'95	'96
❍ WISH	❍ HAVE	$55	55	60	60	60	70

Nephew Fred's Flat

Item #	Intro	Retired	OSRP	GBTru	↑
5557-3	1991	1994	$35	**$70**	8%

Particulars: Addition to "Christmas Carol" grouping. Taiwan piece is darker in color and approx. 1/4" shorter than pieces from China. Four-story home with 3-story turret-like bow windows. Planters flank front door. Overhang window above side door with crow stepped coping in gable rising to two chimneys. Ivy grows up corner area—garlands, wreath, and Christmas greetings decorate facade.

DATE:_______	$:_______	'91	'92	'93	'94	'95	'96
❍ WISH	❍ HAVE	$35	35	36	36	65	65

Old Michaelchurch

Item #	Intro	Retired	OSRP	GBTru	↑
5562-0	1992	1996	$42	**$60**	25%

Particulars: Stone base with lath and plaster filling space between timbered upper portion. Tower rises up front facade with heavy solid look, a simple four sided structure. Double wood doors at rear of church. Early release to Showcase Dealers and Gift Creations Concept (GCC).

DATE:_______	$:_______	'92	'93	'94	'95	'96
❍ WISH	❍ HAVE	$42	46	46	48	4[illegible]

ROWN & CRICKET INN

ITEM #	INTRO	RETIRED	OSRP	GBTRU	↑
5750-9	1992	1992 ANNUAL	$100	**$170**	17%

Particulars: 1st Edition in the Charles Dickens' Signature Series. Special collector box & hang tag. Three-story brick and stone with pillars flanking covered formal entry. Curved canopy roof on Golden Lion Arms Pub. Wrought iron balustrade outlines triple window on second floor. Dressed stone edges walls. Mansard roof with decorative trim and molding. The trim on the early pieces was light; later pieces had a darker gray trim.

DATE:_______ $:_______ ❍ WISH ❍ HAVE

'92	'93	'94	'95	'96
$100	165	175	175	145

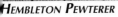

HEMBLETON PEWTERER

ITEM #	INTRO	RETIRED	OSRP	GBTRU	↑
5800-9	1992	1995	$72	**$80**	7%

Particulars: Timber framed with plaster in Elizabethan style. Bay windows create two-story front facade. Chimney Sweep shop with steep pitched roof hugs one side of the pewterer. Early issue has two small additions on right side, later issue has one large addition.

DATE:_______ $:_______ ❍ WISH ❍ HAVE

'92	'93	'94	'95	'96
$72	72	72	72	75

NG'S ROAD POST OFFICE

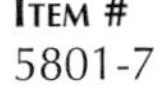

ITEM #	INTRO	RETIRED	OSRP	GBTRU	
5801-7	1992	CURRENT	$45	**$45**	NO CHANGE

Particulars: Simple four-sided stone three-story building with semi-circular turret-like two-story rise out of window area. Entrance door surmounted by pediment just below post office sign. Triple flue chimney rises off back of building.

DATE:_______ $:_______ ❍ WISH ❍ HAVE

'92	'93	'94	'95	'96
$45	45	45	45	45

THE PIED BULL INN

ITEM #	INTRO	RETIRED	OSRP	GBTRU	
5751-7	1993	1993 ANNUAL	$100	**$150**	NO CHANGE

Particulars: 2nd Edition in the Charles Dickens' Signature Series. Special collector box and hang tag. Elizabethan style with wood and plaster upper stories and stone and brick lower levels. Front entry at side of Inn allows public rooms to be of good size to service guests and local folk.

DATE:_______ $:_______ ❍ WISH ❍ HAVE

'93	'94	'95	'96
$100	160	145	150

PUMP LANE SHOPPES

Item #	Intro	Retired	OSRP	GBTru	↑
5808-4	1993	1996	$112	**$145**	29%

Particulars: Set of 3 includes *Bumpstead Nye Cloaks & Canes, #58085, Lomas Ltd. Molasses, #58086* and *W.M Wheat Cakes & Puddings, #58087.*

see below

DATE:_______ $:_______
❍ WISH ❍ HAVE

'93	'94	'95	'9
$112	112	112	11

BUMPSTEAD NYE CLOAKS & CANES

Item #	Intro	Retired	OSRP	GBTru	↑
58085	1993	1996	$37.50	**$45**	20%

Particulars: 1 of the 3-piece set—PUMP LANE SHOPPES. Tall narrow shop with timbered 2nd story. Front gable has design etched into trim. Shop was noted for cloaks and capes as well as canes and walking sticks.

DATE:_______ $:_______
❍ WISH ❍ HAVE

'93	'94	'95	'9
$37.50	37.50	27.50	37.

LOMAS LTD. MOLASSES

Item #	Intro	Retired	OSRP	GBTru	↑
58086	1993	1996	$37.50	**$45**	20%

Particulars: 1 of the 3-piece set—PUMP LANE SHOPPES. Steps lead up to store above stone lower level where molasses and treacles are refined and stored. Double chimneys rise above thatched roof.

DATE:_______ $:_______
❍ WISH ❍ HAVE

'93	'94	'95	'
$37.50	37.50	37.50	37

W.M. WHEAT CAKES & PUDDINGS

Item #	Intro	Retired	OSRP	GBTru	↑
58087	1993	1996	$37.50	**$45**	20%

Particulars: 1 of the 3-piece set—PUMP LANE SHOPPES. Baking chimney rises from center of main shop roof. 2nd-story rooms are dormered with additional chimne at rear. Wreath hangs above curved front door and arched design is repeated above front windows.

DATE:_______ $:_______
❍ WISH ❍ HAVE

'93	'94	'95	'
$37.50	37.50	37.50	37

Boarding & Lodging School (#18)

Item #	Intro	Retired	OSRP	GBTru	↑
5809-2	1993	1993 Annual	$48	**$165**	3%

Particulars: This is the school Scrooge attended as a youngster. Bottomstamp of the Charles Dickens' Heritage Foundation commemorates the 150th Anniversary of *A Christmas Carol.* Address is #18. Special box & hang tag. Early release to Showcase Dealers & select buying groups. An Edition in the Charles Dickens' Signature Collection. Building also available (1994-Current) as Item #5810-6, w/o the commemorative stamp & an address of #43.

DATE:________ $:________
❍ WISH ❍ HAVE

'93	'94	'95	'96
$48	200	200	160

Kingsford's Brew House

Item #	Intro	Retired	OSRP	GBTru	↑
5811-4	1993	1996	$45	**$60**	33%

Particulars: Stone 3-story building with slate roof. Grain was processed into ale by fermentation. Chimneys rise from both sides from ovens & vats where the beverages were brewed. Banner of Tankard hangs outside.

DATE:________ $:________
❍ WISH ❍ HAVE

'93	'94	'95	'96
$45	45	45	45

Great Denton Mill

Item #	Intro	Retired	OSRP	GBTru	No Change
5812-2	1993	Current	$50	**$50**	

Particulars: Both grinding of grain for baking and animal feed as well as preparation of wool combed into yarn took place at Mill. Narrow three-story wood structure with water wheel for power to turn wheels.

DATE:________ $:________
❍ WISH ❍ HAVE

'93	'94	'95	'96
$50	50	50	50

Dedlock Arms

Item #	Intro	Retired	OSRP	GBTru	↑
5752-5	1994	1994 Annual	$100	**$140**	4%

Particulars: 3rd Edition in the Charles Dickens' Signature Series. Special collector box and hang tag. A tavern in Dickens' *Bleak House,* Dickens based his description on Sondes Arms in Rockingham. Stone wall courtyard has metal gate and 2 lanterns. 3-story Inn is brightly lit with Inn sign above front window.

DATE:________ $:________
❍ WISH ❍ HAVE

'94	'95	'96
$100	150	135

Boarding & Lodging School (#43)

Item #	Intro	Retired	OSRP	GBTru	
5810-6	1994	Current	$48	**$48**	No Change

Particulars: Original release in 1993, #5809-2 was a commemorative version with #18 as address. This building has #43 as the address. When both Boarding Schools are side-by-side, the addresses create 1843, the year that *A Christmas Carol* was published.

DATE:_______ $:_______
❍ WISH ❍ HAVE

'94	'95	'96
$48	48	48

Whittlesbourne Church

Item #	Intro	Retired	OSRP	GBTru	
5821-1	1994	Current	$85	**$85**	No Change

Particulars: Midyear release. Stone church with a single fortress-like tower rising off front right side. A masonry brace built against left side supports massive stone wall and provides a walkway.

DATE:_______ $:_______
❍ WISH ❍ HAVE

'94	'95	'96
$85	85	85

Giggelswick Mutton & Ham

Item #	Intro	Retired	OSRP	GBTru	
5822-0	1994	Current	$48	**$48**	No Change

Particulars: Midyear release. The town of Giggleswick is located in North Yorkshire. Butcher shop concentrates on meats from sheep and pigs. Smokehouse on side cures meat and adds special flavoring. Shop has corner wraparound windows.

DATE:_______ $:_______
❍ WISH ❍ HAVE

'94	'95	'96
$48	48	48

Hather Harness

Item #	Intro	Retired	OSRP	GBTru	
5823-8	1994	Current	$48	**$48**	No Change

Particulars: Stone, brick and stucco 3-story shop and family home. Double doors allow entry of horses, oxen, carriages and wagons to be fixed.

DATE:_______ $:_______
❍ WISH ❍ HAVE

'94	'95	'96
$48	48	48

PORTOBELLO ROAD THATCHED COTTAGES

ITEM #	INTRO	RETIRED	OSRP	GBTRU	
5824-6	1994	CURRENT	$120	**$120**	NO CHANGE

Particulars: Set of 3 includes *Mr. & Mrs. Pickle*, #58247, *Cobb Cottage*, #58248 and *Browning Cottage*, #58249.

see below

DATE:_______ $:_______
❍ WISH ❍ HAVE

'94	'95	'96
$120	120	120

MR. & MRS. PICKLE

ITEM #	INTRO	RETIRED	OSRP	GBTRU	
58247	1994	CURRENT	$40	**$40**	NO CHANGE

Particulars: 1 of the 3-piece set—PORTOBELLO ROAD THATCHED COTTAGES. Timbered stucco home with attached Antique Store. Home sign highlights a pickle.

DATE:_______ $:_______
❍ WISH ❍ HAVE

'94	'95	'96
$40	40	40

COBB COTTAGE

ITEM #	INTRO	RETIRED	OSRP	GBTRU	
58248	1994	CURRENT	$40	**$40**	NO CHANGE

Particulars: 1 of the 3-piece set—PORTOBELLO ROAD THATCHED COTTAGES. The thatched roof is being completed on a stucco, timber and brick home. First Heritage Village house without snow on the roof. Unique L-shape with ornate roof ridges.

DATE:_______ $:_______
❍ WISH ❍ HAVE

'94	'95	'96
$40	40	40

BROWNING COTTAGE

ITEM #	INTRO	RETIRED	OSRP	GBTRU	
58249	1994	CURRENT	$40	**$40**	NO CHANGE

Particulars: 1 of the 3-piece set—PORTOBELLO ROAD THATCHED COTTAGES. 2-story brick, timber and stucco home. Original thatch roof replaced by slate to denote increase in family's wealth. Dutch door entry.

DATE:_______ $:_______
❍ WISH ❍ HAVE

'94	'95	'96
$40	40	40

Sir John Falstaff Inn

Item #	Intro	Retired	OSRP	GBTru	No Change
5753-3	1995	1995 Annual	$100	$130	

Particulars: 4th Edition in the Charles Dickens' Signature Series. Special collector box and hang tag. This is based on the inn still located across the street from Gad's Hill Place, Dickens' last home. Three-story Inn of stucco, timber and brick with slate roof. Two-story bay windows frame front entry.

DATE:_______ $:_______

❍ WISH ❍ HAVE

'95	'96
$100	130

Dicken's Village Start A Tradition Set

Item #	Intro	Retired	OSRP	GBTru	↑
5832-7	1995	1996	$85	$120	41%

Particulars: Set of 13. Starter Set was midyear release featured at D56 National Homes For The Holidays Open House Event—Oct/Nov 1995. Special packaging for promotion. Set was also available during Event week of Nov. 7–11, 1996. Set includes *Faversham Lamps & Oil*—2-story shop/home w/stone trim on arched door/windows. Crowsteppped roof edges. *Morston Steak And Kidney Pie*—Meat pies prepared in small 1 ½-story shop/home. *Town Square Carolers* accessory, 5 assorted sisal trees, Cobblestone Road & Bag of Real Plastic Snow.

DATE:_______ $:_______

❍ WISH ❍ HAVE

'95	'96
$85	85

J.D. Nichols Toy Shop

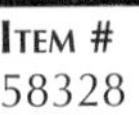

Item #	Intro	Retired	OSRP	GBTru	↑
58328	1995	Current	$48	$50	4%

Particulars: Brightly lit front window, topped by ledge carrying store name, and trimmed with 3 potted trees, highlights toy shop. Tall front gables feature timber design. Brick chimneys rise from steeply pitched roof.

DATE:_______ $:_______

❍ WISH ❍ HAVE

'95	'96
$48	48

Dursley Manor

Item #	Intro	Retired	OSRP	GBTru	↑
58329	1995	Current	$50	$55	10%

Particulars: Two plaques above entry state building name and year cornerstone placed. Brick with stone trim at windows, carriage portico, roof edging and the 3 chimneys.

DATE:_______ $:_______

❍ WISH ❍ HAVE

'95	'96
$50	50

BLENHAM STREET BANK

ITEM #	INTRO	RETIRED	OSRP	GBTRU	
58330	1995	CURRENT	$60	**$60**	NO CHANGE

Particulars: Many windows bring light and openness to squared building design. Strength and fortress-like solidarity promoted by use of stone, columns, and arches above windows. Double entry doors topped by fanlight window arch.

DATE:_______ $:_______
❍ WISH ❍ HAVE

'95	'96
$60	60

WRENBURY SHOPS

ITEM #	INTRO	RETIRED	OSRP	GBTRU	
58331	1995	CURRENT	$100	**$100**	NO CHANGE

Particulars: Set of 3 includes *Wrenbury Baker, #58332, The Chop Shop,* #58333 and *T. Puddlewick Spectacle Shop,* #58334.

see below

DATE:_______ $:_______
❍ WISH ❍ HAVE

'95	'96
$100	100

WRENBURY BAKER

ITEM #	INTRO	RETIRED	OSRP	GBTRU	
58332	1995	CURRENT	$35	**$35**	NO CHANGE

Particulars: 1 of the 3-piece set—WRENBURY SHOPS. Cottage shop houses baker. 1 ½-story with roof line coming down to first floor. Single chimney rises through hand hewn roof. Sign outside by entry.

DATE:_______ $:_______
❍ WISH ❍ HAVE

'95	'96
$35	35

THE CHOP SHOP

ITEM #	INTRO	RETIRED	OSRP	GBTRU	
58333	1995	CURRENT	$35	**$35**	NO CHANGE

Particulars: 1 of the 3-piece set—WRENBURY SHOPS. Large chimney with 4 flue pots rises through rough shingle roof. Sign outside entry advertises wares. Stucco facade.

DATE:_______ $:_______
❍ WISH ❍ HAVE

'95	'96
$35	35

T. Puddlewick Spectacle Shop

Item #	Intro	Retired	OSRP	GBTru	No Change
58334	1995	Current	$35	$35	

Particulars: 1 of the 3-piece set—WRENBURY SHOPS. Ornate timber tudor style shop selling glasses, lorgnettes, looking glasses, monocles, and spyglasses. Sign outside advertises product.

DATE:_______ $:_______
❍ WISH ❍ HAVE

'95	'96
$35	35

The Maltings

Item #	Intro	Retired	OSRP	GBTru	No Change
5833-5	1995	Current	$50	$50	

Particulars: Midyear release. Home, shop and bridge in one construct of stone, stucco and wood. Large doors allow carts to enter. A malting is a building used to roast or malt barley for brewing beer and ale.

DATE:_______ $:_______
❍ WISH ❍ HAVE

'95	'96
$50	50

Dudden Cross Church

Item #	Intro	Retired	OSRP	GBTru	No Change
5834-3	1995	Current	$45	$45	

Particulars: Midyear release. Brick church with stone coping. Bell tower rises on one side through roof. Stone archway to courtyard on other side near entry door.

DATE:_______ $:_______
❍ WISH ❍ HAVE

'95	'96
$45	45

The Grapes Inn

Item #	Intro	Retired	OSRP	GBTru	↑
57534	1996	1996 Annual	$120	$135	11%

Particulars: 5th Edition in Charles Dickens' Signature Series. Inn on the waterfront supplies food, drink and lodging for weary travelers. Rowboats are tied up to rear unloading dock. Two staircases outside lead to inn or to pub and dining areas. Located in Limehouse, this Inn is said to be used as the model for the "Porters" in *Our Mutual Friend*.

DATE:_______ $:_______
❍ WISH ❍ HAVE

'96
$120

Ramsford Palace

Item #	Intro	Retired	OSRP	GBTru	↑
58336	1996	Ltd Ed 27,500	$175	**$495**	183%

Particulars: Midyear release. Set of 17 includes *Ramsford Palace* & Accessories: *Palace Guards,* Set/2, *Palace Gate, Palace Fountain, Wall Hedge,* Set/8, *Corner Wall Topiaries,* Set/4. The building is modeled after Castle Howard in York. The mansion, built by the Earl of Carlisle, was begun in 1700. The south facade comprises a central block surmounted by a dome, between 2 wings. Corinthian pilasters accentuate the height.

DATE:_______ $:_______ **'96**
❍ WISH ❍ HAVE $175

Butter Tub Farmhouse

Item #	Intro	Retired	OSRP	GBTru	
58337	1996	Current	$40	**$40**	No Change

Particulars: Midyear release. Three steeply pitched red roof heights set off tall narrow chimneys. Door and windows have wood frames. High gables match roof heights on front facade. Butter Tub refers to a pass in Yorkshire where cool pools of water known as buttertubs form in potholes.

DATE:_______ $:_______ **'96**
❍ WISH ❍ HAVE $40

Butter Tub Barn

Item #	Intro	Retired	OSRP	GBTru	
58338	1996	Current	$48	**$48**	No Change

Particulars: Midyear release. Two separate barn areas share one steep roof. Wagons can enter through double wood doors or into central loading area.

DATE:_______ $:_______ **'96**
❍ WISH ❍ HAVE $48

The Christmas Carol Cottage (Revisited)

Item #	Intro	Retired	OSRP	GBTru	
58339	1996	Current	$60	**$60**	No Change

Particulars: Midyear release. A new expanded version of home of Bob and Mary Cratchit. Roof has 2 dormer windows. Two fireplaces now heat the house. A log pile against a large chimney holds a built-in Magic Smoking Element powered by a separate transformer that heats a supplied non-toxic liquid allowing smoke to rise out of the chimney.

DATE:_______ $:_______ **'96**
❍ WISH ❍ HAVE $60

Nettie Quin Puppets & Marionettes

Item #	Intro	Retired	OSRP	GBTru
58344	1996	Current	$50	**$50**

Particulars: Front of store features a puppet/marionette stage for performances to passing village folk. Decorations on stage and front facade of 3-story building advertise the wood carving craftsman's talents. This is the first Heritage Village building to feature multiple weathervanes.

DATE:_______ $:_______
❍ WISH ❍ HAVE

Mulberrie Court Brownstones

Item #	Intro	Retired	OSRP	GBTru
58345	1996	Current	$90	**$90**

Particulars: Three identical attached town houses, #5, #6, #7 are three-story brick residences. Each entry door features a glass fanlight and each has a bow window on 1st & 2nd story. Individual room fireplace chimneys are grouped into one roof structure. Railing with gate separates home from passing strollers.

DATE:_______ $:_______
❍ WISH ❍ HAVE

The Olde Camden Town Church (Revisited)

Item #	Intro	Retired	OSRP	GBTru
58346	1996	Current	$55	**$55**

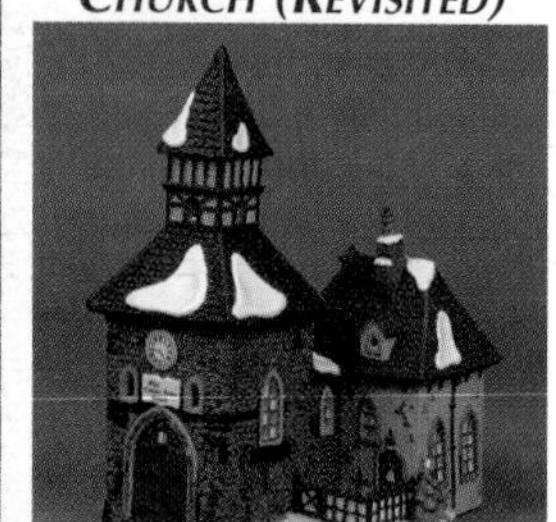

Particulars: This is the church where Bob Cratchit and Tiny Tim spent Christmas morning in *A Christmas Carol.* Dickens may have used St. Stephen's Church in Camden as a model. Piece comes with a miniature storybook created and written by designers which sets scene for piece.

DATE:_______ $:_______
❍ WISH ❍ HAVE

The Melancholy Tavern (Revisited)

Item #	Intro	Retired	OSRP	GBTru
58347	1996	Current	$45	**$45**

Particulars: Tavern where Scrooge ate in *A Christmas Carol.* It is believed that Dickens developed his idea for the tavern from Baker's Chop Shop that once stood along Change Alley in London. Tall narrow timbered tavern offers brew and meals. Piece comes with a miniature storybook created and written by designers which sets scene for piece.

DATE:_______ $:_______
❍ WISH ❍ HAVE

Quilly's Antiques

Item #	Intro	Retired	OSRP	GBTru
58348	1996	Current	$46	**$46**

Particulars: Small town shop with entry and display window built out from front wall. Family lives in cramped upper floor quarters. Walkway crowded with antique objects and small items. Access to side yard through wood door.

DATE:_______ $:_______
❍ WISH ❍ HAVE

Gad's Hill Place

Item #	Intro	Retired	OSRP	GBTru
57535	1997	1997 Annual	$98	**$98**

Particulars: 6th Edition in the Charles Dickens' Signature Series. Located in Kent, this was the last home of Dickens and the only one he ever owned. Three-story red brick home in Queen Anne period style. Balance established by center hall entry highlighted by pediment. Each side of home equals the other in rooms and window treatment. One chimney, bell tower and an attached gazebo displaying Christmas tree.

DATE:_______ $:_______
❍ WISH ❍ HAVE

Dickens' Village Start A Tradition

Item #	Intro	Retired	OSRP	GBTru
58322	1997	Current	$100*	**$100**

Particulars: Set of 13. Starter Set is midyear release to be featured at D56 National Homes For The Holidays Open House Event—11/1/97 to 11/9/97. *SRP reduced to $75 for the Event. Includes 2 lighted buildings *Sudbury Church* and *Old East Rectory*. An accessory set of 3, *The Spirit Of Giving,* a young lady and girl giving gift baskets of food for the poor to the Rector, a Cobblestone Road and Real Plastic Snow complete the set .

DATE:_______ $:_______
❍ WISH ❍ HAVE

Lytes Coal Merchant

Item #	Intro	Retired	OSRP	GBTru
58323	1997	Current	$50	**$50**

Particulars: Midyear release. A very tall building housing a coal merchant. Coverings for the upper windows are metal plates hinged to the window instead of glass panes.

DATE:_______ $:_______
❍ WISH ❍ HAVE

BARMBY MOOR COTTAGE

ITEM #	INTRO	RETIRED	OSRP	GBTRU
58324	1997	CURRENT	$48	**$48**

Particulars: Midyear release. House is 1 ½-story built of stones from the moor. Front of home has one large gabl highlighted by a carved barge-board. Above front door are two small gabled dormer windows. Barmby Moor is village located east of York.

DATE:_______ $:_______
❍ WISH ❍ HAVE

TOWER OF LONDON

ITEM #	INTRO	RETIRED	OSRP	GBTRU
58500	1997	1997 ANNUAL	$165	**$165**

Particulars: 1st Edition in Historical Landmark Series. Midyear release. Set of 5. Lighted main structure, non-lighted gate/ tower, sign, raven master with 2 ravens, wall with 4 ravens. Though the actual Tower Of London has 20 towers, the D56 rendition has only 4. Famous for housing a royal prison as well as the Crown Jewels. Legend says six ravens must be ke at the tower to preserve the monarchy.

DATE:_______ $:_______
❍ WISH ❍ HAVE

THE HUNT AND THE HUNTED

One of the accessories in Dickens' Village is called Tallyho! It is a wonderful piec not only because of the visions that it conjures of hounds running and howling throug the English countryside, but also because it represents "the chase." What could be more appropriate symbol of collecting D56 villages?

As humans we are hunters, gatherers, or both, characteristics passed on by our a cestors. As collectors we exhibit these characteristics, though they are more prevale in some of us. We search for retired pieces, limited editions, or variations. We gather many of the pieces as we like (and quite often some we don't). Over time, howeve many of us have come to realize that the hunt is often as thrilling, if not more so, th the capture.

That's the way it was with Department 56 village collecting just a few years ag Collectors wondered if they would ever see a particular retired piece, never mind t thought of possibly owning it. And limited editions - they were the D56er's personal grail.

Those who have been collecting for four or more years should be able to rememb scouring the shelves, cabinets, and sometimes stockrooms of stores in search of a retir piece, any retired piece. How many collectors remember the hunt while on vacation traveling though areas that you had yet to explore? Did you ever expect to locate an thing? Probably not. But, ah, the hunt...that was the real fun.

It's times like these that collectors seem to remember most fondly when I speak to hem about collecting. They recall the anticipation of the search, the excitement of the ossibilities, the total disregard for the probabilities...the hunt. It is also the aspect of ollecting these houses that many say they miss the most.

Sure, they love the pieces they have. And how could they not be fascinated by the uality and design of the new pieces?

Today things are not quite the same. This is not to say that they are bad or wrong - ust different. The fields have been scoured; the foxes are so plentiful they are as close s a phone call. A limited edition, a retired piece, or a rare variation can be captured in n instant.

This is, however, the natural evolution of a collectible. It is the struggle in our nature etween the hunter and the gatherer. We enjoy the hunt, but we want the trophies, too. Vhen they became too plentiful, we long for the excitement of the search. When it ppears that we may not be able to get all the pieces we desire, we question why they re in such short supply.

So what can we do about it? What can Department 56 do? Do they supply lower uantities making the pieces a little more scarce? How would they satisfy the collectors vho may be upset if they couldn't get a piece when they wanted it? These are easy uestions without easy answers.

After the '95 retirements were announced, I spoke with a number of collectors who vere surprised to see so many pieces on that list still available on dealers' shelves. This ad not been the case in previous years. Could this be an indicator that the demand for ew pieces has decreased? At first you would think so. But the demand has seemed to ncrease, if anything. The unusual scene of recently retired pieces still on a dealer's helf could be the result of dealers ordering in larger quantities than they had in previ-us years.

Would I like to see fewer pieces being made because the fewer there are, the more aluable they will become? No, though this is the sentiment of many collectors, and I nderstand it. I would like to see less of each building produced because I believe the ompany's management can build into the pieces that one quality the designers, the ulptors, and the painters cannot...that special aspect of collecting...the hunt. Tallyho!

the ***Village Chronicle.***

NEW ENGLAND VILLAGE

The second porcelain village to be introduced by Department 56 was New England Village in 1986. It immediately captured the spirit and character of the six state region. The coastline, farmlands, mountains, and valleys were all represented

Throughout the years, there has been one limited edition, *Smythe Woolen Mil* Surprisingly, there have been introductions inspired by areas other than New England itself. These include two Pennsylvania farms, Jannes Mullet and A. Bieler and the New York-based story, *The Legend of Sleepy Hollow*. Most recently, th well-received designs of coastal homes and businesses have propelled New England Village's popularity to an all-time high.

THE BOTTOM LINE:

Cost of all pieces introduced to New England Village through the 1997 midyea introductions including accessories: (This does not include variations, or speci pieces.) **$1,760**

Greenbook TruMarket Value of all pieces through the 1997 midyear introduc tions including accessories: (This does not include variations, special pieces.) **$6,00**

ıEW ENGLAND VILLAGE SINCE ⱳE LAST MET...

... NEW FOR SALE LISTINGS

HUDSON STOVEWORKS - 1996

ıe villagers of New England will be able to stay warm now that there a shop specializing in the production, repairing, and selling of oves. The piece features the shop with attached foundry.

ıAVIGATIONAL CHARTS & MAPS - 1996

ıe captains and pilots of the vessels leaving the docks of the village ·ill use the charts and maps sold at this shop to safely navigate their ·ay to other ports.

OBWHITE COTTAGE - 1996

you wanted to have a cottage down by the seashore, this would be ıe one. With its gingerbread designs, double entrances, and soft ɔlors, it would certainly be one of the most desired properties.

'AN GUILDER'S ORNAMENTAL IRONWORKS - 1997

ıis newest shop is also the latest foundry-based building. It joins *ankee Jud Bell Casting* and *J. Hudson Stoveworks* in creating ·roducts out of metals. It's the first multi-vaned building in the village.

. NO LONGER ON THE MARKET

642-1 Bluebird Seed And Bulb
648-0 A. BIELER FARM, Set of 2
- 56481 Pennsylvania Dutch Farmhouse
- 56482 Pennsylvania Dutch Barn

947-1 Captain's Cottage

WHAT GOES WHERE

THE LEGEND OF SLEEPY HOLLOW

Considered by many to be America's first highly praised writer, Washingtc Irving is best remembered for two tales that take place in the Hudson Valley, "R Van Winkle" and "The Legend of Sleepy Hollow." Both of these stories appeared i Irving's *The Sketch Book* published in 1819.

"The Legend of Sleepy Hollow" is often incorrectly referred to as "The Legen of the Headless Horseman." This is because it is the mysterious rider who, with h head perched on the pommel of his saddle, sticks in the mind of the reader whe all is said and done, not the main character, Ichabod Crane.

Crane, a schoolmaster from Connecticut, was teaching in the nearby town i New York. This tall, lanky fellow had aspirations to wed Katrina Van Tassel, c more accurately, what she would inherit. He had competition, however, in th likes of Brom Bones, a worthy suitor, indeed.

After attending a party at the Van Tassel farmhouse, Ichabod heads home in th dark of night. Along the way, just where it is said that goblins can be encountere he is confronted by the headless horseman. A chase ensues, and, just as Ichabo reaches the point where the ghosts do not pass, he is knocked from his horse by pumpkin that hits him in the head. Ichabod was never seen again, and the reaso for his disappearance was never learned. Was it a ghost or Brom Bones?

Buildings:

SLEEPY HOLLOW, Set of 3 • Sleepy Hollow School • Van Tassel Manor • Ichabod Crane's Cottage	5954-4	1990-1993
Sleepy Hollow Church	5955-2	1990-1993

Accessories:

Sleepy Hollow Characters, Set of 3	5956-0	1990-1992

ETIRED BUILDINGS

540-5	1995	McGrebe-Cutters & Sleighs
542-1	1996	Bluebird Seed And Bulb
543-0	1995	Yankee Jud Bell Casting
544-8	1995	Stoney Brook Town Hall
548-0	1996	A. BIELER FARM
5481	1996	Pennsylvania Dutch Farmhouse
5482	1996	Pennsylvania Dutch Barn
930-7	1994	Craggy Cove Lighthouse
931-5	1989	Weston Train Station
939-0	1990	CHERRY LANE SHOPS
939-0	1990	Ben's Barbershop
939-0	1990	Otis Hayes Butcher Shop
939-0	1990	Anne Shaw Toys
940-4	1991	Ada's Bed And Boarding House
942-0	1991	Berkshire House
943-9	1992	Jannes Mullet Amish Farm House
944-7	1992	Jannes Mullet Amish Barn
946-3	1994	Shingle Creek House
947-1	1996	Captain's Cottage
954-4	1993	SLEEPY HOLLOW
954-4	1993	Sleepy Hollow School
954-4	1993	Van Tassel Manor
954-4	1993	Ichabod Crane's Cottage
955-2	1993	Sleepy Hollow Church
530-7	1989	NEW ENGLAND VILLAGE
530-7	1989	Apothecary Shop
530-7	1989	General Store
530-7	1989	Nathaniel Bingham Fabrics
530-7	1989	Livery Stable & Boot Shop
530-7	1989	Steeple Church
530-7	1989	Brick Town Hall
530-7	1989	Red Schoolhouse
538-2	1989	Jacob Adams Farmhouse And Barn
539-0	1990	Steeple Church
544-7	1990	Timber Knoll Log Cabin

IMITED EDITION

543-9	Smythe Woolen Mill	7,500

NEW ENGLAND VILLAGE

ITEM #	INTRO	RETIRED	OSRP	GBTRU	↑
6530-7	1986	1989	$170	**$1275**	4%

Particulars: Set of 7 includes *Apothecary Shop, General Store, Nathaniel Bingham Fabrics, Livery Stable & Boo Shop, Steeple Church, Brick Town Hall* and *Red Schoolhouse.*
(*In 1994, Set of 7 could be purchased for approximate 15% less than the sum of the individual pieces.)

see below

DATE:_______ $:_______ ❍ WISH ❍ HAVE

'91	'92	'93	'94	'95	'9
$650	950	1125	*	1250	12

APOTHECARY SHOP

ITEM #	INTRO	RETIRED	OSRP	GBTRU	↑
6530-7	1986	1989	$25	**$105**	5%

Particulars: 1 of the 7-piece set—NEW ENGLAND VILLAGE. Variegated fieldstone with white wood bay window. Gable and lean-to are blue clapboard.

DATE:_______ $:_______ ❍ WISH ❍ HAVE

'91	'92	'93	'94	'95	'9
$70	80	88	92	100	1(

GENERAL STORE

ITEM #	INTRO	RETIRED	OSRP	GBTRU	↑
6530-7	1986	1989	$25	**$345**	6%

Particulars: 1 of the 7-piece set—NEW ENGLAND VILLAGE. Round columns support full length covered porc Two small dormers on roof with central chimney.

DATE:_______ $:_______ ❍ WISH ❍ HAVE

'91	'92	'93	'94	'95	'9
$185	250	360	360	350	3:

NATHANIEL BINGHAM FABRICS

ITEM #	INTRO	RETIRED	OSRP	GBTRU	
6530-7	1986	1989	$25	**$160**	NO CHANC

Particulars: 1 of the 7-piece set—NEW ENGLAND VILLAGE. Clapboard saltbox design fabric store and Post Office. Each shop has own chimney. Living quarters above larger fabric store.

DATE:_______ $:_______ ❍ WISH ❍ HAVE

'91	'92	'93	'94	'95	'9
$85	125	150	150	150	1(

Livery Stable & Boot Shop

Item #	Intro	Retired	OSRP	GBTru	↑
6530-7	1986	1989	$25	**$155**	3%

Particulars: 1 of the 7-piece set—NEW ENGLAND VILLAGE. Two-story painted clapboard house with wood planked wing contains tannery and livery stable. Stable has stone chimney, double doors.

DATE:_______ $:_______ ❍ WISH ❍ HAVE

'91	'92	'93	'94	'95	'96
$70	105	112	142	145	150

Steeple Church— "First Version"

Item #	Intro	Retired	OSRP	GBTru	↓
6530-7	1986	1989	$25	**$180**	3%

Particulars: 1 of the 7-piece set—NEW ENGLAND VILLAGE. Variations in this piece affect GBTru$. This is the First Version where the tree is attached with porcelain slip. Reissued in 1989 as #6539-0 when #6530-7 retired with the rest of the Original NEV Set.

DATE:_______ $:_______ ❍ WISH ❍ HAVE

'91	'92	'93	'94	'95	'96
$65	130	155	175	175	185

Steeple Church— "Second Version"

Item #	Intro	Retired	OSRP	GBTru	↑
6530-7	1986	1989	$25	**$100**	5%

Particulars: 1 of the 7-piece set—NEW ENGLAND VILLAGE. This is the Second Version where the tree is attached with glue. Building is a white clapboard church w/tier-2 steeple. Windows have molding above and below. Simple design.

DATE:_______ $:_______ ❍ WISH ❍ HAVE

'91	'92	'93	'94	'95	'96
$-	-	-	100	100	95

Left to right: Second Version, First Version. When viewed straight on, the First version's tree does not touch the ground and appears level with first step.

Brick Town Hall

Item #	Intro	Retired	OSRP	GBTru	↑
6530-7	1986	1989	$25	**$225**	2%

Particulars: 1 of the 7-piece set—NEW ENGLAND VILLAGE. Mansard roof over two-story Town Hall. Cupola centered on roof ridge between two brick chimneys. Windows trimmed with ornamental molding.

DATE:_______ $:_______ ❍ WISH ❍ HAVE

'91	'92	'93	'94	'95	'9
$150	190	212	215	210	22

Red Schoolhouse

Item #	Intro	Retired	OSRP	GBTru	↑
6530-7	1986	1989	$25	**$280**	10%

Particulars: 1 of the 7-piece set—NEW ENGLAND VILLAGE. Red one-room wood school with stone chimney and open belfry. Generally heated by wood stove. Han powered water pump by front door.

DATE:_______ $:_______ ❍ WISH ❍ HAVE

'91	'92	'93	'94	'95	'9
$150	210	240	270	260	25

Jacob Adams Farmhouse

Item #	Intro	Retired	OSRP	GBTru	↑
6538-2	1986	1989	$65	**$565**	8%

Particulars: Set of 5. 2 buildings, 3 animals. Buildings light. Re multi-level wood barn atop a stone foundation. Stone silo attached. Home features front porch, small front bay windov butter churn by door, simple design. It is very unusual for these buildings to be sold separately. Because the animals were simply wrapped and placed in the box with no separat compartments, they are often damaged.

DATE:_______ $:_______ ❍ WISH ❍ HAVE

'91	'92	'93	'94	'95	'9
$250	375	510	575	575	52

Jacob Adams Barn

Craggy Cove Lighthouse

Item #	Intro	Retired	OSRP	GBTru	↑
5930-7	1987	1994	$35	**$70**	17%

Particulars: Keeper lives in small white clapboard home attached to lighthouse. Front porch of home features holiday decorated columns. Stone house foundation, whitewashed brick light tower.

DATE:_______	$:_______	'91	'92	'93	'94	'95	'96
❍ WISH	❍ HAVE	$44	45	45	45	60	60

Veston Train Station

Item #	Intro	Retired	OSRP	GBTru	↑
5931-5	1987	1989	$42	**$280**	8%

Particulars: Luggage ramps lead to platform, where you purchase tickets and wait inside or on benches outside. Wheeled luggage cart stands on side of building. This station looks very much like the now-dilapidated station in Weston, MA.

DATE:_______	$:_______	'91	'92	'93	'94	'95	'96
❍ WISH	❍ HAVE	$165	215	248	265	275	260

Smythe Woolen Mill

Item #	Intro	Retired	OSRP	GBTru	↑
6543-9	1987	Ltd Ed 7,500	$42	**$1085**	3%

Particulars: Fabric woven for manufacturing into clothing, yard goods. Hydro powered by water wheel. Stone base with wood upper stories. Bales of wool stacked outside office door. Lower windows each with shutter.

DATE:_______	$:_______	'91	'92	'93	'94	'95	'96
❍ WISH	❍ HAVE	$1100	1235	1255	1255	1150	1050

mber Knoll Log Cabin

Item #	Intro	Retired	OSRP	GBTru	↑
6544-7	1987	1990	$28	**$175**	6%

Particulars: Two stone chimneys and fireplace provide heat and cooking facilities for rustic log cabin. Wood shakes comprise roof. One wing rises two stories.

DATE:_______	$:_______	'91	'92	'93	'94	'95	'96
❍ WISH	❍ HAVE	$75	95	130	150	165	165

OLD NORTH CHURCH

ITEM #	INTRO	RETIRED	OSRP	GBTRU	↑
5932-3	1988	CURRENT	$40	**$48**	7%

Particulars: This design is based on the famous historic landmark, Christ Church in Boston, where sexton Robert Newman hung lanterns in its steeple to warn colonists in Charlestown that the British were on their way to Lexington and Concord. Red brick church. First- and second-floor windows feature sunburst and/or spoke tops. Steeple rises from main entry. Belfry has tiered design.

DATE:_______	$:_______	'91	'92	'93	'94	'95	'9
❍ WISH	❍ HAVE	$42	44	45	45	45	4

CHERRY LANE SHOPS

ITEM #	INTRO	RETIRED	OSRP	GBTRU	↑
5939-0	1988	1990	$80	**$345**	5%

Particulars: Set of 3 includes *Ben's Barbershop, Otis Haye Butcher Shop* and *Anne Shaw Toys.*

see below

DATE:_______	$:_______	'91	'92	'93	'94	'95	'9
❍ WISH	❍ HAVE	$175	215	275	NE	325	33

BEN'S BARBERSHOP

ITEM #	INTRO	RETIRED	OSRP	GBTRU	↑
5939-0	1988	1990	$27	**$115**	5%

Particulars: 1 of the 3-piece set—CHERRY LANE SHOPS. barber pole hangs from front house corner next to a bench for customers. Water tower on roof supplies the shop's needs. Upstairs office used by a lawyer.

DATE:_______	$:_______	'91	'92	'93	'94	'95	'9
❍ WISH	❍ HAVE	$60	75	85	85	95	11

OTIS HAYES BUTCHER SHOP

ITEM #	INTRO	RETIRED	OSRP	GBTRU	↑
5939-0	1988	1990	$27	**$90**	13%

Particulars: 1 of the 3-piece set—CHERRY LANE SHOPS. Dutch door entry, stone side walls, brick front. Small si and thick walls plus river/lake ice helped keep meat fresh.

DATE:_______	$:_______	'91	'92	'93	'94	'95	'9
❍ WISH	❍ HAVE	$55	65	68	75	75	8(

Anne Shaw Toys

Item #	Intro	Retired	OSRP	GBTru	⬆
5939-0	1988	1990	$27	**$175**	13%

Particulars: 1 of the 3-piece set—CHERRY LANE SHOPS. Large front windows with window boxes allow a look at toys for sale. Molding beneath floor edge and squared shape give roof a turret look and feel.

DATE:_______ $:_______ ❍ WISH ❍ HAVE

'91	'92	'93	'94	'95	'96
$80	115	125	150	160	155

Ada's Bed And Boarding House—"Version 1"

Item #	Intro	Retired	OSRP	GBTru	⬇
5940-4	1988	1991	$36	**$285**	8%

Particulars: There are three color and mold variations that affect GBTru$. The first version is lemon yellow in color, the rear steps are part of the building's mold, and there are alternating yellow panes on the second-story windows. Building is a large family home converted to a bed and breakfast for travelers. Double chimneys. Central cupola and wraparound front porch.

DATE:_______ $:_______ ❍ WISH ❍ HAVE

'91	'92	'93	'94	'95	'96
$37.50	310	300	300	325	310

Ada's Bed And Boarding House—"Version 2"

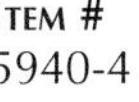

Item #	Intro	Retired	OSRP	GBTru	⬇
5940-4	1988	1991	$36	**$155**	6%

Particulars: The second version is a paler yellow but the same mold as Version 1—the rear steps are part of the building's mold.

DATE:_______ $:_______ ❍ WISH ❍ HAVE

'91	'92	'93	'94	'95	'96
$37.50	150	160	195	150	165

Ada's Bed And Boarding House—"Version 3"

Item #	Intro	Retired	OSRP	GBTru	⬆
5940-4	1988	1991	$36	**$130**	4%

Particulars: The third version is pale yellow in color and a different mold where the rear steps are an add on—not part of the the building's mold. In this version the second-story windows have yellow panes in the top half only.

DATE:_______ $:_______ ❍ WISH ❍ HAVE

'91	'92	'93	'94	'95	'96
$37.50	85	105	125	125	125

Berkshire House—"Original Blue"

Item #	Intro	Retired	OSRP	GBTru	
5942-0	1989	1991	$40	**$160**	NO CHANG

Particulars: Variations in color affect GBTru$: "Original Blue," "Teal," or "Forest Green." This is the "Original Blue." Building is a Dutch colonial inn with two front entries, half porch, five dormered windows on front, second-story mansard roof.

DATE:________ $:________

❍ WISH ❍ HAVE

'91	'92	'93	'94	'95	'96
$40	125	140	150	150	16(

Berkshire House—"Teal"

Item #	Intro	Retired	OSRP	GBTru	
5942-0	1989	1991	$40	**$110**	NO CHANGI

Particulars: This is the "Teal" house.

DATE:________ $:________

❍ WISH ❍ HAVE

'91	'92	'93	'94	'95	'96
$40	95	95	95	100	11(

Berkshire House—"Forest Green"

Item #	Intro	Retired	OSRP	GBTru
5942-0	1989	1991	$40	**NE**

Particulars: This is the "Forest Green" house.

DATE:________ $:________

❍ WISH ❍ HAVE

'91	'92	'93	'94	'95	'96
-	-	-	-	NE	NE

Jannes Mullet Amish Farm House

Item #	Intro	Retired	OSRP.	GBTru	↑
5943-9	1989	1992	$32	**$115**	5%

Particulars: White frame house, fenced yard on side, two chimneys, gutter and leader to barrel to collect rain water. Along with the *Jannes Mullet Amish Barn*, this is the first "non-New England" piece to be added to New England Village.

DATE:________ $:________

❍ WISH ❍ HAVE

'91	'92	'93	'94	'95	'96
$32	32	85	100	110	110

Jannes Mullet Amish Barn

Item #	Intro	Retired	OSRP	GBTru	↑
5944-7	1989	1992	$48	**$95**	6%

Particulars: Wood and fieldstone with attached sheds and silo, Amish family black buggy stands at barn entrance. Along with the *Jannes Mullet Amish Farm House*, this is the first "non-New England" piece to be added to New England Village.

DATE:________ $:________

❍ WISH ❍ HAVE

'91	'92	'93	'94	'95	'96
$48	48	86	98	90	90

Steeple Church

Item #	Intro	Retired	OSRP	GBTru	↓
6539-0	1989	1990	$30	**$80**	11%

Particulars: Reissue—see 1986 *Steeple Church*, #6530-7. White clapboard church with steeple. Windows have molding above and below. Simple design.

DATE:________ $:________

❍ WISH ❍ HAVE

'91	'92	'93	'94	'95	'96
$65	85	85	85	90	90

Shingle Creek House

Item #	Intro	Retired	OSRP	GBTru	↑
5946-3	1990	1994	$37.50	**$60**	9%

Particulars: Saltbox design with chimney rising from mid-roof. Windows have shutters and molding on top and base. Attached shed on one side, with storm cellar doors and fenced side entrance. Early release to Showcase Dealers and the National Association Of Limited Edition Dealers (NALED).

DATE:________ $:________

❍ WISH ❍ HAVE

'91	'92	'93	'94	'95	'96
$37.50	40	40	40	45	55

Captain's Cottage

Item #	Intro	Retired	OSRP	GBTru	↑
5947-1	1990	1996	$40	**$55**	22%

Particulars: 2 ½-story has balcony full length of 2nd story. Enclosed staircase on house side to second floor. A connected double dormer is centered on front roof between two ridge chimneys.

DATE:________ $:________

❍ WISH ❍ HAVE

'91	'92	'93	'94	'95	'96
$40	40	42	42	44	45

SLEEPY HOLLOW

ITEM #	INTRO	RETIRED	OSRP	GBTRU	↑
5954-4	1990	1993	$96	**$195**	11%

Particulars: Set of 3 includes *Sleepy Hollow School, Van Tassel Manor,* and *Ichabod Crane's Cottage.* This set wa inspired by Washington Irving's classic, *The Legend of Sleepy Hollow.* The story takes place along the Hudson River in N. Tarrytown, NY.

see below

DATE:_______ $:_______ ❍ WISH ❍ HAVE

'91	'92	'93	'94	'95	'9(
$96	96	96	180	170	17

SLEEPY HOLLOW SCHOOL

ITEM #	INTRO	RETIRED	OSRP	GBTRU	NO
5954-4	1990	1993	$32	**$90**	CHANG

Particulars: 1 of the 3-piece set—SLEEPY HOLLOW. Framed stone chimney warms log cabin school. Brick and wood belfry houses bell. Wood pile and bench wit bucket near front door. School teacher Ichabod Crane taught in this one-room schoolhouse.

DATE:_______ $:_______ ❍ WISH ❍ HAVE

'91	'92	'93	'94	'95	'9(
$32	32	32	78	80	9C

VAN TASSEL MANOR

ITEM #	INTRO	RETIRED	OSRP	GBTRU	NO
5954-4	1990	1993	$32	**$60**	CHANG

Particulars: 1 of the 3-piece set—SLEEPY HOLLOW. Yello house with mansard roof with two front dormers. Wood corner posts support porch. Stone lean-to on one side. Double chimneys rise off roof ridge. Four ears of corn decorate front entry. After attending a party at the Van Tassel residence, Ichabod Crane set out for home, but never got there.

DATE:_______ $:_______ ❍ WISH ❍ HAVE

'91	'92	'93	'94	'95	'96
$32	32	32	65	60	60

ICHABOD CRANE'S COTTAGE

ITEM #	INTRO	RETIRED	OSRP	GBTRU	↑
5954-4	1990	1993	$32	**$65**	18%

Particulars: 1 of the 3-piece set—SLEEPY HOLLOW. Stone first story topped by wood second story. Rough shingled roof with dip in the middle between two brick chimneys This is the modest home provided for the village school master.

DATE:_______ $:_______ ❍ WISH ❍ HAVE

'91	'92	'93	'94	'95	'96
$32	32	32	60	55	55

EEPY HOLLOW CHURCH

ITEM #	INTRO	RETIRED	OSRP	GBTRU	↑
5955-2	1990	1993	$36	**$65**	8%

Particulars: Wood church with steeple rising off front. Arched windows with prominent sills. Front steps lead to double doors with ornate hinges and molding.

DATE:_______ $:_______ ❍ WISH ❍ HAVE

'91	'92	'93	'94	'95	'96
$36	36	36	65	60	60

McGREBE-CUTTERS & SLEIGHS

ITEM #	INTRO	RETIRED	OSRP	GBTRU	NO CHANGE
5640-5	1991	1995	$45	**$65**	

Particulars: Builders of carriages, sleighs, and sleds to move people and goods in snowy New England. A cutter is a small sleigh that seats one person. Stone and wood building. Large doors in front and side to allow movement of vehicles. Stone half has short tower atop roof. Large loft doors above entry.

DATE:_______ $:_______ ❍ WISH ❍ HAVE

'91	'92	'93	'94	'95	'96
$45	45	48	48	48	65

LUEBIRD SEED AND BULB

ITEM #	INTRO	RETIRED	OSRP	GBTRU	↑
5642-1	1992	1996	$48	**$55**	15%

Particulars: Covered storage area near entry door has open storage bins. Small shuttered arched window adjacent to door. Outside stairs lead to other storage areas. Two stories with stone block lower level and fieldstone chimney.

DATE:_______ $:_______ ❍ WISH ❍ HAVE

'92	'93	'94	'95	'96
$48	48	48	48	48

'ANKEE JUD BELL CASTING

ITEM #	INTRO	RETIRED	OSRP	GBTRU	↓
5643-0	1992	1995	$44	**$55**	8%

Particulars: Red brick foundry with steeply pitched gable roof. Projecting side doors on second and third story for lifting heavy, large castings. Tall circular brick chimney rises off rear of foundry.

DATE:_______ $:_______ ❍ WISH ❍ HAVE

'92	'93	'94	'95	'96
$44	44	44	44	60

Stoney Brook Town Hall

Item #	Intro	Retired	OSRP	GBTru	
5644-8	1992	1995	$42	**$60**	NO CHAN

Particulars: Rectangular brick building serves as meeting hall for town governance. Side entry with a latch gate, cellar windows with shutters, roof dormers and two chimneys, and many windows on long sides of buildin complete structure.

DATE:_______ $:_______
❍ WISH ❍ HAVE

'92	'93	'94	'95	'9
$42	42	42	42	6

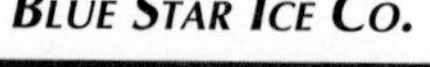

Blue Star Ice Co.

Item #	Intro	Retired	OSRP	GBTru	
5647-2	1993	Current	$45	**$48**	NO CHAN

Particulars: Stone 1st story with insulated wood upper storage level. Wooden chute enabled ice block to be pulled up where sawdust or salt hay insulated each block.

DATE:_______ $:_______
❍ WISH ❍ HAVE

'93	'94	'95	'9
$45	45	48	4

A. Bieler Farm

Item #	Intro	Retired	OSRP	GBTru	↑
5648-0	1993	1996	$92	**$115**	21%

Particulars: Set of 2 includes *Pennsylvania Dutch Farmhouse,* #56481 and *Pennsylvania Dutch Barn,* #56482.

see below

DATE:_______ $:_______
❍ WISH ❍ HAVE

'93	'94	'95	'9
$92	92	95	95

Pennsylvania Dutch Farmhouse

Item #	Intro	Retired	OSRP	GBTru	↑
56481	1993	1996	$42	**$65**	49%

Particulars: 1 of the 2-piece set—A. BIELER FARM. Two-story clapboard home. Many windowed to let in light, colorful trim on all windows, roof and wall moldings.

DATE:_______ $:_______
❍ WISH ❍ HAVE

'93	'94	'95	'96
$42	42	43.50	43.5

PENNSYLVANIA DUTCH BARN

ITEM #	INTRO	RETIRED	OSRP	GBTRU	↑
56482	1993	1996	$50	**$65**	26%

Particulars: 1 of the 2-piece set—A. BIELER FARM. Red barn with green mansard roof. Two stone silos on one corner. Double door entry reached by stone supported ramp. Hex signs hung on barn outer walls.

DATE:_______ $:_______
❍ WISH ❍ HAVE

'93	'94	'95	'96
$50	50	51.50	51.50

LINGTON FALLS CHURCH

ITEM #	INTRO	RETIRED	OSRP	GBTRU	NO CHANGE
5651-0	1994	CURRENT	$40	**$42**	

Particulars: Midyear release. Wood church with steeple rising in tiers above main entry. Pillars at front doors are wrapped in garlands. Double tier of windows on side of church to let in daylight. Simple structure with a country look.

DATE:_______ $:_______
❍ WISH ❍ HAVE

'94	'95	'96
$40	42	42

APE KEAG FISH CANNERY

ITEM #	INTRO	RETIRED	OSRP	GBTRU	NO CHANGE
5652-9	1994	CURRENT	$48	**$48**	

Particulars: Lobster pots, buoys are stacked on wharf along building front. Brick tower rising on side of factory cannery allow visual check of fishing boats.

DATE:_______ $:_______
❍ WISH ❍ HAVE

'95	'96
$48	48

GEONHEAD LIGHTHOUSE

ITEM #	INTRO	RETIRED	OSRP	GBTRU	NO CHANGE
5653-7	1994	CURRENT	$50	**$50**	

Particulars: Light shines from porthole windows. Tower connects to keeper's home. Steps lead down from rocks to water.

DATE:_______ $:_______
❍ WISH ❍ HAVE

'95	'96
$50	50

BREWSTER BAY COTTAGES

ITEM #	INTRO	RETIRED	OSRP	GBTRU	
5657-0	1995	CURRENT	$90	**$90**	NO CHAN

Particulars: Set of 2 includes *Jeremiah Brewster House,* #56568 and *Thomas T. Julian House,* #56569.

see below

DATE:_______ $:_______
❍ WISH ❍ HAVE

'95	'9
$90	9

THOMAS T. JULIAN HOUSE

ITEM #	INTRO	RETIRED	OSRP	GBTRU	
56569	1995	CURRENT	$45	**$45**	NO CHAN

Particulars: 1 of the 2-piece set—BREWSTER BAY COTTAGES. Midyear release. Central chimney rises where 4 gabled roof meets. 2-story bay windowed turret next to covered porch entry. The boxes of the first pieces shipped read "Jeremiah Brewster House." When the mistake was noticed, D56 applied a sticker with the correct name over the incorrect one. Later shipments have the correct name printed directly on the box.

DATE:_______ $:_______
❍ WISH ❍ HAVE

'95	'9
$45	4

JEREMIAH BREWSTER HOUSE

ITEM #	INTRO	RETIRED	OSRP	GBTRU	
56568	1995	CURRENT	$45	**$45**	NO CHAN

Particulars: 1 of the 2-piece set—BREWSTER BAY COTTAGE Midyear release. Shed roof side addition attached to main square 2-story house. Shuttered windows, widow's walk on roof. The boxes of the first pieces shipped read "Thomas T. Julian House." When the mistake was noticed, D56 applied sticker with the correct name over the incorrect one. Later shipments have the correct name printed directly on the box

DATE:_______ $:_______
❍ WISH ❍ HAVE

'95	'9
$45	4

CHOWDER HOUSE

ITEM #	INTRO	RETIRED	OSRP	GBTRU	
56571	1995	CURRENT	$40	**$40**	NO CHAN

Particulars: Small cozy eating establishment sits on fieldstone base. Small boats can tie up to one side while another entry serves walk-ins. Blue clapboard with a mansard roof.

DATE:_______ $:_______
❍ WISH ❍ HAVE

'95	'9
$40	4(

Woodbridge Post Office

Item #	Intro	Retired	OSRP	GBTru	
56572	1995	Current	$40	**$40**	No Change

Particulars: Two-story brick post office serves village for mail, stamps, parcels and postal cards. Windows flank double entry doors.

DATE:_______ $:_______
❍ WISH ❍ HAVE

'95	'96
$40	40

Pierce Boat Works

Item #	Intro	Retired	OSRP	GBTru	
56573	1995	Current	$55	**$55**	No Change

Particulars: Boats for lobstermen and fishermen are built at the boat works. Wooden building with double doors allow boats to be pulled or rolled down ramp. Rowboat held on winch and pulley rig on side of building.

DATE:_______ $:_______
❍ WISH ❍ HAVE

'95	'96
$55	55

Apple Valley School

Item #	Intro	Retired	OSRP	GBTru	
56172	1996	Current	$35	**$35**	No Change

Particulars: Midyear release. Small squared brick and stone village school. Tall central chimney connects to stove to keep schoolrooms heated. Bell tower in front gable.

DATE:_______ $:_______
❍ WISH ❍ HAVE

'96
$35

. Hudson Stoveworks

Item #	Intro	Retired	OSRP	GBTru
56574	1996	Current	$60	**$60**

Particulars: Manufacturer of stoves combines shop and foundry. Stone and brick factory attached to office. Stoves are on display outside front door. Foundry is powered by coal and wood furnaces.

DATE:_______ $:_______
❍ WISH ❍ HAVE

Navigational Charts & Maps

Item #	Intro	Retired	OSRP	GBTru
56575	1996	Current	$48	**$48**

Particulars: Business provides information for sea and rive vessels to travel the waterways safely. 2 1/2-story with stone base and clapboard upper levels. Double stairs hu front facade with door entry on second story. Seagulls rest on roof which also has weathervane

DATE:_______ $:_______
❍ WISH ❍ HAVE

Bobwhite Cottage

Item #	Intro	Retired	OSRP	GBTru
56576	1996	Current	$50	**$50**

Particulars: 1 1/2-story home with front and side porches. Porch design features square and octagonal fretwork. Steep pitched roof has front dormer. Upper side bedroo has door to sunporch protected by balustrade railing. Th house is named for a North American Quail or Partridge native to this area.

DATE:_______ $:_______
❍ WISH ❍ HAVE

Van Guilder's Ornamental Ironworks

Item #	Intro	Retired	OSRP	GBTru
56577	1997	Current	$50	**$50**

Particulars: Midyear release. Third building in the village that pertains to metal craftsmanship. A sign on the front of the building announces that weathervanes are available. It is the first New England building with multiple weathervanes.

DATE:_______ $:_______
❍ WISH ❍ HAVE

THE QUINTESSENTIAL NEW ENGLAND COTTAGE

Quaint is the first word that comes to my mind when thinking about cottages. These smal functional houses can be located in many regions of the country, but New England is where th "American" Cottage was born.

In the mid-1800's, when the steam powered saw came into use, lumber became the mate rial of choice for many home builders. Not only was lumber plentiful, it was easier to work wit than stone. New forms of style, structure, and creativity were now available. In fact, the cottag gave birth to an entirely new phenomenon, the American front porch.

Until this time, the popular style of cottages was Gothic–a direct result of the need to us stone. Wood, however, allowed builders to branch out to other styles–Carpenter Gothic an en Gingerbread Carpenter Gothic among them. The term "gingerbread," by the way, comes m the word gingimbrat meaning preserved ginger. It became gingerbread when the last syl-ble was mistranslated to bread. This term was first used to describe the ornate decorations of iling ships and then the architectural ornamentation of homes in coastal areas.

Loosely based on the Swiss chalet's design, the cottage is characterized by a steep roof, nall rooms, a porch or porches, and is usually one or one and a half stories high. The upper vel, if finished, often allows space for only one or two rooms.

As cottages gained praise and acceptance, they began to dot the rugged New England oreline. Some islands such as Martha's Vineyard and Nantucket off Massachusetts' Cape Cod ecame known for their colorful homes.

The cottages on Nantucket are known for their picturesque style and the rose gardens that rround them, creating an unequaled charm. The island has maintained its flavor of a whaling y from the last century, and a walk down its white, clam shell-covered streets allows one to nagine the lives of the cottages' residents.

Martha's Vineyard, or the Vineyard as it is referred to, has been home to more than 300 ndy-colored cottages. Aside from their vivid colors, these homes feature decorative moldings, tterned shingles, and delicate details. Though it would appear that they were part of an intri-te nineteenth century plan to beautify the island's streets, they are actually the results of home ilders trying to outdo each other.

It all started in 1835 when week-long religious meetings were held in the area of Oak Bluffs–iginally part of Edgartown. The attendees of the Methodist Camp Meetings pitched tents for elter during their stay. Martha's Vineyard Camp Ground had exploded into a summer seaside sort with "wooden tents" standing where the original tents used to be. At this time, the town parated from Edgartown, and its citizens named it Cottage City. The name remained until 907.

The cottages' designs were often based on the Victorian style that was then all the rage, pecially along Newport, Rhode Island's Bellevue Avenue where many of the nation's wealthi-t citizens were building their cottages. The only thing Newport and Vineyard homes had in mmon, however, was their proximity to the ocean. Newport's "summer cottages," as their vners called them, had as many as seventy rooms.

Many of the Vineyard's cottages were actually constructed in Rhode Island and shipped to e island. And there is another Rhode Island connection to the Cottage City's history. The most pensive cottage built on the island during the nineteenth century was for Rhode Island's vernor during the Civil War, William Sprague. Known as the Ark, it cost $3,500 to complete.

People from all over the world now visit or vacation on Nantucket and Martha's Vineyard. me even have the opportunity to stay in cottages, others simply admire them. We have such home for the residents of our village.

Though not the first cottage introduced, D56 has produced possibly its most delightful little ttage yet–*Bobwhite Cottage*. A hit with New England Village collectors as soon as it was troduced, it's certain to be a "Cross-over" building as well—purchased and displayed by llectors of other villages.

Along with this attractive color scheme and soft-spoken charm, one of the highlights of the esign is the side entrance complete with a love seat on the porch and a balcony with an open or. I wouldn't be a bit surprised to see this entrance used as the front of the house in many splays. In either case, there's little doubt that this building will continue the success D56 has njoyed and the realism it has captured with the New England Village introductions of the past w years. Now how about a Newport Cottage?

the Village Chronicle.

ALPINE VILLAGE

Alpine Village, the third porcelain village, was introduced in 1986. It represer a Bavarian town featuring businesses, farms, and homes that dot the mountainsid and valleys throughout the Alps.

This slow-to-grow village has never had a limited edition. In fact, it wasn't un 1997 that it first received a midyear introduction. The attractiveness of i latest introductions, as well as its slow growth, has captured the interest of mar collectors.

THE BOTTOM LINE:

Cost of all pieces introduced to Alpine Village through the 1997 midyear intr ductions including accessories: (This does not include variations, or special piece **$694**

Greenbook TruMarket Value of all pieces through the 1997 midyear introdu tions including accessories: (This does not include variations, special pieces.) **$2,1**

ALPINE VILLAGE SINCE WE LAST MET...

... NEW FOR SALE LISTINGS

***Danube Music Publisher* - 1996**

This ornamental building is home to the area's music publisher. From here, the sounds of Bavarian music are made available to the world.

***Bernhardiner Hundchen* - 1997**

This is Alpine Village's first midyear introduction. Translated as St. Bernard Puppies, the name of this building implies that the large dogs are bred and sold from this house/kennel.

... NO LONGER ON THE MARKET

ALPINE VILLAGE

- 65405 Bessor Bierkeller
- 65406 Gasthof Eisl
- 65409 Milche-Kase

Note: 65407 Apotheke & 65408 E. Staubr Backer have not been retired.

ETIRED BUILDINGS

615-4 1993 Bahnhof (Train Station)
952-8 1989 Josef Engel Farmhouse
5405 1996 Bessor Bierkeller*
5406 1996 Gasthof Eisl*
5409 1996 Milch-Kase*
541-2 1991 Alpine Church

Note: Only 3 of the 5 buildings in LPINE VILLAGE, Set of 5, were retired. 5407, Apotheke, and 65408, E. Staubr acker, have not been retired.

QUIKREFERENCE

ALPINE VILLAGE

ITEM #	INTRO	RETIRED	OSRP	GBTRU
6540-4	1986	*	$150	$*

see below

Particulars: Set of 5 includes *Bessor Bierkeller, #65405, Gasthof Eisl, #65406, Apotheke, #65407, E. Staubr Backer, #65408, Milch-Kase, #65409.* Early release to National Association Of Limited Edition Dealers (NALED), 1987. *In 1996, three of the five buildings were retired. Two are still current.

DATE:_______	$:_______	'91	'92	'93	'94	'95	'9
❍ WISH	❍ HAVE	$185	185	185	185	195	19

BESSOR BIERKELLER

ITEM #	INTRO	RETIRED	OSRP	GBTRU	↑
65405	1986	1996	$25	**$45**	15%

Particulars: 1 of the 5-piece set—ALPINE VILLAGE. (Beer Cellar) Window boxes on second story hung with colorful banners. Third story rustic timbered enclosed balcony has garland decoration. Early release to National Association Of Limited Edition Dealers (NALED), 1987.

DATE:_______	$:_______	'91	'92	'93	'94	'95	'9
❍ WISH	❍ HAVE	$37	37	37	37	39	3

GASTHOF EISL

ITEM #	INTRO	RETIRED	OSRP	GBTRU	↑
65406	1986	1996	$25	**$45**	15%

Particulars: 1 of the 5-piece set—ALPINE VILLAGE. (Guest House) Rustic inn, fieldstone first floor with two stories of stucco topped by orange/red roof. A third-story balcony is decorated with greenery and banners. Window boxes also decorate other rooms. Early release to National Association Of Limited Edition Dealers (NALED), 1987.

DATE:_______	$:_______	'91	'92	'93	'94	'95	'96
❍ WISH	❍ HAVE	$37	37	37	37	39	39

APOTHEKE

ITEM #	INTRO	RETIRED	OSRP	GBTRU	NO
65407	1986	CURRENT	$25	**$39**	CHANG

Particulars: 1 of the 5-piece set—ALPINE VILLAGE. (Apothecary) Cream walls topped by blue roof. Banners flying from attic window. Prescriptions and drugstore supplies available from store on ground floor. Building shared with tobacconist. Early release to National Association Of Limited Edition Dealers (NALED), 1987. This building did not retire in 1996.

DATE:_______	$:_______	'91	'92	'93	'94	'95	'96
❍ WISH	❍ HAVE	$37	37	37	37	39	39

E. Staubr Backer

Item #	Intro	Retired	OSRP	GBTru	NO CHANGE
65408	1986	Current	$25	**$39**	

Particulars: 1 of the 5-piece set—ALPINE VILLAGE. (Bakery) Only building in which bulb is inserted in the side. Three stories with bakery on ground level. Third story has some timbering design and an oriel window. Tiled roof and two chimneys. Early release to National Association Of Limited Edition Dealers (NALED), 1987. This building did not retire in 1996.

DATE:_______	$:_______	'91	'92	'93	'94	'95	'96
❍ WISH	❍ HAVE	$37	37	37	37	39	39

Milch-Kase

Item #	Intro	Retired	OSRP	GBTru	⬆
65409	1986	1996	$25	**$45**	15%

Particulars: 1 of the 5-piece set—ALPINE VILLAGE. (Milk & Cheese Shop) Milk cans by door denotes shop that sells milk and cheese. Rough slate roof tops blue walls and wood planking exterior. Double wood doors allow wagons to bring supplies in/out. Early release to National Association Of Limited Edition Dealers (NALED), 1987.

DATE:_______	$:_______	'91	'92	'93	'94	'95	'96
❍ WISH	❍ HAVE	$37	37	37	37	39	39

osef Engel Farmhouse

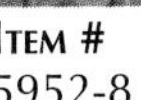

Item #	Intro	Retired	OSRP	GBTru	⬆
5952-8	1987	1989	$33	**$970**	5%

Particulars: House and barn are connected. Stucco over stone. Barn has hayloft above animal and equipment area. Shutters swing overhead. Home has balcony above front entry with herringbone planking. Red roof, capped chimneys.

DATE:_______	$:_______	'91	'92	'93	'94	'95	'96
❍ WISH	❍ HAVE	$225	450	610	960	975	925

Alpine Church— "White Trim"

Item #	Intro	Retired	OSRP	GBTru	⬆
6541-2	1987	1991	$32	**$385**	10%

Particulars: Variations in color affect GBTru$—"White Trim" or "Dark Trim." This is the "White Trim." Onion dome tops steeple which also features a clock on all sides of the tower.

DATE:_______	$:_______	'91	'92	'93	'94	'95	'96
❍ WISH	❍ HAVE	$36	85	112	155	295	350

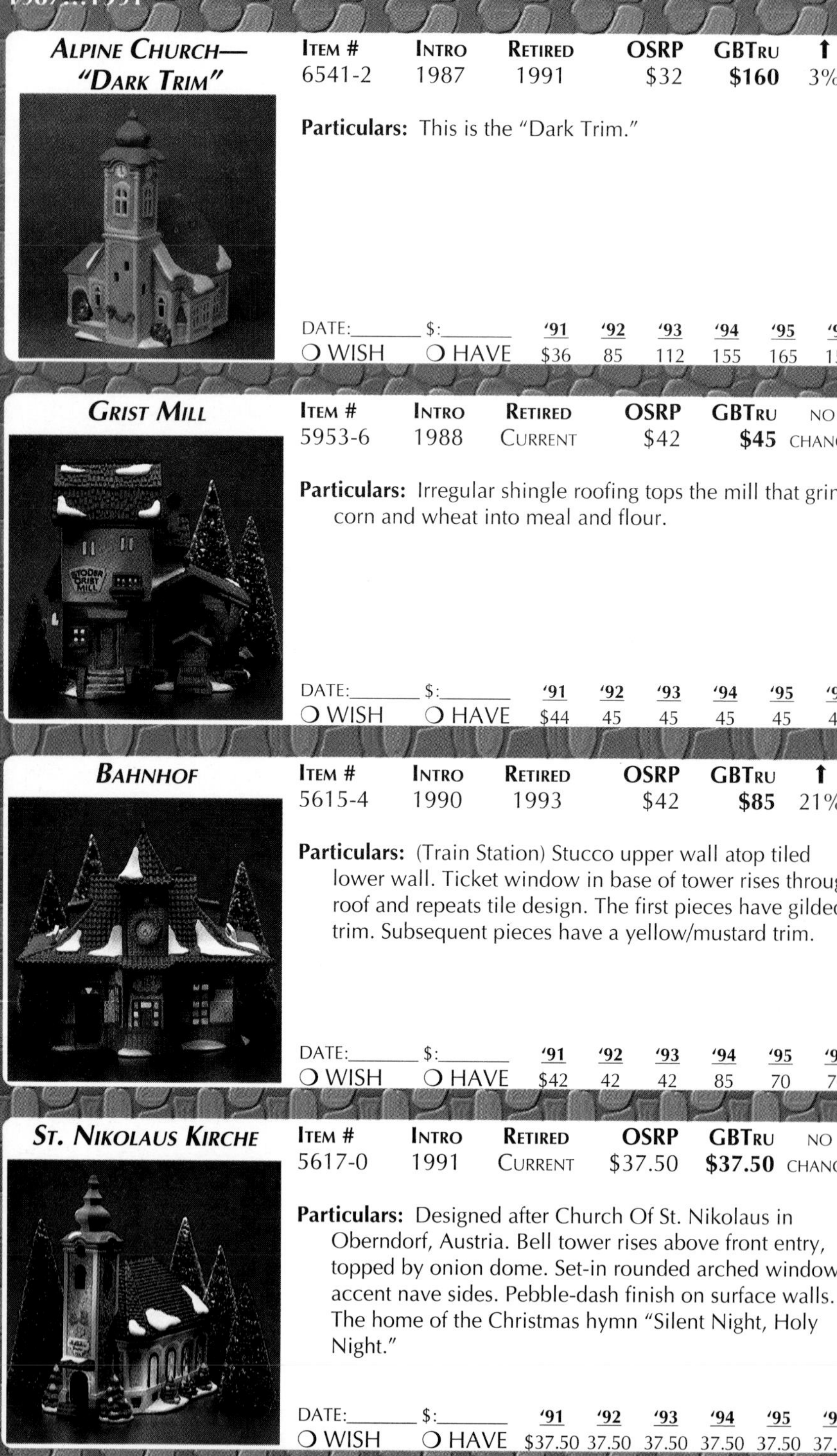

Alpine Church— "Dark Trim"

Item #	Intro	Retired	OSRP	GBTru	↑
6541-2	1987	1991	$32	**$160**	3%

Particulars: This is the "Dark Trim."

DATE:________ $:________

❍ WISH ❍ HAVE

'91	'92	'93	'94	'95	'9
$36	85	112	155	165	15

Grist Mill

Item #	Intro	Retired	OSRP	GBTru	No
5953-6	1988	Current	$42	**$45**	Chanc

Particulars: Irregular shingle roofing tops the mill that grin corn and wheat into meal and flour.

DATE:________ $:________

❍ WISH ❍ HAVE

'91	'92	'93	'94	'95	'9
$44	45	45	45	45	4

Bahnhof

Item #	Intro	Retired	OSRP	GBTru	↑
5615-4	1990	1993	$42	**$85**	21%

Particulars: (Train Station) Stucco upper wall atop tiled lower wall. Ticket window in base of tower rises throug roof and repeats tile design. The first pieces have gilded trim. Subsequent pieces have a yellow/mustard trim.

DATE:________ $:________

❍ WISH ❍ HAVE

'91	'92	'93	'94	'95	'9
$42	42	42	85	70	7

St. Nikolaus Kirche

Item #	Intro	Retired	OSRP	GBTru	No
5617-0	1991	Current	$37.50	**$37.50**	Chanc

Particulars: Designed after Church Of St. Nikolaus in Oberndorf, Austria. Bell tower rises above front entry, topped by onion dome. Set-in rounded arched window accent nave sides. Pebble-dash finish on surface walls. The home of the Christmas hymn "Silent Night, Holy Night."

DATE:________ $:________

❍ WISH ❍ HAVE

'91	'92	'93	'94	'95	'9
$37.50	37.50	37.50	37.50	37.50	37.

SILENT NIGHT ... HOLY NIGHT

The most beloved Christmas hymn is "Silent Night." It is sung around the world and ıs been translated to all but a few known languages. Like many great things, however, is wonderful song grew from very humble beginnings. In fact, the creator of the words, ıther Josef Mohr died never knowing what a wonderful gift he and Franz Gruber had ven to the world.

Along with Mohr and Gruber, the other key player in the story of "Silent Night" and e St. Nikolaus Kirche is the Salzach River. It was this river that caused the rust in the gan of the church. (To this day a popular notion states that hungry mice ate through e bellows of the organ.) It was also this river that later weakened the foundation of the ıurch requiring that it be torn down.

The St. Nikolaus Kirche was located in Oberndorf, Austria about 10 miles northwest Salzburg. Mohr, the assistant priest at this church, was out of favor with his superiors ıd was moved frequently. He would only spend two years here. But while at this ıurch, he was confronted with the possibility of not having music for the Christmas ve service because of the organ's condition. It was on that day that he wrote the words ıd asked Gruber, a school teacher who played the church organ for extra money, to ompose the music on his guitar. That night in 1818 the two men and a choir sang the ng. Once they made it through the service, the story ended–at least as far as they ıew.

A few months later, an organ builder went to the church to repair the organ. While was there the song was brought to his attention. He copied the song and sang it as he ade his rounds repairing organs throughout the countryside. It was heard and admired y others, and in 1834 it was sung for the king of Prussia, though the name of the song ad been changed to "Song from Heaven." Five years later, it made its way across the tlantic to America.

No one knew who had written the song, though many claimed that it came directly om God. When Gruber claimed that he wrote it, he was scorned and ridiculed. Though e still possessed the original copy of the song, few believed that a "mere" teacher ould have penned such music.

Mohr's fate was even more sad. Prior to his death in 1848 in Wagrain, Austria, he ontinued to be transferred, usually staying in one town for less than a year. He died a oor man, though befittingly on St. Nicholas' Day. In the thirty years that followed his riting the most famous Christmas hymn, he never heard it again or knew of its popu- rity.

The D56 *St. Nikolaus Kirche* is a tribute to a small church in a small town where two ıodest men gave a special gift to the world. The D56 piece has transcended villages ith non-Alpine collectors placing it in their village. It has also transcended collecting ith people buying it solely because it symbolizes a song that has meant much in their ves.

the Village Chronicle.

ALPINE SHOPS

Item #	Intro	Retired	OSRP	GBTru	
5618-9	1992	Current	$75	$75	NO CHANC

Particulars: Set of 2 includes *Metterniche Wurst,* #56190 and *Kukuck Uhren,* #56191.

see below

DATE:_______ $:_______

❍ WISH ❍ HAVE

'92	'93	'94	'95	'9
$75	75	75	75	75

Metterniche Wurst

Item #	Intro	Retired	OSRP	GBTru	
56190	1992	Current	$37.50	$37.50	NO CHANC

Particulars: 1 of the 2-piece set—ALPINE SHOPS. (Sausage Shop) Stucco over stone and brick with steeply pitched roof coming down to first floor on sides. Front facade framed by ornamental curved coping.

DATE:_______ $:_______

❍ WISH ❍ HAVE

'92	'93	'94	'95	'9
$37.50	37.50	37.50	37.50	37.5

Kukuck Uhren

Item #	Intro	Retired	OSRP	GBTru	
56191	1992	Current	$37.50	$37.50	NO CHANC

Particulars: 1 of the 2-piece set—ALPINE SHOPS. (Clock Shop) Franc Schiller displays his trademark clock on shop sign above recessed entry door. Small shop has wood timbers that outline the stone, brick and stucco exterior.

DATE:_______ $:_______

❍ WISH ❍ HAVE

'92	'93	'94	'95	'96
$37.50	37.50	37.50	37.50	37.5

Sport Laden

Item #	Intro	Retired	OSRP	GBTru	
5612-0	1993	Current	$50	$50	NO CHANG

Particulars: Shop for skiing and winter sports equipment. Small shop tucked away on one side. Roof overhangs protect facade and chimneys are capped to keep out snow, ice and rain.

DATE:_______ $:_______

❍ WISH ❍ HAVE

'93	'94	'95	'96
$50	50	50	50

ONDITOREI SCHOKOLADE

ITEM #	INTRO	RETIRED	OSRP	GBTRU	NO
5614-6	1994	CURRENT	$37.50	**$37.50**	CHANGE

Particulars: (Bakery & Chocolate Shop) Garland and banners hang down from the second-story balcony. The extended eaves protect the building from heavy snows.

DATE:________ $:________
❍ WISH ❍ HAVE

'94	'95	'96
$37.50	37.50	37.50

KAMM HAUS

ITEM #	INTRO	RETIRED	OSRP	GBTRU	NO
56171	1995	CURRENT	$42	**$42**	CHANGE

Particulars: "House On The Crest" is the translation of this Alpine building's name. Long stairs lead up to the main balcony and front door of the skiers' inn. Roof overhangs offer protection from icing. Large fireplace at rear of roof has a cap to keep snow from falling in.

DATE:________ $:________
❍ WISH ❍ HAVE

'95	'96
$42	42

ANUBE MUSIC PUBLISHER

ITEM #	INTRO	RETIRED	OSRP	GBTRU
56173	1996	CURRENT	$55	**$55**

Particulars: The Donau Musik Verlag continues onion dome roof motif on store facade and attached music studio which announces violin lessons. Dressed stone outlines windows, doorways and corners on main facade while pargeting carved in ornamental patterns highlights studio.

DATE:________ $:________
❍ WISH ❍ HAVE

ERNHARDINER HUNDCHEN

ITEM #	INTRO	RETIRED	OSRP	GBTRU
56174	1997	CURRENT	$50	**$50**

Particulars: Midyear release. Kennels and training center for St. Bernard puppies and dogs. The breed is known for endurance and ability to track and rescue people lost or injured in snowy mountainous regions.

DATE:________ $:________
❍ WISH ❍ HAVE

CHRISTMAS IN THE CITY

The hustle and bustle of Christmas in the big city was made available to colle tors when Department 56 introduced its fourth porcelain village, Christmas in tl City, in 1987. This representation of a large city instantly brought collectors back the days of holiday shopping before the advent of sprawling suburban malls. Mar collectors imagined that Christmas in the City represented New York City, but D partment 56 never confirmed this, not until 1996, anyway. It was then that Gran Central Railway Station was introduced.

Christmas in the City has had two limited editions, *Dorothy's Dress Shop* ar the *Cathedral Church of St. Mark*. It was the *Cathedral Church of St. Mark* that dre attention when its planned production of 17,500 was curtailed at 3,024 due production problems.

For collectors who want to "hear" the cars, trains, and Christmas songs, and see Santas on the street corners and shoppers hustling on sidewalks, Christmas the City is the series.

THE BOTTOM LINE:

Cost of all pieces introduced to Christmas in the City through the 1997 midye introductions including accessories: (This does not include variations, or speci pieces.) **$2,336**

Greenbook TruMarket Value of all pieces through the 1997 midyear introdu tions including accessories: (This does not include variations, special pieces.) **$7,70**

CHRISTMAS IN THE CITY SINCE WE LAST MET...

... NEW FOR SALE LISTINGS

Grand Central Railway Station - 1996

When this railway station was announced, Department 56 confirmed for the first time that Christmas in the City is its rendition of New York City. Painted on the back of the building are two train tunnels. Now the villagers can escape the city quickly for a holiday vacation.

Cafe Caprice French Restaurant - 1996

The City has expanded its flavorful dining with its third ethnic restaurant. Now the villagers can choose from Chinese, Italian, or French cuisine.

The City Globe - 1997

This formidable building houses the first newspaper publisher for the City. The City Globe building features half a globe above the front entrance and a globe that actually spins perched atop its tower.

Ii-De-Ho Nightclub - 1997

osters on three-story red brick nightclub highlight present and future lub acts. Marquee over double door entry. Club name highlights a ab Calloway jazz riff.

..NO LONGER ON THE MARKET

531-0 UPTOWN SHOPPES, Set of 3
- 55311 Haberdashery
- 55312 Music Emporium
- 55313 City Clockworks

880-7 WEST VILLAGE SHOPS, Set of 2
- 58808 Potter's Tea Seller
- 58809 Spring St. Coffee House

ETIRED BUILDINGS

531-0	1996	UPTOWN SHOPPES
5311	1996	Haberdashery
5312	1996	Music Emporium
5313	1996	City Clockworks
536-0	1995	Red Brick Fire Station
537-9	1994	Wong's In Chinatown
538-7	1995	"Little Italy" Ristorante
543-3	1993	Arts Academy
544-1	1994	The Doctor's Office
880-7	1996	WEST VILLAGE SHOPS
8808	1996	Potter's Tea Seller
8809	1996	Spring St. Coffee House
961-7	1989	Sutton Place Brownstones
962-5	1990	The Cathedral
963-3	1989	Palace Theatre
968-4	1991	Chocolate Shoppe
969-2	1991	City Hall
970-6	1992	Hank's Market
972-2	1990	Variety Store
973-0	1994	Ritz Hotel
977-3	1992	5607 Park Avenue Townhouse
978-1	1992	5609 Park Avenue Townhouse
512-9	1990	CHRISTMAS IN THE CITY
512-9	1990	Toy Shop And Pet Store
512-9	1990	Bakery
512-9	1990	Tower Restaurant

LIMITED EDITIONS

5549-2	Cathedral Church Of St. Mark	3,024
5974-9	Dorothy's Dress Shop	12,500

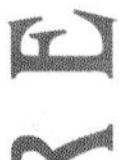

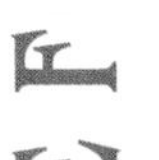

Sutton Place Brownstones

Item #	Intro	Retired	OSRP	GBTru	↑
5961-7	1987	1989	$80	**$875**	4%

Particulars: Three multi-storied homes, attached via shared common walls. Three shops occupy semi-below ground-level space. Attic dormer windows have iron grillwork. "Sutton Plac Rowhouse" is inscribed on the bottom, not "Sutton Place Brownstones." It's common for a piece to have a concave bac wall, however, one with a relatively straight wall can be found and is generally considered to be more valuable.

DATE:_______ $:_______ ❍ WISH ❍ HAVE

'91	'92	'93	'94	'95	'9
$425	760	775	825	825	84

The Cathedral

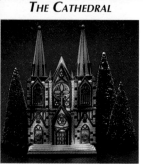

Item #	Intro	Retired	OSRP	GBTru	↑
5962-5	1987	1990	$60	**$355**	4%

Particulars: Twin spires, early Gothic design and decorate windows set this Cathedral apart. Stone church incorpo rates a fortress-like solidness. The first version is smalle darker, and has snow on the steps. The second version larger, lighter, and has no snow on the steps.

DATE:_______ $:_______ ❍ WISH ❍ HAVE

'91	'92	'93	'94	'95	'9
$220	285	305	330	335	34

Palace Theatre

Item #	Intro	Retired	OSRP	GBTru	↑
5963-3	1987	1989	$45	**$935**	5%

Particulars: Mask of Comedy & Tragedy are bas-reliefs on brick building featuring Christmas Show of Nutcracker. Stage entrance side of building. The first version is smaller and has more snow o the roof. The first version has gilded trim; the second version has yellow/mustard trim. It's not unusual for a piece to have concave convex walls, however, a piece with relatively straight walls can found and is generally considered to be more valuable.

DATE:_______ $:_______ ❍ WISH ❍ HAVE

'91	'92	'93	'94	'95	'9
$450	1100	1025	925	925	89

Christmas in the City

Item #	Intro	Retired	OSRP	GBTru	↑
6512-9	1987	1990	$112	**$590**	4%

Particulars: Set of 3 includes *Toy Shop And Pet Store, Bakery* and *Tower Restaurant.*

see next page

DATE:_______ $:_______ ❍ WISH ❍ HAVE

'91	'92	'93	'94	'95	'9
$250	290	335	375	475	56

Y SHOP AND PET STORE

ITEM #	INTRO	RETIRED	OSRP	GBTRU	↑
6512-9	1987	1990	$37.50	**$275**	17%

Particulars: 1 of the 3-piece set—CHRISTMAS IN THE CITY. Side by side Pet Store and Toy Shop. Tucked in at side is Tailor Shop. Ground floor has extra high ceiling with half circle windows. Individual pieces may vary in color. The earlier pieces are very dark, later ones are lighter.

DATE:_______ $:_______

❍ WISH ❍ HAVE

'91	'92	'93	'94	'95	'96
$85	115	120	150	220	235

BAKERY

ITEM #	INTRO	RETIRED	OSRP	GBTRU	↑
6512-9	1987	1990	$37.50	**$115**	15%

Particulars: 1 of the 3-piece set—CHRISTMAS IN THE CITY. Four-story building with Bakery on first two levels. Iron grill work for safety and decor on smaller windows. Two different height chimneys. Individual pieces may vary in color. The earlier pieces are light, later ones are darker.

DATE:_______ $:_______

❍ WISH ❍ HAVE

'91	'92	'93	'94	'95	'96
$80	80	95	95	95	100

TOWER RESTAURANT

ITEM #	INTRO	RETIRED	OSRP	GBTRU	↑
6512-9	1987	1990	$37.50	**$275**	17%

Particulars: 1 of the 3-piece set—CHRISTMAS IN THE CITY. Multi-sided tower structure is integral part of residential building. Double door entry to restaurant/cafe. Iron grillwork on upper tower windows. Individual pieces may vary in color. The earlier pieces are very dark, later one are lighter.

DATE:_______ $:_______

❍ WISH ❍ HAVE

'91	'92	'93	'94	'95	'96
$110	130	165	175	200	235

CHOCOLATE SHOPPE

ITEM #	INTRO	RETIRED	OSRP	GBTRU	↑
5968-4	1988	1991	$40	**$150**	11%

Particulars: Paneled roof between first and second story extends to shop signs. Building over Shoppe rises three stories plus attic. Above Brown Brothers Bookstore is one short story plus attic. Stone facade has heart panels at base while bookstore has sign and canopy over window. Individual pieces may vary in color. The earlier pieces are dark, later ones are lighter. The roof of the attached bookstore is most often not level. None of the variations affect GBTru$.

DATE:_______ $:_______

❍ WISH ❍ HAVE

'91	'92	'93	'94	'95	'96
$45	90	90	110	100	135

City Hall—"Proof"

Item #	Intro	Retired	OSRP	GBTru	NO
5969-2	1988	1991	$65	**$195**	CHAN

Particulars: This piece is smaller than the regular City Hal It came in a foam box with no sleeve or lightcord.

DATE:_______ $:_______ ❍ WISH ❍ HAVE

'91	'92	'93	'94	'95	'9
$-	225	215	200	185	1

City Hall

Item #	Intro	Retired	OSRP	GBTru	↑
5969-2	1988	1991	$65	**$170**	6%

Particulars: Imposing fortress with four towers at corners plus repeat design on clock tower. Broad steps plus lar columns establish entry doors. Stone arches accent first floor windows plus tower window. Planters with evergreens on either side of steps.

DATE:_______ $:_______ ❍ WISH ❍ HAVE

'91	'92	'93	'94	'95	'9
$75	150	150	150	155	1(

Hank's Market

Item #	Intro	Retired	OSRP	GBTru	NO
5970-6	1988	1992	$40	**$85**	CHAN

Particulars: This piece is also referred to as "Corner Grocer." Boxes and barrels of produce are on display. Rolled awnings over sign. Brick building with painted brick on upper sections of second story. Two upper windows are multi-paned with half-circle sunburst, oth window has awning. Two chimneys on steeply pitched roof.

DATE:_______ $:_______ ❍ WISH ❍ HAVE

'91	'92	'93	'94	'95	'9
$45	45	78	78	80	8

Variety Store

Item #	Intro	Retired	OSRP	GBTru	↑
5972-2	1988	1990	$45	**$180**	9%

Particulars: The mold used for this building is the same one us for the *Drugstore,* #672-6, in the Bachman's Hometown Series. The design was based on a building in Stillwater, MN Corner store in two-story brick building. Garland decorated awnings extend out to shelter display windows and shopper Separate door for upper story. Next door shop is barbershop with striped pole outside. Small eyeglass shop completes tric

DATE:_______ $:_______ ❍ WISH ❍ HAVE

'91	'92	'93	'94	'95	'9
$100	105	108	135	150	16

RITZ HOTEL

ITEM #	INTRO	RETIRED	OSRP	GBTRU	↑
5973-0	1989	1994	$55	**$80**	7%

Particulars: Red doors complete columned entryway, red window canopy over each second story French window. Stone, block, and brick building. Cupola on attic window. Slate roof.

DATE:_______	$:_______	'91	'92	'93	'94	'95	'96
❍ WISH	❍ HAVE	$55	55	55	55	65	75

OROTHY'S DRESS SHOP

ITEM #	INTRO	RETIRED	OSRP	GBTRU	↑
5974-9	1989	LTD ED 12,500	$70	**$380**	1%

Particulars: Bright green door and awning, bay windows on first and second floor, mansard roof.

DATE:_______	$:_______	'91	'92	'93	'94	'95	'96
❍ WISH	❍ HAVE	$350	355	370	370	350	375

DOROTHY'S DRESS SHOP

Arguably the most neglected, rejected, misunderstood and ignored numbered lim-d edition that has been produced by Department 56 is *Dorothy's Dress Shop. Green ate Cottage* could possibly be a close contender, but I would place my vote for orothy's.

Issued in 1989, the first limited edition building for Christmas In The City is limited only 12,500 pieces. Its suggested retail price was $70. The amazing part of this piece's story though is its current secondary price. Having been retired since 1991, it still only lls for approximately $350 - $400.

Before going any further, let's take a look at this wonderful city building. Three city ories high, Dorothy's is a very colorful and vivid piece. This, however, is one of the aracteristics that many collectors do not like about it. Others feels that it is the com-nation of reds, greens, blues and grays that give it its fine quality.

How could you not include it in your city? It offers the ladies of the City a place to rchase finely made dresses and have hats made. The adjacent building, though not as gh and rather thin, is where the citizens can purchase gifts or treat themselves to quisite jewelry. This piece is definitely the upscale shop in any collector's display of e City. Should you decide to add one to your village, make sure that you check the airs that lead to the second floor. Often the stairs are pulling away from the building or e railing is glued on at an odd angle.

continued next page

DOROTHY'S DRESS SHOP (*continued from pg189*)

Now, let's compare Dorothy's to the history of two other limited editions. Though is not truly accurate to compare it with Dickens' Village pieces, *C. Fletcher Pub House* and *Ruth Marion Scotch Woolens* are the two pieces that have the most in co mon with it. First, the Public House, issued in 1988, is also a limited edition of 12,5 pieces. With higher demand created by a greater number of collectors for its village, now sells for roughly $600. Ruth Marion, issued the same year as the City piece, limited to 17,500 pieces yet sells for the same secondary price, or thereabout.

Other than the fact that there are not as many CIC collectors as there are Dicker Village collectors, you would think that this building would be selling for a price clos to that of the Public House. It actually makes Dorothy's look like a very good buy.

If you are a City collector and do not have the Dress Shop, take another look a maybe you will agree.

the **Village Chronicl**

5607 PARK AVENUE TOWNHOUSE

ITEM #	INTRO	RETIRED	OSRP	GBTRU	↑
5977-3	1989	1992	$48	**$85**	6%

Particulars: Four stories with ground floor card and gift shop, curved corner turret, blue canopy over double French door entry. Earlier pieces had gilded trim at top building, later production had dull gold colored paint. This does not affect secondary market value.

DATE:_______ $:_______ ❍ WISH ❍ HAVE

'91	'92	'93	'94	'95	'9
$48	50	78	81	80	8

5609 PARK AVENUE TOWNHOUSE

ITEM #	INTRO	RETIRED	OSRP	GBTRU	↑
5978-1	1989	1992	$48	**$85**	6%

Particulars: Four stories with ground floor art gallery, dou wood doors lead to apartments, blue canopy over entr Earlier pieces had gilded trim at top of building, later production has dull gold colored paint. This does not affect secondary market value.

DATE:_______ $:_______ ❍ WISH ❍ HAVE

'91	'92	'93	'94	'95	'9
$48	50	78	82	80	8

ED BRICK FIRE STATION

ITEM #	INTRO	RETIRED	OSRP	GBTRU	↑
5536-0	1990	1995	$55	**$80**	7%

Particulars: Brick Station House for Hook & Ladder Company. Large wood doors lead to equipment with separate door for upper level. Stone block detailing on turret and above upper floor windows. Formal pediment at front gate.

DATE:_______ $:_______ ❍ WISH ❍ HAVE

'91	'92	'93	'94	'95	'96
$55	55	55	55	55	75

'ONG'S IN CHINATOWN

ITEM #	INTRO	RETIRED	OSRP	GBTRU	↑
5537-9	1990	1994	$55	**$80**	14%

Particulars: Chinese restaurant and a laundry in brick building. Canopy over entry and at roof feature pagoda shape. Fire escape for second- and third-story tenants. Chinese characters highlight signs and entry. In the first version the top window is red. In the second version the top window is gold.

DATE:_______ $:_______ ❍ WISH ❍ HAVE

'91	'92	'93	'94	'95	'96
$55	55	55	55	70	70

OLLYDALE'S DEPARTMENT STORE

ITEM #	INTRO	RETIRED	OSRP	GBTRU	
5534-4	1991	CURRENT	$75	**$85**	NO CHANGE

Particulars: First shipments are from Taiwan and have holly on the first floor canopies only. The second version is from China and has holly on all canopies. The third version is from the Philippines. Building has corner curved front with awnings on windows, domed cupola, skylights on roof, and carved balustrade design on second story windows highlight store.

DATE:_______ $:_______ ❍ WISH ❍ HAVE

'91	'92	'93	'94	'95	'96
$75	75	85	85	85	85

ITTLE ITALY" RISTORANTE

ITEM #	INTRO	RETIRED	OSRP	GBTRU	↑
5538-7	1991	1995	$50	**$85**	13%

Particulars: Three-story tall, narrow, stucco finish upper level above brick street level entry. Outdoor cafe serving pizza is on side.

DATE:_______ $:_______ ❍ WISH ❍ HAVE

'91	'92	'93	'94	'95	'96
$50	50	52	52	52	75

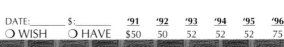

All Saints Corner Church

Item #	Intro	Retired	OSRP	GBTru	NC
5542-5	1991	Current	$96	**$110**	CHAN

Particulars: Gothic style. Carved support frame arched windows, tall steeple with corners capped by small steeple design. Large windows exhibit tracery pattern.

DATE:_______ $:_______ ❍ WISH ❍ HAVE

'91	'92	'93	'94	'95
$96	96	105	105	110

Arts Academy

Item #	Intro	Retired	OSRP	GBTru	↑
5543-3	1991	1993	$45	**$80**	7%

Particulars: Two-story brick building has classrooms and practice halls. Curved canopy over entrance repeats design of arched triple window, skylight & small towe window.

DATE:_______ $:_______ ❍ WISH ❍ HAVE

'91	'92	'93	'94	'95
$45	45	46	80	75

The Doctor's Office

Item #	Intro	Retired	OSRP	GBTru	↑
5544-1	1991	1994	$60	**$80**	7%

Particulars: Four-story brick building for Doctor, Dentist, and office space. Bow window is first level Doctor. Dentist windows have broad awning.

DATE:_______ $:_______ ❍ WISH ❍ HAVE

'91	'92	'93	'94	'95
$60	60	60	60	75

Cathedral Church Of St. Mark

Item #	Intro	Retired	OSRP	GBTru	↓
5549-2	1991	Ltd Ed 3,024*	$120	**$1850**	1%

Particulars: Commonly referred to as "St. Mark's." *Announced Edition 17,500—closed at 3,024 pieces due to production problems. Early rele to Gift Creations Concepts (GCC), Fall 1992. This building is subject to firing cracks and should be inspected closely while lighted. Front has lc of fortification with two towers rising next to entry. Moldings are richly carved above double doors. Stone and brick with accented stone work framing walls and towers. Triple windows on each upper tower side.

DATE:_______ $:_______ ❍ WISH ❍ HAVE

'91	'92	'93	'94	'95
$120	120	2900	2850	2300

'PTOWN SHOPPES

ITEM #	INTRO	RETIRED	OSRP	GBTRU	↑
5531-0	1992	1996	$150	**$175**	17%

Particulars: Set of 3 includes *Haberdashery, #55311*, *Music Emporium, #55312* and *City Clockworks, #55313.*

see below

DATE:________ $:________

❍ WISH ❍ HAVE

'92	'93	'94	'95	'96
$150	150	150	150	150

HABERDASHERY

ITEM #	INTRO	RETIRED	OSRP	GBTRU	↑
55311	1992	1996	$40	**$55**	38%

Particulars: 1 of the 3-piece set—UPTOWN SHOPPES. Squared corner of three-story building is men's clothier entry. First-story front window topped by canopy and store sign. 2nd-floor triple windows topped by ornamental molding and side windows have triangular canopies. Brick, stone, and roughcast pepple-dash facade.

DATE:________ $:________

❍ WISH ❍ HAVE

'92	'93	'94	'95	'96
$40	40	40	40	40

MUSIC EMPORIUM

ITEM #	INTRO	RETIRED	OSRP	GBTRU	↑
55312	1992	1996	$54	**$65**	20%

Particulars: 1 of the 3-piece set—UPTOWN SHOPPES. Brick store decorates side wall with a musical score. Store name is superimposed and trimmed for holidays. Other signs advertise violins, flutes, and horns. Tallest of the three shops, building has 3 floors and attic dormer. The music on the side of the building was inspired by a similar idea on the side of Schmitt Music Center in Minneapolis, MN.

DATE:________ $:________

❍ WISH ❍ HAVE

'92	'93	'94	'95	'96
$54	54	54	54	54

CITY CLOCKWORKS

ITEM #	INTRO	RETIRED	OSRP	GBTRU	↑
55313	1992	1996	$56	**$70**	25%

Particulars: 1 of the 3-piece set—UPTOWN SHOPPES. Triangular shaped building. Front angle blunted by semi-circular windows above entry to shop. Large clock hangs at right angles to store between sign and windows. Second clock next to entrance.

DATE:________ $:________

❍ WISH ❍ HAVE

'92	'93	'94	'95	'96
$56	56	56	56	56

WEST VILLAGE SHOPS

ITEM #	INTRO	RETIRED	OSRP	GBTRU	↑
5880-7	1993	1996	$90	**$120**	33

Particulars: Set of 2 includes *Potter's Tea Seller,* #58808 *Spring St. Coffee House,* #58809.

see below

DATE:_______ $:_______

❍ WISH ❍ HAVE

'93	'94	'95
$90	90	90

POTTER'S TEA SELLER

ITEM #	INTRO	RETIRED	OSRP	GBTRU	↑
58808	1993	1996	$45	**$60**	33

Particulars: 1 of the 2-piece set—WEST VILLAGE SHOPS Stone 3-story shop serves tea by the cup or pot. Stone arches decorate windows. Green awning covers uppe window above entry. Sign hangs in front of door to al shoppers.

DATE:_______ $:_______

❍ WISH ❍ HAVE

'93	'94	'95
$45	45	45

SPRING ST. COFFEE HOUSE

ITEM #	INTRO	RETIRED	OSRP	GBTRU	↑
58809	1993	1996	$45	**$65**	44

Particulars: 1 of the 2-piece set—WEST VILLAGE SHOPS Four-story narrow building. Steps lead to entry door covered by small pillared portico. Buy beans ground t order & blended for taste, or have a cup at the shop. Lower level is brick, upper stories are stucco.

DATE:_______ $:_______

❍ WISH ❍ HAVE

'93	'94	'95
$45	45	45

BROKERAGE HOUSE

ITEM #	INTRO	RETIRED	OSRP	GBTRU	NO
5881-5	1994	CURRENT	$48	**$48**	CHAN

Particulars: Stone building gives impression of invincibili Four pillars support large entry pediment which has name of Exchange carved into stone. Feeling of wealth reinforced by gold embellishments. "18" is symbolic o initial D56 stock offering at $18.00. "Price & Price" is honor of Mr. & Mrs. Price. Judith Price is Department 56's Ms. Lit Town.

DATE:_______ $:_______

❍ WISH ❍ HAVE

'94	'95
$48	48

IRST METROPOLITAN BANK

ITEM #	INTRO	RETIRED	OSRP	GBTRU	NO CHANGE
5882-3	1994	CURRENT	$60	**$60**	

Particulars: Domed, three-story building presents solid edifice. Four columns reach to third story and create covered entry and area for name inscription. Bank has gilt trim on dome, windows and door.

DATE:_______ $:_______
❍ WISH ❍ HAVE

'94	'95	'96
$60	60	60

HERITAGE MUSEUM OF ART

ITEM #	INTRO	RETIRED	OSRP	GBTRU	NO CHANGE
5883-1	1994	CURRENT	$96	**$96**	

Particulars: A stately, symmetrical structure with large windows. Names of famous artists are displayed around the top of the building and Thomas Nast's rendition of Santa Claus is on display above the entrance.

DATE:_______ $:_______
❍ WISH ❍ HAVE

'94	'95	'96
$96	96	96

VY TERRACE APARTMENTS

ITEM #	INTRO	RETIRED	OSRP	GBTRU	NO CHANGE
5887-4	1995	CURRENT	$60	**$60**	

Particulars: Midyear release. 3-story brick building with two canopy covered entries. 3rd-floor apartment has terrace with wrought iron enclosure.

DATE:_______ $:_______
❍ WISH ❍ HAVE

'95	'96
$60	60

HOLY NAME CHURCH

ITEM #	INTRO	RETIRED	OSRP	GBTRU	NO CHANGE
58875	1995	CURRENT	$96	**$96**	

Particulars: Brick church with entry and steeple with ornate pediment and molding topped by golden dome and cross. Stained glass fills rose window and lancet windows. Niche for statuary in steeple. Ribbed roof with carved design in ridge edging. Design adaptation—Cathedral of the Immaculate Conception, Kansas City, MO.

DATE:_______ $:_______
❍ WISH ❍ HAVE

'95	'96
$96	96

Brighton School

Item #	Intro	Retired	OSRP	GBTru	N
58876	1995	Current	$52	**$52**	CHA

Particulars: Brick school with small flag flying atop cloc tower. Stone foundation with steps that lead to front doors. School name above doors. Banner over windo tells children date of winter recess.

DATE:_______ $:_______
❍ WISH ❍ HAVE

'95
$52

BROWNSTONES ON THE SQUARE

Item #	Intro	Retired	OSRP	GBTru	NO
58877	1995	Current	$90	**$90**	CHA

Particulars: Set of 2 includes *Beekman House,* #58878 a *Pickford Place,* #58879.

see below

DATE:_______ $:_______
❍ WISH ❍ HAVE

'95
$90

Beekman House

Item #	Intro	Retired	OSRP	GBTru	NO
58878	1995	Current	$45	**$45**	CHA

Particulars: 1 of the 2-piece set—BROWNSTONES ON SQUARE. Four-story walk-up with entry canopy, decorated with script "B." Building name above pane first level window with lamp close by. 2nd-story arch window has wrought iron ornamentation, while other front windows are canopied. Date appears on ornate molding.

DATE:_______ $:_______
❍ WISH ❍ HAVE

'95
$45

Pickford Place

Item #	Intro	Retired	OSRP	GBTru	NO
58879	1995	Current	$45	**$45**	CHA

Particulars: 1 of the 2-piece set.—BROWNSTONES ON THE SQUARE. Four-story walk-up with entry canopy, decorated with script "P." Building name above pane first level window with lamp close by. 2nd-story arch window has potted plant while other front windows h wrought iron ornamentation. Date appears on ornate molding.

DATE:_______ $:_______
❍ WISH ❍ HAVE

'95
$45

Washington Street Post Office

Item #	Intro	Retired	OSRP	GBTru	
58880	1996	Current	$52	**$52**	No Change

Particulars: Midyear release. Three story brick with roof and edges of building finished in dressed stone. This office can receive and send letters, packages and airmail as well as sell stamps.

DATE:_______ $:_______
❍ WISH ❍ HAVE

'96
$52

Grand Central Railway Station

Item #	Intro	Retired	OSRP	GBTru
58881	1996	Current	$90	**$90**

Particulars: Two-story rendition of New York City's Grand Central Terminal. Arched colonnade entry topped by balustrade. Access to platforms from side entrances. Brick building with formal elegant trim topped by clock.

DATE:_______ $:_______
❍ WISH ❍ HAVE

Cafe Caprice French Restaurant

Item #	Intro	Retired	OSRP	GBTru	
58882	1996	Current	$45	**$45**	No Change

Particulars: Blue roof and shutters trim three-story building housing French restaurant. Onion dome tower rises at front. French/English tutor lives and works on third floor.

DATE:_______ $:_______
❍ WISH ❍ HAVE

The City Globe

Item #	Intro	Retired	OSRP	GBTru
58883	1997	Current	$65	**$65**

Particulars: Midyear release. Newspaper publishing company for the City. Globe that tops the tower actually spins.

DATE:_______ $:_______
❍ WISH ❍ HAVE

Hi-De-Ho Nightclub

Item #	Intro	Retired	OSRP	GBTru
58884	1997	Current	$52	**$52**

Particulars: Midyear release. Posters on three-story red bric nightclub highlight present and future club acts. Marque over double door entry. Club name highlights a Cab Calloway jazz riff.

DATE:_______ $:_______
❍ WISH ❍ HAVE

WHEN WAS THE LAST TIME YOU WENT TO A DOG SHOW?

When I speak at different events such as Gatherings, open houses and club meetings, one of the questions that I ask the collectors in the audience is, "How many village pieces do the majority of Department 56 consumers purchase per year?" Some collectors catch on and realize that the question is a trick one and offer answers that are very close, if not correct. They notice that the key word in the question is consumers. The collectors who do not catch on right away call out answers ranging anywhere from 10 pieces to 50 pieces.

The answer is ... Well, let's leave that alone for a minute. We can continue based on the fact that if the answer wasn't a surprisingly low number I wouldn't be writing about it. The fun I have when I ask this question comes from the conversations and comments that follow my answer. Usually there is a bit of laughter followed by more than one collector's commenting, "I guess we're not average!" You must remember, however, that the question concerns consumers of D56 villages in general, not just fanatics like us.

Consumers are a broad-based group which includes those who may purchase only one piece in their lifetime, perhaps as a night light. It includes someone who may buy a fire station as a gift for a fire fighter, for instance. It includes those who add to their village with only a piece or two a year. Keep in mind that the chances are very high that consumers such as these will probably never know of the "collectibility" of Department 56 villages.

Then there is the opposite end of the spectrum, the end at which you and I reside. This group includes all of us who have been bitten by the D56 bug. Though very visible, this group isn't as large as that of the "everyday" consumer. The number of people buying a couple of pieces a year far outweighs those who buy every piece of every village.

It is because our group is so visible that it is difficult for us to visualize how many people do not know or care that the villages are collectible. We have, in fact, been too close to the collectibility status for too long to be able to think in such terms. But, there is a way to put yourself in the shoes of non-collectors and think as they do. All you have to do is answer a few questions.

continued page 216

Little Town Of Bethlehem

The Little Town of Bethlehem is the only village to be sold as a complete set. The fifth porcelain village by Department 56, it comes complete with twelve pieces—no individual pieces have ever been added or retired.

LITTLE TOWN OF BETHLEHEM

ITEM #	INTRO	RETIRED	OSRP	GBTRU	
5975-7	1987	CURRENT	$150	**$150**	NO CHANG

Particulars: Set of 12. Replica of Holy Family Manger Scen with Three Wise Men and Shepherd. Stone and sun-drie brick homes and shelters add Mid-East simplicity. Animals attentive to Holy Family. The first version has snow on the manger. The second version does not.

see below

DATE:_______ $:_______	'91	'92	'93	'94	'95	'96
❍ WISH ❍ HAVE	$150	150	150	150	150	15(

LITTLE TOWN OF BETHLEHEM

LITTLE TOWN OF BETHLEHEM

LITTLE TOWN OF BETHLEHEM

The North Pole Village

How could have Department 56 introduced a more appropriate Christmas se-s than North Pole? The sixth porcelain series features the make believe world of nta's village complete with his workshop, toy shops, candy makers, elves, and ndeer.

North Pole was an instant hit when it debuted in 1990. Collectors of other lages added it to their collections and non-collectors became collectors. This ies, with its universal appeal, may someday be the most popular village offered Department 56.

THE BOTTOM LINE:

Cost of all pieces introduced to North Pole through the 1997 midyear introduc-ns including accessories: (This does not include variations, or special pieces.) **,527**

Greenbook TruMarket Value of all pieces through the 1997 midyear introduc-ns including accessories: (This does not include variations, special pieces.) **$2,040**

The North Pole Village Since We Last Met...

... NEW FOR SALE LISTINGS

Route 1, North Pole, Home of Mr. & Mrs. Claus - 1996

Since Santa's Workshop retired in 1993, many collectors felt that Santa and Mrs. Claus didn't have a home. That situation was remedied when this building was announced. Its colors and design are such to complement the Workshop.

Hall of Records - 1996

Your name is in this building, but is it on the list of good children or naughty children? Santa must use microfilm to keep all of the names in such an average sized building.

Christmas Bread Bakers - 1996

Breads from all over the world are baked in this bakery at the North Pole. Some of the more popular kinds are listed on the front of the building.

The Glacier Gazette - 1997

The news of events taking place at the North Pole can be read daily in the village's one and only publication.

... NO LONGER ON THE MARKET

56016	NORTH POLE–Elf Bunkhouse*
5624-3	Obbie's Books & Letrinka's Candy
5625-1	Elfie's Sleds & Skates
5628-6	Santa's Woodworks
56390	North Pole Start A Tradition Set
	• Candy Cane & Peppermint Shop
	• Gift Wrap & Ribbons

*Note: 56015, Reindeer Barn has not been retired.

TIRED BUILDINGS

00-6	1993	Santa's Workshop
016	1996	Elf Bunkhouse*
20-0	1995	NeeNee's Dolls And Toys
21-9	1995	NORTH POLE SHOPS
21-9	1995	Orly's Bell & Harness Supply
21-9	1995	Rimpy's Bakery
22-7	1995	Tassy's Mitten & Hassel's Woolies
24-3	1996	Obbie's Books & Letrinka's Candy
25-1	1996	Elfie's Sleds & Skates
28-6	1996	Santa's Woodworks
390	1996	North Pole Start A Tradition Set
390	1996	Candy Cane & Peppermint Shop
390	1996	Gift Wrap & Ribbons

lote: Only 1 of the 2 buildings in ORTH POLE, Set of 2, was retired. 015, Reindeer Barn, has not been tired.

OMES FOR THE HOLIDAYS

390 North Pole Start A Tradition Set, 1996
CANDY CANE LANE, Set of 2

- Candy Cane Lane & Peppermint Shop Building
- Gift Wrap & Ribbons Building
- Candy Cane Elves Accessory

Santa's Workshop

Item #	Intro	Retired	OSRP	GBTru	
5600-6	1990	1993	$72	**$420**	13

Particulars: Multi-chimnied, many gabled home and workshop. Stone foundation with stucco and timber upper stories. Balconies extend off windows and holc garlands. Mailbox by front door.

DATE:_______ $:_______ ❍ WISH ❍ HAVE

'91	'92	'93	'94	'95
$72	75	75	150	375

NORTH POLE

Item #	Intro	Retired	OSRP	GBTru
5601-4	1990	*	$70	*

Particulars: Set of 2 includes *Reindeer Barn,* #56015 anc *Elf Bunkhouse,* #56016. *Set is split between Current Retired—the *Elf Bunkhouse* was retired from this set i 1996.

see below

DATE:_______ $:_______ ❍ WISH ❍ HAVE

'91	'92	'93	'94	'95
$70	75	80	80	80

Reindeer Barn

Item #	Intro	Retired	OSRP	GBTru	
56015	1990	Current	$35	**$40**	NC CHAN

Particulars: 1 of the 2-piece set—NORTH POLE. Stone a stucco has stalls for all reindeer. Steeply pitched roof cupola on ridge and step design on front of dormers. Roof vents and Dutch stall doors provide ventilation. common variation is a name duplicated, another omi on reindeer stalls.

DATE:_______ $:_______ ❍ WISH ❍ HAVE

'91	'92	'93	'94	'95
$35	37.50	40	40	40

Elf Bunkhouse

Item #	Intro	Retired	OSRP	GBTru	
56016	1990	1996	$35	**$60**	↑ 50

Particulars: 1 of the 2-piece set—NORTH POLE. Home f Santa's helpers, 3 stories with steeply pitched roof anc protected chimney. Made of wood, stone, and stucco featuring bay windows, dormers, and a balcony. The and inscription on the bottom of the building both rea "Elf Bunkhouse," while the sign on the front of the building reads "Elves Bunkhouse."

DATE:_______ $:_______ ❍ WISH ❍ HAVE

'91	'92	'93	'94	'95
$35	37.50	40	40	40

NeeNee's Dolls And Toys

Item #	Intro	Retired	OSRP	GBTru	↑
5620-0	1991	1995	$36	**$60**	9%

Particulars: Rough finish stucco and stone house. Steeply pitched rear roof, red shuttered lattice-paned front second-story windows. Early release to Showcase Dealers and Gift Creations Concepts (GCC). Ⓝ monogram within wreath begins spelling out of N-O-R-T-H P-O-L-E.

DATE:________ $:________ ❍ WISH ❍ HAVE

'91	'92	'93	'94	'95	'96
$36	37.50	37.50	37.50	37.50	55

North Pole Shops

see below

Item #	Intro	Retired	OSRP	GBTru	↑
5621-9	1991	1995	$75	**$130**	24%

Particulars: Set of 2 includes *Orly's Bell & Harness Supply* and *Rimpy's Bakery.*

DATE:________ $:________ ❍ WISH ❍ HAVE

'91	'92	'93	'94	'95	'96
$75	75	75	75	75	105

Orly's Bell & Harness Supply

Item #	Intro	Retired	OSRP	GBTru	↑
5621-9	1991	1995	$37.50	**$65**	18%

Particulars: 1 of the 2-piece set—NORTH POLE SHOPS. Stone steps lead to bell shop doorway with brick work design to frame it. Sleigh strap with bells above sign. Harness area has large wood doors that open to allow horse drawn carriage or wagon to enter. Window with balcony above, on 2nd story. Monogram within wreath. Ⓞ

DATE:________ $:________ ❍ WISH ❍ HAVE

'91	'92	'93	'94	'95	'96
$37.50	37.50	37.50	37.50	37.50	55

Rimpy's Bakery

Item #	Intro	Retired	OSRP	GBTru	↑
5621-9	1991	1995	$37.50	**$70**	27%

Particulars: 1 of the 2-piece set—NORTH POLE SHOPS. Three storied, half wood timbered narrow building. Hipped-roof with gable on facade. Large eight paned front window with wood crib in front and on side. Monogram within wreath. Ⓡ

DATE:________ $:________ ❍ WISH ❍ HAVE

'91	'92	'93	'94	'95	'96
$37.50	37.50	37.50	37.50	37.50	55

Tassy's Mitten & Hassel's Woolies

Item #	Intro	Retired	OSRP	GBTru	↑
5622-7	1991	1995	$50	**$80**	7%

Particulars: Two shops in connected buildings. Hassel's ha corner turret window and oriel turret upper window. Tassy's has angled front window at ground and three arched windows on overhang second story. Gable has carved bough and berry design—roof angles steeply pitched. Monograms within wreaths. (T) & (H)

DATE:_______ $:_______ ❍ WISH ❍ HAVE

'91	'92	'93	'94	'95	'96
$50	50	50	50	50	75

Post Office

Item #	Intro	Retired	OSRP	GBTru	No
5623-5	1992	Current	$45	**$50**	Chanc

Particulars: Basis for building is turret with what appears to be a half-house on one side of main tower. Second floo features multi-paned windows, small curved turret between second and third floor could hold staircase and take up little wall space. Third floor has low balcony outside windows. Monogram within wreath. Early relea to Showcase Dealers. (P)

DATE:_______ $:_______ ❍ WISH ❍ HAVE

'92	'93	'94	'95	'96
$45	50	50	50	50

Obbie's Books & Letrinka's Candy

Item #	Intro	Retired	OSRP	GBTru	↑
5624-3	1992	1996	$70	**$90**	29%

Particulars: The tall narrow book and toy shop contrasts sharply with the shorter, wider, candy shop. Both shops have steep pitched roofs. A bay window on Obbie's side wall plus a numbe of dormer windows reinforce the angular look of the shop. Onio dome shaped chimney and cupola on roof ridge are unique to Letrinka's which also has a vertical timbered ground level design Both shops have lettered wreaths by front entries. (O) & (L)

DATE:_______ $:_______ ❍ WISH ❍ HAVE

'92	'93	'94	'95	'96
$70	70	70	70	70

Elfie's Sleds & Skates

Item #	Intro	Retired	OSRP	GBTru	↑
5625-1	1992	1996	$48	**$60**	25%

Particulars: Distinctive roof design with chimneys that are only visible outside from the second story. Roof hood projects out from walls to protect windows on house sides as well as sweeping down to help form large front window. Wreath with letter "E" in addition to to shop signs. (E)

DATE:_______ $:_______ ❍ WISH ❍ HAVE

'92	'93	'94	'95	'96
$48	48	48	48	48

North Pole Chapel

Item #	Intro	Retired	OSRP	GBTru	No Change
5626-0	1993	Current	$45	**$45**	

Particulars: Spire, containing brass bell, rises at rear of Chapel. Fieldstone topped by timbered upper story. Double door front entry flanked by evergreens. Side chimney rises through roof with flue pipe capped by onion cap. Large wreath encircled clock above entry. Early release to Showcase Dealers and select buying groups.

DATE:_______ $:_______
❍ WISH ❍ HAVE

'93	'94	'95	'96
$45	45	45	45

North Pole Express Depot

Item #	Intro	Retired	OSRP	GBTru	No Change
5627-8	1993	Current	$48	**$48**	

Particulars: Receiving area for people and deliveries in and out of North Pole not going by Santa's sled. Roof line at lowest point is pagoda-like with an A-frame gable transversing a ridge. Stone chimney rises at rear of roof. Separate doors for passengers and freight.

DATE:_______ $:_______
❍ WISH ❍ HAVE

'93	'94	'95	'96
$48	48	48	48

Santa's Woodworks

Item #	Intro	Retired	OSRP	GBTru	↑
5628-6	1993	1996	$42	**$60**	33%

Particulars: Lower level contains heavy equipment for sawing, debarking and trimming wood. Main level reached by wood stairs at side of open porch. Structure is a log house.

DATE:_______ $:_______
❍ WISH ❍ HAVE

'93	'94	'95	'96
$42	42	45	45

Santa's Lookout Tower

Item #	Intro	Retired	OSRP	GBTru	No Change
5629-4	1993	Current	$45	**$48**	

Particulars: Pennants fly above door and top of tower which rises above trees to give Santa a clear picture of flight conditions. Balcony around highest story lets Santa check wind velocity.

DATE:_______ $:_______
❍ WISH ❍ HAVE

'93	'94	'95	'96
$45	45	48	48

Elfin Snow Cone Works

Item #	Intro	Retired	OSRP	GBTru	NO
5633-2	1994	Current	$40	**$40**	CHAN

Particulars: Snow cones on shutters and sign of steep roof shop. Roof molding trim resembles icing. Oriole windo extends from 3rd floor to rooftop.

DATE:_______ $:_______
❍ WISH ❍ HAVE

'94	'95	'9
$40	40	4

Beard Barber Shop

Item #	Intro	Retired	OSRP	GBTru	NO
5634-0	1994	Current	$27.50	**$27.50**	CHAN

Particulars: Small shop with 3 tall front windows allowing light to enter. Barber pole at entry and banner of shears establish function of shop.

DATE:_______ $:_______
❍ WISH ❍ HAVE

'94	'95	'9
$27.50	27.50	27.

North Pole Dolls & Santa's Bear Works

Item #	Intro	Retired	OSRP	GBTru	NO
5635-9	1994	Current	$96	**$96**	CHAN

Particulars: Set of 3 consists of *North Pole Dolls, Santa's Bear Works* and *Entrance.* Entrance is non-lit. Two 3-story mirror image buildings with 2-story center connec ing entrance way. Shops have signs by doors. A "NP" pennant flies from the cupola in the center.

DATE:_______ $:_______
❍ WISH ❍ HAVE

'94	'95	'9
$96	96	9

Tin Soldier Shop

Item #	Intro	Retired	OSRP	GBTru	NO
5638-3	1995	Current	$42	**$42**	CHAN

Particulars: Midyear release. Tall, narrow shop with garlar draped balcony. Toy soldiers decorate base of 2-story turret at side of entry.

DATE:_______ $:_______
❍ WISH ❍ HAVE

'95	'9
$42	4

Elfin Forge & Assembly Shop

Item #	Intro	Retired	OSRP	GBTru	NO
56384	1995	Current	$65	**$65**	CHANGE

Particulars: North Pole folks make all the necessary iron works at the forge. Steps lead up to entry that connects two building wings. The forge furnaces are housed in the 3-story building with the tall furnace pipes. Design and assembly takes place in attached turret, with finished product exiting through large double doors.

DATE:_______ $:_______
❍ WISH ❍ HAVE

'95	'96
$65	65

Weather & Time Observatory

Item #	Intro	Retired	OSRP	GBTru	NO
56385	1995	Current	$50	**$50**	CHANGE

Particulars: Santa has to know all time zones and prevailing climate to plan his big sleigh trip as well as conditions for visiting folk, elves and animals. Telescope located in rooftop observatory, clocks are set for all time zones. Satellite dish brings in news on weather. Fortress-like turret for astronomy and smaller attached areas for offices.

DATE:_______ $:_______
❍ WISH ❍ HAVE

'95	'96
$50	50

ita's Rooming House

Item #	Intro	Retired	OSRP	GBTru	NO
56386	1995	Current	$50	**$50**	CHANGE

Particulars: Visitors to the North Pole stay at this red clapboard inn. Stairs lead up to entry door for bedrooms. Lower level houses kitchen, dining and sitting rooms, as well as the cloak room.

DATE:_______ $:_______
❍ WISH ❍ HAVE

'95	'96
$50	50

lves' Trade School

Item #	Intro	Retired	OSRP	GBTru	NO
56387	1995	Current	$50	**$50**	CHANGE

Particulars: All Toy Workshop, Forge & Assembly, Astronomy and Charting skills are taught at the school for elves. Stone pillars form part of sturdy base to support wood structure. Hammer holds school sign above red door.

DATE:_______ $:_______
❍ WISH ❍ HAVE

'95	'96
$50	50

Popcorn & Cranberry House

Item #	Intro	Retired	OSRP	GBTru	N
56388	1996	Current	$45	$45	CHA

Particulars: Midyear release. Tall chimney separates fro part of house from rear work area. Elves work on the berries and corn preparing them for stringing into garlands and creation of holiday trim. Berries trim fro sign accented by red roof, door and windows.

DATE:_______ $:_______
❍ WISH ❍ HAVE

Santa's Bell Repair

Item #	Intro	Retired	OSRP	GBTru	N
56389	1996	Current	$45	$45	CHA

Particulars: Midyear release. Bells that no longer ring, chime or jingle are sent to the repair shop to be fixed shined. Brass bells over entry, tall fieldstone chimney and combination bell tower dormer set this design ap

DATE:_______ $:_______
❍ WISH ❍ HAVE

North Pole Start A Tradition Set

Item #	Intro	Retired	OSRP	GBTru	1
56390	1996	1996	$85	$105	24

Particulars: Set of 12 includes CANDY CANE LANE, Set of 2—*Ca Cane & Peppermint Shop* and *Gift Wrap & Ribbons*. Accessories: of 2—*Candy Cane Elves*, 6 Trees and a Bag of Snow. Starter Set w midyear release featured at D56 National Homes For The Holiday Open House Event, November 7–11, 1996. Special packaging fo promotion. Starter Set was priced at $65.00 during the Event. GBT for buildings separately is $55.00 each.

DATE:_______ $:_______
❍ WISH ❍ HAVE

Route 1, North Pole, Home of Mr. & Mrs. Claus

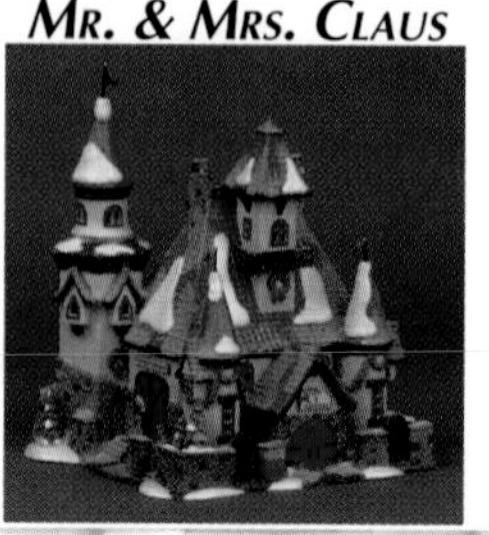

Item #	Intro	Retired	OSRP	GBTru
56391	1996	Current	$110	$110

Particulars: Steep red rooftop, double turrets flank entry door. Rear turret flies a North Pole banner. Mailbox o front stone wall. The first shipments came with the gr gates separate in the box. A short time later, the piece arrived with the gates already inserted into the fence.

DATE:_______ $:_______
❍ WISH ❍ HAVE

Hall of Records

Item #	Intro	Retired	OSRP	GBTru
56392	1996	Current	$50	**$50**

Particulars: Central fortress-like tower with clock provides record-keeping on naughty and nice files for Santa and elves. Side wings of building have bright red rooftops with green struts and saw-toothed trim. Staff out for hot chocolate break.

DATE:________ $:________
❍ WISH ❍ HAVE

Christmas Bread Bakers

Item #	Intro	Retired	OSRP	GBTru
56393	1996	Current	$55	**$55**

Particulars: Bright blue curved roof with wheat grain symbols on red trim. Domed awnings cover front windows and door. Special treats listed on facade above bay window.

DATE:________ $:________
❍ WISH ❍ HAVE

The Glacier Gazette

Item #	Intro	Retired	OSRP	GBTru
56394	1997	Current	$48	**$48**

Particulars: Midyear release. North Pole newspaper and telegraph office.

DATE:________ $:________
❍ WISH ❍ HAVE

Notes: ____

DISNEY PARKS VILLAGE

To non-Department 56 collectors, the most significant aspect of the company' seventh porcelain village is its association with the Disney theme parks. To Depar ment 56 collectors, the most significant aspect is the fact that Disney Parks Villa is the only village to be retired in its entirety.

Introduced in 1994, it was retired in 1996 after only six buildings and fo accessories were produced. This is the village for collectors who want to have entire village on display all year long.

THE BOTTOM LINE:

Cost of all pieces introduced to Disney Parks Village through the 1995 intr ductions including accessories: (This does not include variations, or special piece **$389**

Greenbook TruMarket Value of all pieces through the 1995 introductions i cluding accessories: (This does not include variations, special pieces.) **$765**

RETIRED BUILDINGS

5350-3	1996	Mickey's Christmas Carol
5351-1	1996	OLDE WORLD ANTIQUES SHOPS
5351-1	1996	Olde World Antiques I
5351-1	1996	Olde World Antiques II
5352-0	1996	Disneyland Fire Department #105
53521	1996	Silversmith
53522	1996	Tinker Bell's Treasures

Quikreference

MICKEY'S CHRISTMAS CAROL—"10 POINTS"

ITEM #	INTRO	RETIRED	OSRP	GBTRU	
5350-3	1994	1996	$144	**$144**	NO CHANGE

Particulars: Set of 2. This is the first version with small gold spires at the lower corners of the roof dormers as well as at their peaks. Replica of the building in Fantasyland at Disney World in Orlando, Florida. Gold trim and blue roof along with multiple turrets and gables make this a very distinctive building. Item #742-0, sold by the Disney Theme Parks has the "Holiday Collection" bottomstamp and a GBTru of $250.

DATE:________ $:________
❍ WISH ❍ HAVE

'94	'95	'96
$144	144	144

MICKEY'S CHRISTMAS CAROL—"6 POINTS"

ITEM #	INTRO	RETIRED	OSRP	GBTRU	
5350-3	1994	1996	$144	**$144**	NO CHANGE

Particulars: Set of 2. This is the second version—small gold spires are no longer at the lower corners of the roof dormers.

DATE:________ $:________
❍ WISH ❍ HAVE

'94	'95	'96
$144	144	144

OLDE WORLD ANTIQUES SHOPS

ITEM #	INTRO	RETIRED	OSRP	GBTRU	
5351-1	1994	1996	$90	**$90**	NO CHANGE

Particulars: Set of 2 includes *Olde World Antiques I* and *Olde World Antiques II*. Item #743-9, sold by the Disney Theme Parks has the "Holiday Collection" bottomstamp and a GBTru of $150.

see below

DATE:________ $:________
❍ WISH ❍ HAVE

'94	'95	'96
$90	90	90

OLDE WORLD ANTIQUES I

ITEM #	INTRO	RETIRED	OSRP	GBTRU	
5351-1	1994	1996	$45	**$45**	NO CHANGE

Particulars: 1 of the 2-piece set—OLDE WORLD ANTIQUES SHOPS. Similar building can be seen in Disney World's Liberty Square. Windows vary from arched to rectangular. Item #743-9, sold by the Disney Theme Parks has the "Holiday Collection" bottomstamp and a GBTru of $75.

DATE:________ $:________
❍ WISH ❍ HAVE

'94	'95	'96
$45	45	45

OLDE WORLD ANTIQUES II

ITEM #	INTRO	RETIRED	OSRP	GBTRU	NO CHANGE
5351-1	1994	1996	$45	**$45**	

Particulars: 1 of the 2-piece set—OLDE WORLD ANTIQUES SHOPS. Replica of the building in Liberty Square in Orlando's Disney World. Long staircase in front leads to second floor. Item #743-9, sold by the Disney Theme Parks has the "Holiday Collection" bottomstamp and a GBTru of $75.

DATE:________ $:________
❍ WISH ❍ HAVE

'94	'95	'96
$45	45	45

DISNEYLAND FIRE DEPARTMENT #105

ITEM #	INTRO	RETIRED	OSRP	GBTRU	NO CHANGE
5352-0	1994	1996	$45	**$45**	

Particulars: Inspired by the fire station on Main Street in Disneyland. Brick station's large front doors allow fire equipment in and out. Item #744-7, sold by the Disney Theme Parks has the "Holiday Collection" bottomstamp and a GBTru of $75.

DATE:________ $:________
❍ WISH ❍ HAVE

'94	'95	'96
$45	45	45

SILVERSMITH

ITEM #	INTRO	RETIRED	OSRP	GBTRU	↑
53521	1995	1996	$50	**$225**	350%

Particulars: Five-sided building of fieldstone. Many windows on all sides. Dormers in each roof section. Hanging sign above double entry doors. Potted trees flank door. Item #7448, sold by the Disney Theme Parks has the "Holiday Collection" bottomstamp and a GBTru of $245.

DATE:________ $:________
❍ WISH ❍ HAVE

'95	'96
$50	50

TINKER BELL'S TREASURES

ITEM #	INTRO	RETIRED	OSRP	GBTRU	↑
53522	1995	1996	$60	**$225**	375%

Particulars: Timbered and stucco building with twin chimneys. Porcelain trees in raised stone garden beds flank front and sides. Roof line slopes down to trees to frame front entry. Item #7449, sold by the Disney Theme Parks has the "Holiday Collection" bottomstamp and a GBTru of $245.

DATE:________ $:________
❍ WISH ❍ HAVE

'95	'96
$60	60

WHEN WAS THE LAST TIME... continued from page 198

Do you own a cat or a dog? If so, when was the last time that you entered the pet in a show? Would you ever even dream of owning a show animal? For most of you, this would not be something in which you would have an interest. The average pet owners are just that ... pet owners. They are not part of that relatively small group of owners of show animals. Just as you have a cat, dog or other pet and are quite happy to leave it at that, many consumers feel the same way about their villages. The buildings are simply something they enjoy, and they would not entertain the idea of making it something more.

I am a prime example. I love basset hounds, (That's right, the low, long dog with soulful eyes, and ears that hang to the ground) probably more than I love D56 villages. My dream is to have a number of them. It is not my desire, though, nor will it ever be, to show them. I just want to enjoy them.

So the next time you are trying to determine how small the group is that you belong to, the group of incredibly enthusiastic collectors, think of all the animal owners whom you have met and how few of them show their animals.

Oh, yes, the answer! Before that, though, let me tell you that the answer comes from a portion of the Letter from the Chairman in Department 56's 1994 Annual Report. If you find it hard to believe, even after reading this article, it came right from the source, so to speak. Without any further ado, just ... two or three. Can you believe it? I guess we're not average!

the Village Chronicle.

NOTES:

TIRED ACCESSORIES

53-8	1996	Mickey & Minnie
53-9	1996	Balloon Seller
54-6	1996	Disney Parks Family
55-4	1996	Olde World Antiques Gate
16-6	1992	Boulevard
17-4	1990	Mailbox & Fire Hydrant
32-8	1995	Don't Drop The Presents!
33-6	1995	Welcome Home
35-2	1992	Busy Sidewalks
39-5	1994	'Tis The Season
45-0	1993	All Around The Town
46-8	1995	The Fire Brigade
47-6	1995	"City Fire Dept." Fire Truck
51-4	1992	David Copperfield Characters
54-9	1993	Oliver Twist Characters
56-5	1996	Playing In The Snow
59-0	1995	Poultry Market
60-3	1994	Come Into The Inn
70-0	1993	Carolers On The Doorstep
72-7	1994	Village Sign With Snowman
78-6	1992	Royal Coach
79-4	1991	Constables
80-8	1992	Violet Vendor/Carolers/ Chestnut Vendor
02-2	1995	Toymaker Elves
03-0	1995	Baker Elves
04-9	1994	Letters For Santa
08-1	1993	Trimming The North Pole
10-3	1993	Santa's Little Helpers
19-7	1995	Buying Baker's Bread
30-8	1995	Woodsmen Elves
41-3	1993	Market Day
45-6	1995	Harvest Seed Cart
46-4	1995	Town Tinker
49-9	1996	Knife Grinder
02-5	1995	The Old Puppeteer
03-3	1995	The Bird Seller
04-1	1994	Village Street Peddlers
17-3	1996	Vision Of A Christmas Past
18-1	1996	C. Bradford, Wheel-wright & Son
5832-7	1996	Town Square Carolers
5865-3	1996	Village Express Van
5901-3	1989	Farm People & Animals
5903-0	1991	Childe Pond And Skaters
5928-5	1990	Fezziwig And Friends
5929-3	1991	Nicholas Nickleby Characters
5934-0	1990	Blacksmith
5938-2	1994	Snow Children
5941-2	1991	Village Harvest People
5945-5	1991	Farm Animals
5948-0	1992	Amish Family
5949-8	1992	Amish Buggy
5950-1	1989	Silo & Hay Shed
5951-0	1989	Ox Sled
5956-0	1992	Sleepy Hollow Characters
5957-9	1991	Organ Grinder
5958-7	1992	Popcorn Vendor
5959-5	1991	River Street Ice House Cart
5960-9	1993	Christmas In The City Sign
5964-1	1996	Automobiles
5965-0	1990	City People
5966-8	1988	Shopkeepers
5967-6	1988	City Workers
5971-4	1991	City Newsstand
5980-3	1996	Village Express Train
5981-1	1990	Village Train Trestle
5982-0	1993	One Horse Open Sleigh
5983-8	1991	City Bus & Milk Truck
5985-4	1991	Salvation Army Band
5986-2	1990	Woodcutter And Son
5987-0	1994	Red Covered Bridge
5997-8	1988	Village Express Train–Black
6501-3	1990	Christmas Carol Figures
6510-2	1989	Lighted Tree W/Children And Ladder
6511-0	1990	Sleighride
6526-9	1990	Carolers
6527-7	1986	Village Train
6531-5	1990	Covered Wooden Bridge
6532-3	1990	New England Winter Set
6537-4	1992	Porcelain Trees
6542-0	1992	Alpine Villagers
6545-5	1990	Skating Pond

6546-3	1990	Stone Bridge
6547-1	1989	Village Well & Holy Cross
6569-2	1993	Dickens' Village Sign
6570-6	1993	New England Village Sign
6571-4	1993	Alpine Village Sign
6589-7	1989	Maple Sugaring Shed
6590-0	1990	Dover Coach
9953-8	1990	HV Promotional Sign

LIMITED EDITION

58404	"A Christmas Carol Reading" by Charles Dickens	42,500

CLASSIC ORNAMENT SERIES

98733	Dickens' "Village Mill" Ornament	1997
98734	North Pole "Santa's Workshop" Ornament	1997

HOMES FOR THE HOLIDAYS EVENT PIECES

98711	Christmas Bells	1996
56100	The Holly & The Ivy	1997

CAROLERS— "WHITE POST"

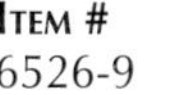

ITEM #	INTRO	RETIRED	OSRP	GBTRU	⬇
6526-9	1984	1990	$10	**$110**	8%

Particulars: Set of 3. Dickens' Village accessory. 3 versions of set exist. Version 1—White Post, Viola is very light with dark brown trim, little detail in figures, made in Taiwan. This version is the more difficult version to find. Group of village people sing or listen to carols.

DATE:_______	$:_______	'91	'92	'93	'94	'95	'96
❍ WISH	❍ HAVE	$135	120	152	120	120	120

CAROLERS— "BLACK POST"

ITEM #	INTRO	RETIRED	OSRP	GBTRU	⬇
6526-9	1984	1990	$10	**$37**	8%

Particulars: Version 2—Black post, viola is one color, more detail in figures, made in Taiwan. Version 3—Black post, viola has dark trim, largest set, made in Philippines.

DATE:_______	$:_______	'91	'92	'93	'94	'95	'96
❍ WISH	❍ HAVE	$25	28	45	36	38	40

VILLAGE TRAIN

ITEM #	INTRO	RETIRED	OSRP	GBTRU	⬆
6527-7	1985	1986	$12	**$410**	4%

Particulars: Set of 3. Dickens' Village accessory. Known as the "Brighton Train" because of the name on the side of the middle car. Three-car porcelain train, with engine, passenger car and caboose mail/freight car.

DATE:_______	$:_______	'91	'92	'93	'94	'95	'96
❍ WISH	❍ HAVE	$450	475	455	455	475	395

HRISTMAS CAROL FIGURES

ITEM #	INTRO	RETIRED	OSRP	GBTRU	
6501-3	1986	1990	$12.50	**$85**	NO CHANGE

Particulars: Set of 3. Dickens' Village accessory. Ebenezer Scrooge, Bob Cratchit carrying Tiny Tim and young boy with poulterer/goose.

DATE:_______	$:_______	'91	'92	'93	'94	'95	'96
❍ WISH	❍ HAVE	$20	28	42	65	80	85

Lighted Tree W/ Children & Ladder

Item #	Intro	Retired	OSRP	GBTru	⬇
6510-2	1986	1989	$35	**$305**	5%

Particulars: Set of 3. Lighted. Christmas In The City accessory. Children climb ladder to decorate tree. The tree is battery operated. Many have been sold on the secondary market as defective, but it's usually just a matter of crossed wires. Once they are switched, the unit works nicely. Check the boy on the ladder carefully as he often falls off the ladder and gets damaged. The sleeve of the first shipments read "Christmas In The City" though that village didn't make its debut for another year.

DATE:_______	$:_______	'91	'92	'93	'94	'95	'9
❍ WISH	❍ HAVE	$225	285	290	350	350	32

Sleighride

Item #	Intro	Retired	OSRP	GBTru	
6511-0	1986	1990	$19.50	**$50**	NO CHANG

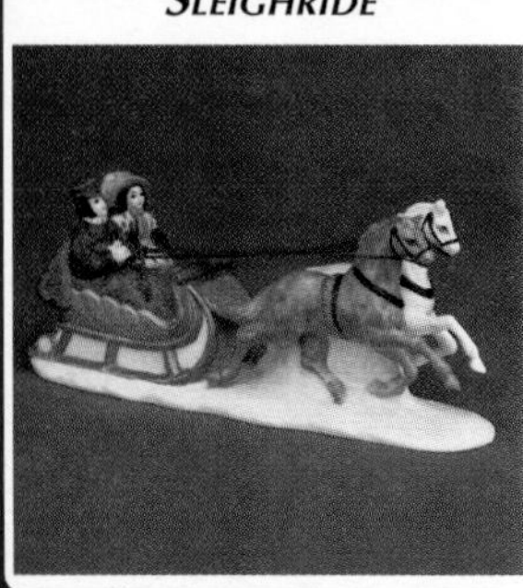

Particulars: Dickens' and New England Village accessory. Couple enjoys ride in old fashioned sleigh drawn by two horses. Inspired by a Nathaniel Currier print. The Sleighride has 2 versions. Version 1—Original sleeve reads, "Dickens Sleighride"—man has narrow white scarf with red polka dot Version 2—Man's scarf and lapels are white with red polka dots. Gray horse is more spotted.

DATE:_______	$:_______	'91	'92	'93	'94	'95	'9
❍ WISH	❍ HAVE	$35	38	50	58	50	5

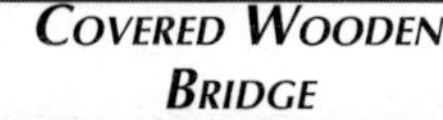

Covered Wooden Bridge

Item #	Intro	Retired	OSRP	GBTru	⬆
6531-5	1986	1990	$10	**$40**	5%

Particulars: New England Village accessory. Simple wood bridge with shingle roof, protects travelers from weathe while crossing river. Variations in color from light to dark. Variations do not affect secondary market value.

DATE:_______	$:_______	'91	'92	'93	'94	'95	'
❍ WISH	❍ HAVE	$25	28	32	32	35	3

New England Winter Set

Item #	Intro	Retired	OSRP	GBTru	⬆
6532-3	1986	1990	$18	**$50**	6%

Particulars: Set of 5. Stone well, man pushes sleigh as woman rides, snow covered trees, man pulls cut tree.

DATE:_______	$:_______	'91	'92	'93	'94	'95	'
❍ WISH	❍ HAVE	$35	35	50	46	45	

TRIMMING THE TREE

One of the most popular Heritage Village accessories to be introduced throughout the years is *Lighted Tree With Children And Ladder* (6510-2). The popularity of this piece should be no surprise. Think of all the towns, villages and cities that have a tree in a square or town green. With so many of us having grown up with this tradition, it is a natural for us to want a grand, lighted tree in our villages.

Issued in 1986, the tree originally sold for $35. For years now, it has been considered a Christmas In The City accessory, though many use it in Dickens', New England, Alpine and even North Pole. For those of you who cannot picture it anywhere but in the City, realize one thing. Christmas In The City was not issued until 1987, one year after the tree itself. Therefore, it must have been produced for Dickens', New England or Alpine, right? Come on, now. That would be too simple.

Though the tree was issued before the City, the original box signified that it was a City piece. Right across the lower portion of the front panel of the box it states in large letters, "Christmas In The City" with "Lighted Tree Accessory" in smaller print. Imagine how confusing this must have been to a collector back then.

When the trees began to show up on dealers' shelves, there were a few problems. One arose when it came time for dealers to sell their last piece off the shelf; the child on the ladder and the ladder itself often were missing. More often, however, the lights just did not work. Because of this, many were sold at a discount or returned to the company.

When news got out that the problem was usually only a matter of reversed wires, some collectors took advantage of the discounted "defective" pieces. They bought one, brought it home and re-soldered the wires. This still happens on the secondary market today. Sellers will reduce their selling price significantly because the piece does not light. I have spoken to collectors who have paid $100 or less for one. A few minutes' work and they have a wonderful accessory worth $300 or more.

The problem with the lights is not the only thing to be aware of if you are looking for one on the secondary. Because the boy climbing the ladder rests precariously upon it, many have been knocked off and broken. Make sure that it is included and that it is in fine condition. You'll be surprised how many have this problem.

If you would rather not pay secondary prices for a tree, you still have the opportunity to purchase the Town Tree (5565-4). Either is a great tree to have in your display; one just has a little bit of history that goes with it. But then again, if you have more than one village, wouldn't it be great to have a tree in each?

the **Village Chronicle.**

Porcelain Trees

Item #	Intro	Retired	OSRP	GBTru	NO
6537-4	1986	1992	$14	**$35**	CHANGE

Particulars: Set of 2. Two different size snow covered evergreens.

DATE:________	$:________	'91	'92	'93	'94	'95	'96
❍ WISH	❍ HAVE	$16	17	25	36	35	35

Alpine Villagers

Item #	Intro	Retired	OSRP	GBTru	NO
6542-0	1986	1992	$13	**$38**	CHANGE

Particulars: Set of 3. Seated man, walking woman carrying book, dog pulling wagon with milk cans. Figurines got thinner in later years of production. This does not affect secondary market value.

DATE:________	$:________	'91	'92	'93	'94	'95	'96
❍ WISH	❍ HAVE	$15	15	36	36	35	38

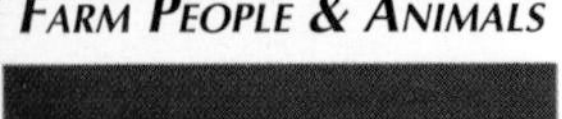

Farm People & Animals

Item #	Intro	Retired	OSRP	GBTru	↑
5901-3	1987	1989	$24	**$100**	6%

Particulars: Set of 5. Dickens' Village accessory. Man hauling logs. Woman and girl feeding geese. Goat pulls wagon and deer eat winter hay.

DATE:________	$:________	'91	'92	'93	'94	'95	'96
❍ WISH	❍ HAVE	$55	60	72	80	90	94

Blacksmith

Item #	Intro	Retired	OSRP	GBTru	↑
5934-0	1987	1990	$20	**$80**	7%

Particulars: Set of 3. Dickens' Village accessory. One man tends fire while smithy shoes horse. Boy holds pail of nails.

DATE:________	$:________	'91	'92	'93	'94	'95	'96
❍ WISH	❍ HAVE	$35	42	46	55	70	75

Silo & Hay Shed

Item #	Intro	Retired	OSRP	GBTru	↑
5950-1	1987	1989	$18	**$175**	9%

Particulars: Set of 2. Dickens' Village accessories. Stone and stucco grain storage silo and elevated wood hay building. There are two color variations: First Version—silo roof has stripes of rust, gold and brown, Second Version—silo roof is almost solid brown. This does not affect secondary market price.

DATE:_______ $:_______ ❍ WISH ❍ HAVE

'91	'92	'93	'94	'95	'96
$70	85	125	140	160	160

Ox Sled—"Tan Pants"

Item #	Intro	Retired	OSRP	GBTru	No Change
5951-0	1987	1989	$20	**$250**	

Particulars: Dickens' Village accessory. Ox team pulls wood wagon on sled runners. Driver and a small boy holding a Christmas tree. Variations in color affect GBTru$: "Tan Pants" or "Blue Pants." In this "Tan Pants" Version, the driver wears tan pants and sits on a green seat cushion. The mound of snow under the oxen is attached to the hind legs.

DATE:_______ $:_______ ❍ WISH ❍ HAVE

'91	'92	'93	'94	'95	'96
$65	85	112	225	250	250

Ox Sled—"Blue Pants"

Item #	Intro	Retired	OSRP	GBTru	↑
5951-0	1987	1989	$20	**$160**	14%

Particulars: In this version the driver has blue pants and sits on a black seat cushion. The mound of snow under the oxen is attached to the hind legs.

DATE:_______ $:_______ ❍ WISH ❍ HAVE

'91	'92	'93	'94	'95	'96
$65	85	112	135	145	140

Ox Sled—"Blue Pants/ Mold Change"

Item #	Intro	Retired	OSRP	GBTru	↑
5951-0	1987	1989	$20	**$160**	14%

Particulars: In this version the driver has blue pants and sits on a black seat cushion. The mound of snow under the oxen is not attached to the hind legs.

DATE:_______ $:_______ ❍ WISH ❍ HAVE

'91	'92	'93	'94	'95	'96
$65	85	112	135	145	140

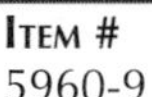

Christmas In The City Sign

Item #	Intro	Retired	OSRP	GBTru	↑
5960-9	1987	1993	$6	**$18**	20%

Particulars: Christmas In The City Collection sign.

DATE:_______ $:_______ ❍ WISH ❍ HAVE

'91	'92	'93	'94	'95	'96
$6.50	6.50	8.50	12	15	15

Automobiles

Item #	Intro	Retired	OSRP	GBTru	↑
5964-1	1987	1996	$15	**$27**	23%

Particulars: Set of 3. Christmas In The City accessory. City delivery truck, checkered taxi, and roadster. Size: 3".

DATE:_______ $:_______ ❍ WISH ❍ HAVE

'91	'92	'93	'94	'95	'96
$20	20	22	22	22	22

City People

Item #	Intro	Retired	OSRP	GBTru	
5965-0	1987	1990	$27.50	**$55**	NO CHANGE

Particulars: Set of 5. Christmas In The City accessory. Police officer, man walking dog, pretzel man with pushcart, mother and daughter with shopping bag, and woman collecting for the needy.

DATE:_______ $:_______ ❍ WISH ❍ HAVE

'91	'92	'93	'94	'95	'96
$45	50	50	50	50	55

Shopkeepers

Item #	Intro	Retired	OSRP	GBTru	↑
5966-8	1987	1988	$15	**$40**	5%

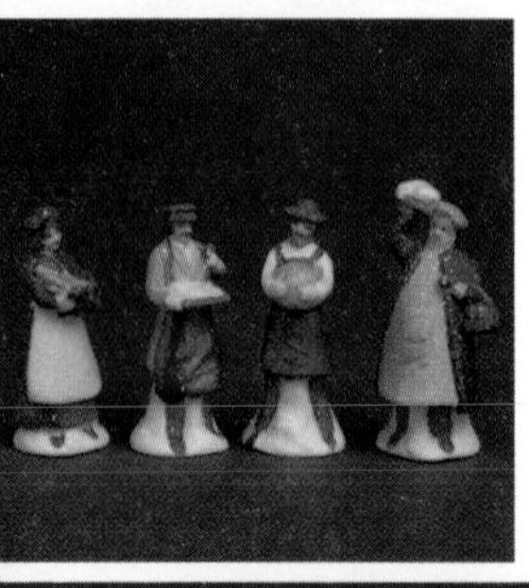

Particulars: Set of 4. Dickens' Village accessory. *Shopkeepers* and *City Workers* are the only figures to have "snow" sprinkled on them. Vendors of fruits, vegetables, breads, cakes.

DATE:_______ $:_______ ❍ WISH ❍ HAVE

'91	'92	'93	'94	'95	'96
$35	30	35	35	38	38

City Workers

Item #	Intro	Retired	OSRP	GBTru	↑
5967-6	1987	1988	$15	**$45**	29%

Particulars: Set of 4. Dickens' Village accessory. *Shopkeepers* and *City Workers* are the only figures to have "snow" sprinkled on them. Some boxes read "City People." Police constable, nurse, driver, tradesman with packages.

DATE:_______	$:_______	'91	'92	'93	'94	'95	'96
❍ WISH	❍ HAVE	$35	35	38	38	40	35

'llage Express Train— Black

Item #	Intro	Retired	OSRP	GBTru	↑
5997-8	1987	1988	$90	**$300**	13%

Particulars: Set of 22. Manufactured by Tyco. Black locomotive pulls a coal car, two passenger cars and a caboose.

DATE:_______	$:_______	'91	'92	'93	'94	'95	'96
❍ WISH	❍ HAVE	$-	-	300	300	300	265

Skating Pond

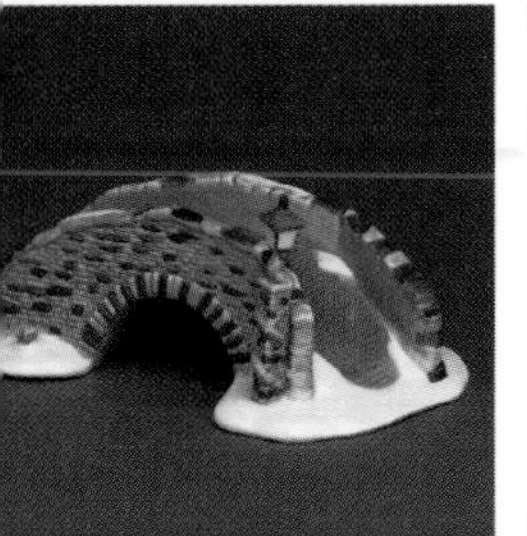

Item #	Intro	Retired	OSRP	GBTru	No Change
6545-5	1987	1990	$24	**$75**	

Particulars: Dickens', New England & Christmas In The City accessory. There are two color variations. Version 1 is made in Taiwan, the ice has generally very light blue streaks. Version 2 is made in the Philippines, blue covers most of ice surface. Variations do not affect secondary market price. Low stone wall circles pond. One child watches other child skating. Two snowy trees.

DATE:_______	$:_______	'91	'92	'93	'94	'95	'96
❍ WISH	❍ HAVE	$65	60	60	75	75	75

Stone Bridge

Item #	Intro	Retired	OSRP	GBTru	↓
6546-3	1987	1990	$12	**$75**	6%

Particulars: Variegated fieldstone arches over river. Corner post has lamp. Variations in color from light to dark do not affect secondary market price.

DATE:_______	$:_______	'91	'92	'93	'94	'95	'96
❍ WISH	❍ HAVE	$40	60	70	80	80	80

Village Well & Holy Cross

Item #	Intro	Retired	OSRP	GBTru	⬇
6547-1	1987	1989	$13	**$150**	9%

Particulars: Set of 2. Dickens' Village accessory. There are two variations in color. The first version has blue water and dark birds. The second version has colorless water and the birds are light in color. Variations do not affect secondary market price. Old fashioned hand pump for water housed in small gazebo. Cross upon pedestal on stone step base.

DATE:________ $:________

		'91	'92	'93	'94	'95	'9
❍ WISH	❍ HAVE	$70	98	145	130	160	16

Dickens' Village Sign

Item #	Intro	Retired	OSRP	GBTru	NO
6569-2	1987	1993	$6	**$18**	CHANC

Particulars: The village signs are the only pieces to identify the actual manufacturer of the piece. The bottomstamp reads "Handcrafted by Jiean Fung Porcelains, Taiwan." The early signs have a dark background. This does not affect secondary market value.

DATE:________ $:________

		'91	'92	'93	'94	'95	'9
❍ WISH	❍ HAVE	$6.50	6.50	6.50	18	20	1

New England Village Sign

Item #	Intro	Retired	OSRP	GBTru	⬆
6570-6	1987	1993	$6	**$17**	6%

Particulars: The village signs are the only pieces to identify the actual manufacturer of the piece. The bottomstamp reads "Handcrafted by Jiean Fung Porcelains, Taiwan." The early signs are more detailed and have richer color. This does not affect secondary market value.

DATE:________ $:________

		'91	'92	'93	'94	'95	'9
❍ WISH	❍ HAVE	$6.50	6.50	6.50	14	15	1

Alpine Village Sign

Item #	Intro	Retired	OSRP	GBTru	⬆
6571-4	1987	1993	$6	**$18**	6%

Particulars: The village signs are the only pieces to identify the actual manufacturer of the piece. The bottomstamp reads "Handcrafted by Jiean Fung Porcelains, Taiwan." The early signs are more detailed and have richer color. This does not affect secondary market value.

DATE:________ $:________

		'91	'92	'93	'94	'95	'9
❍ WISH	❍ HAVE	$6.50	6.50	6.50	28	20	1

Maple Sugaring Shed

Item #	Intro	Retired	OSRP	GBTru	↑
6589-7	1987	1989	$19	**$255**	19%

Particulars: Set of 3. New England Village accessory. Two tapped trees, sled with bucket of syrup, and open walled shed with cooking vat.

DATE:_______	$:_______	'91	'92	'93	'94	'95	'96
❍ WISH	❍ HAVE	$125	130	165	210	245	215

Dover Coach— "First Version"

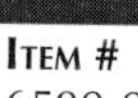

Item #	Intro	Retired	OSRP	GBTru	↑
6590-0	1987	1990	$18	**$100**	2%

Particulars: Dickens' Village accessory. Passenger coach with one horse, driver, and coachman. There are 3 versions that affect GBTru$. This First Version is made in Taiwan, the coachman is clean shaven and the coach wheels are very crude.

DATE:_______	$:_______	'91	'92	'93	'94	'95	'96
❍ WISH	❍ HAVE	$45	55	58	125	110	98

Dover Coach— "Second Version"

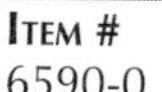

Item #	Intro	Retired	OSRP	GBTru	↑
6590-0	1987	1990	$18	**$75**	25%

Particulars: This Second Version is also made in Taiwan, the coachman has a mustache, the coach wheels are more round and there are two recesses on the underside of the base.

DATE:_______	$:_______	'91	'92	'93	'94	'95	'96
❍ WISH	❍ HAVE	$45	55	58	65	65	60

Dover Coach— "Third Version"

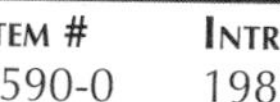

Item #	Intro	Retired	OSRP	GBTru	↓
6590-0	1987	1990	$18	**$60**	6%

Particulars: This Third Version is made in Sri Lanka, the coachman has a mustache, and the coach wheels are round.

DATE:_______	$:_______	'91	'92	'93	'94	'95	'96
❍ WISH	❍ HAVE	$45	55	58	75	75	64

Childe Pond And Skaters

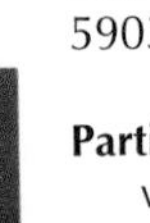

Item #	Intro	Retired	OSRP	GBTru	No
5903-0	1988	1991	$30	**$80**	Change

Particulars: Set of 4. Dickens' Village accessory. Brick warming house, shutters latch against wind, wooden benches for skaters, birdhouse above door. Color of warming hut varies. This does not affect secondary market price.

DATE:_______ $:_______ ❍ WISH ❍ HAVE

'91	'92	'93	'94	'95	'96
$32	65	72	85	80	80

Fezziwig And Friends

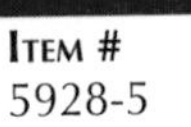

Item #	Intro	Retired	OSRP	GBTru	↓
5928-5	1988	1990	$12.50	**$50**	4%

Particulars: Set of 3. Dickens' Village accessory. Addition t *Christmas Carol* grouping. Husband and wife bringing food to elderly neighbors.

DATE:_______ $:_______ ❍ WISH ❍ HAVE

'91	'92	'93	'94	'95	'96
$30	30	42	48	50	52

Nicholas Nickleby Characters

Item #	Intro	Retired	OSRP	GBTru	↑
5929-3	1988	1991	$20	**$38**	19%

Particulars: Set of 4. Dickens' Village accessory. Misspelle as Nicholas Nick**el**by on sleeve. Nicholas and sister Kat Wackford Squeers with schoolbook, three children playing, and four-wheeled wagon.

DATE:_______ $:_______ ❍ WISH ❍ HAVE

'91	'92	'93	'94	'95	'9
$20	45	40	35	36	3

Snow Children

Item #	Intro	Retired	OSRP	GBTru	↑
5938-2	1988	1994	$15	**$30**	7%

Particulars: Set of 3. Girl finishes snowman while dog watches. Two boys push off on sled, another belly flop on his sled.

DATE:_______ $:_______ ❍ WISH ❍ HAVE

'91	'92	'93	'94	'95	'
$16	16	17	17	22	2

Village Harvest People

Item #	Intro	Retired	OSRP	GBTru	↑
5941-2	1988	1991	$27.50	**$50**	11%

Particulars: Set of 4. New England Village accessory. Sleeve reads "Harvest Time." Woman with butter churn, man loads pumpkins on cart, corn shocks, and pumpkins.

DATE:_______	$:_______	'91	'92	'93	'94	'95	'96
❍ WISH	❍ HAVE	$28	50	55	45	45	45

City Newsstand

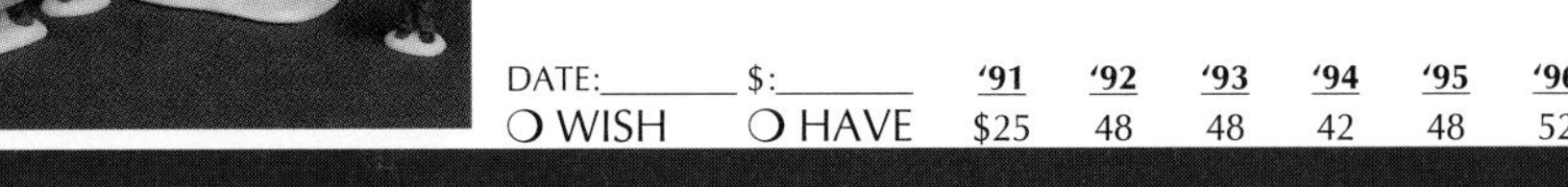

Item #	Intro	Retired	OSRP	GBTru	↑
5971-4	1988	1991	$25	**$60**	15%

Particulars: Set of 4. Christmas In The City accessory. News vendor, magazine and newspaper wooden stand, woman reading paper, newsboy showing headlines.

DATE:_______	$:_______	'91	'92	'93	'94	'95	'96
❍ WISH	❍ HAVE	$25	48	48	42	48	52

Village Express Train

Item #	Intro	Retired	OSRP	GBTru	
5980-3	1988	1996	$95	**$100**	NO CHANGE

Particulars: Set of 22. Manufactured by Bachmann Trains. Red, black and silver locomotive pulls the cars around the track.

DATE:_______	$:_______	'91	'92	'93	'94	'95	'96
❍ WISH	❍ HAVE	$95	95	100	100	100	100

Village Train Trestle

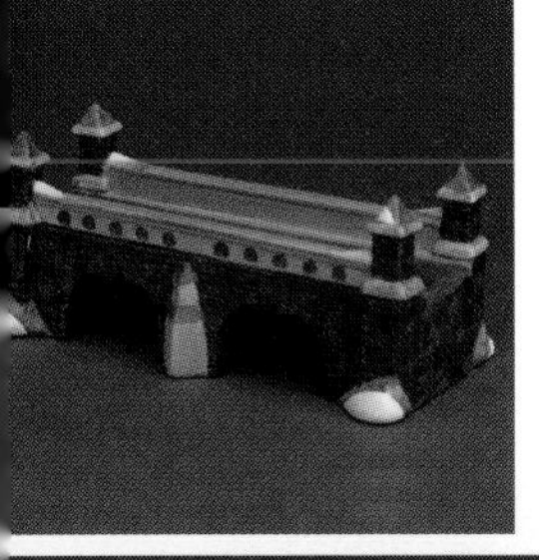

Item #	Intro	Retired	OSRP	GBTru	
5981-1	1988	1990	$17	**$70**	NO CHANGE

Particulars: Double arch trestle spans river. Single track on stone train overpass. Sleeve reads "Stone Train Trestle."

DATE:_______	$:_______	'91	'92	'93	'94	'95	'96
❍ WISH	❍ HAVE	$35	42	60	60	60	70

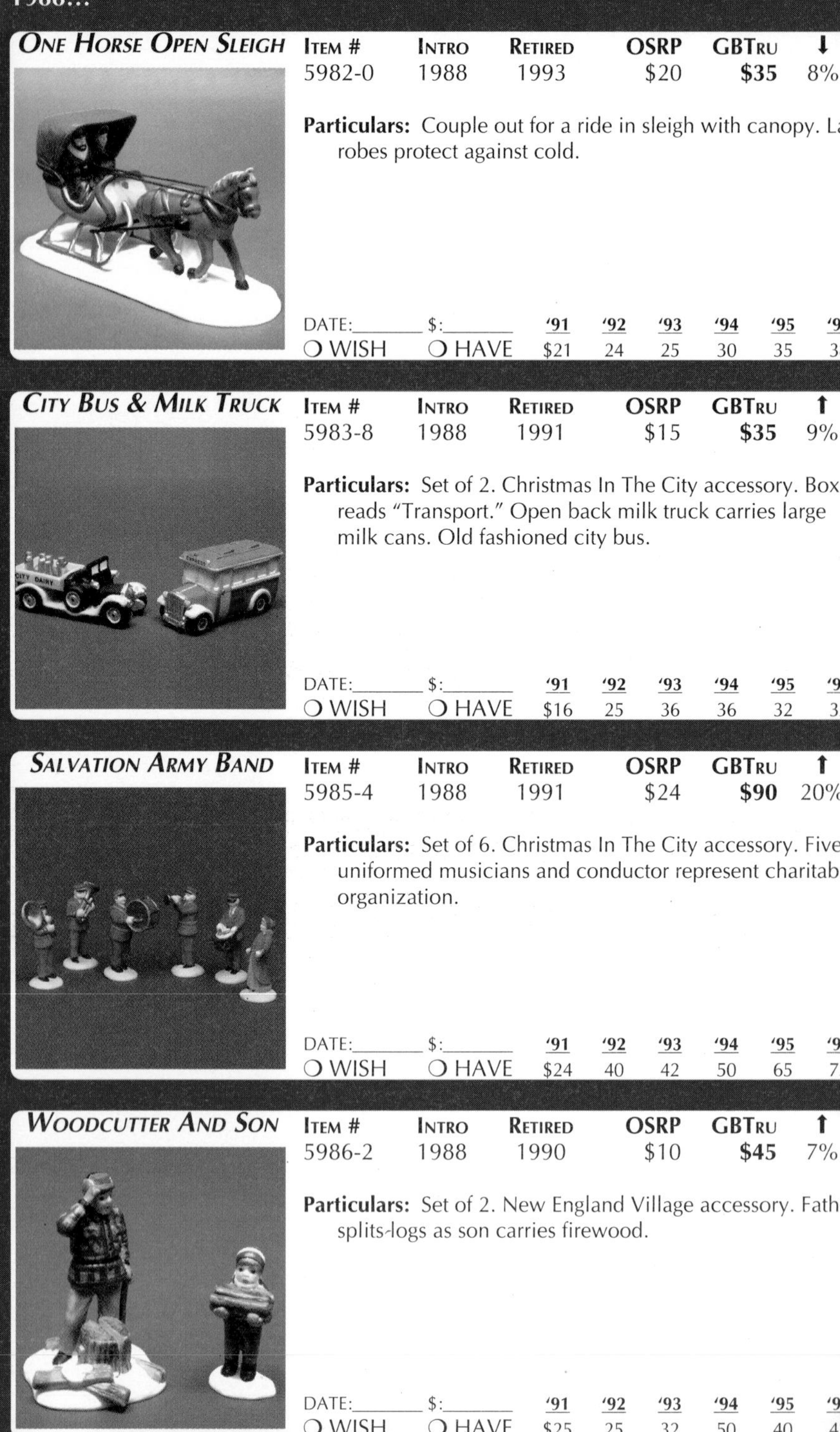

ONE HORSE OPEN SLEIGH

ITEM #	INTRO	RETIRED	OSRP	GBTRU	↓
5982-0	1988	1993	$20	**$35**	8%

Particulars: Couple out for a ride in sleigh with canopy. La robes protect against cold.

DATE:_______	$:_______	'91	'92	'93	'94	'95	'9
❍ WISH	❍ HAVE	$21	24	25	30	35	3

CITY BUS & MILK TRUCK

ITEM #	INTRO	RETIRED	OSRP	GBTRU	↑
5983-8	1988	1991	$15	**$35**	9%

Particulars: Set of 2. Christmas In The City accessory. Box reads "Transport." Open back milk truck carries large milk cans. Old fashioned city bus.

DATE:_______	$:_______	'91	'92	'93	'94	'95	'9
❍ WISH	❍ HAVE	$16	25	36	36	32	3

SALVATION ARMY BAND

ITEM #	INTRO	RETIRED	OSRP	GBTRU	↑
5985-4	1988	1991	$24	**$90**	20%

Particulars: Set of 6. Christmas In The City accessory. Five uniformed musicians and conductor represent charitab organization.

DATE:_______	$:_______	'91	'92	'93	'94	'95	'9
❍ WISH	❍ HAVE	$24	40	42	50	65	7

WOODCUTTER AND SON

ITEM #	INTRO	RETIRED	OSRP	GBTRU	↑
5986-2	1988	1990	$10	**$45**	7%

Particulars: Set of 2. New England Village accessory. Fath splits-logs as son carries firewood.

DATE:_______	$:_______	'91	'92	'93	'94	'95	'9
❍ WISH	❍ HAVE	$25	25	32	50	40	4

Red Covered Bridge

Item #	Intro	Retired	OSRP	GBTru	↑
5987-0	1988	1994	$15	**$25**	4%

Particulars: New England Village accessory. Wooden bridge spans Maple Creek supported by stone bases.

DATE:_______ $:_______

❍ WISH ❍ HAVE

'91	'92	'93	'94	'95	'96
$16	16	17	17	22	24

Town Square Gazebo

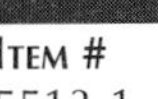

Item #	Intro	Retired	OSRP	GBTru	
5513-1	1989	Current	$19	**$19**	No Change

Particulars: Eight posts support the roof that rises to a spire. Stone work on floor follows the shape of the roof. Resin.

DATE:_______ $:_______

❍ WISH ❍ HAVE

'91	'92	'93	'94	'95	'96
$19	19	19	19	19	19

Boulevard

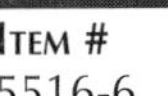

Item #	Intro	Retired	OSRP	GBTru	
5516-6	1989	1992	$25	**$50**	No Change

Particulars: Set of 14. Christmas In The City accessory. 4 sidewalk pieces, 4 removable 5" trees, 2 benches, 4 hitching posts. Forms a tree-lined sidewalk. Trees provide shade at benches.

DATE:_______ $:_______

❍ WISH ❍ HAVE

'91	'92	'93	'94	'95	'96
$25	25	25	-	50	50

Mailbox & Fire Hydrant

Item #	Intro	Retired	OSRP	GBTru	↓
5517-4	1989	1990	$6	**$20**	9%

Particulars: Christmas In The City accessory. U.S. Post Office colors of red, white and blue mailbox features "U.S. Mail" sign and eagle logo. Replaced in 1990 by *Mailbox & Fire Hydrant,* #5214-0, a green and red HV mailbox.

DATE:_______ $:_______

❍ WISH ❍ HAVE

'95	'96
$20	22

David Copperfield Characters

Item #	Intro	Retired	OSRP	GBTru	⬇
5551-4	1989	1992	$32.50	**$42**	5%

Particulars: Set of 5. Dickens' Village accessory. David Copperfield, Agnes, Mr. Wickfield, Peggotty with young David and Emily, Betsy Trotwood with Mr. Dick.

DATE:________ $:________ ❍ WISH ❍ HAVE

'91	'92	'93	'94	'95	'96
$32.50	32.50	44	44	48	44

Village Sign With Snowman

Item #	Intro	Retired	OSRP	GBTru	⬇
5572-7	1989	1994	$10	**$17**	15%

Particulars: Snowman with top hat and scarf next to brick pillars and Heritage Village Sign. Size: 3".

DATE:________ $:________ ❍ WISH ❍ HAVE

'91	'92	'93	'94	'95	'96
$10	10	10	10	12	20

Lamplighter With Lamp

Item #	Intro	Retired	OSRP	GBTru	
5577-8	1989	Current	$9	**$10**	No Change

Particulars: Set of 2. Dickens' Village accessory. Man carries lit torch to light street lamps at dusk. Old fashioned lamp post, small tree by post. Size: 3 1/2".

DATE:________ $:________ ❍ WISH ❍ HAVE

'91	'92	'93	'94	'95	'96
$10	10	10	10	10	10

Royal Coach

Item #	Intro	Retired	OSRP	GBTru	
5578-6	1989	1992	$55	**$75**	No Chang

Particulars: Dickens' Village accessory. Gold filigree decorates red coach with Royal Coat Of Arms on door. Wheel base and undercarriage are cast metal, four gray horses have red and gold harnesses. Early release to National Association Of Limited Edition Dealers (NALED).

DATE:________ $:________ ❍ WISH ❍ HAVE

'91	'92	'93	'94	'95	'9
$55	56	86	75	75	75

Constables

Item #	Intro	Retired	OSRP	GBTru	↑
5579-4	1989	1991	$17.50	**$65**	5%

Particulars: Set of 3. Dickens' Village accessory. One holds club, one with seated dog, one tips hat and stands by lamppost.

DATE:_______	$:_______	**'91**	**'92**	**'93**	**'94**	**'95**	**'96**
❍ WISH	❍ HAVE	$17.50	35	42	55	60	62

olet Vendor/Carol-s/Chestnut Vendor

Item #	Intro	Retired	OSRP	GBTru	↑
5580-8	1989	1992	$23.00	**$45**	13%

Particulars: Set of 3. Dickens' Village accessory. Elderly woman sells bunches of violets from basket, man sells fresh roasted nuts, and two women singing carols.

DATE:_______	$:_______	**'91**	**'92**	**'93**	**'94**	**'95**	**'96**
❍ WISH	❍ HAVE	$23	24	52	45	40	40

King's Road Cab

Item #	Intro	Retired	OSRP	GBTru	No
5581-6	1989	Current	$30	**$30**	Change

Particulars: Dickens' Village accessory. Two-wheeled horse drawn carriage. Driver sits high and behind cab. Passengers protected from weather.

DATE:_______	$:_______	**'91**	**'92**	**'93**	**'94**	**'95**	**'96**
❍ WISH	❍ HAVE	$30	30	30	30	30	30

hristmas Morning Figures

Item #	Intro	Retired	OSRP	GBTru	No
5588-3	1989	Current	$18	**$18**	Change

Particulars: Set of 3. Dickens' Village accessory. Scrooge transformed—smiling, small boy by fence and lamp-post—waving, couple carrying presents. Early release to National Association Of Limited Edition Dealers (NALED). Addition to *Christmas Carol* grouping.

DATE:_______	$:_______	**'91**	**'92**	**'93**	**'94**	**'95**	**'96**
❍ WISH	❍ HAVE	$18	18	18	18	18	18

Christmas Spirits Figures

Item #	Intro	Retired	OSRP	GBTru	NO
5589-1	1989	Current	$27.50	**$27.50**	CHAN

Particulars: Set of 4. Dickens' Village accessory. Scrooge with Ghost of...1) Christmas Past, 2) Christmas Present, and 3) Future...&...Marley. Addition to *Christmas Caro* grouping.

DATE:_______	$:_______	'91	'92	'93	'94	'95	'9
❍ WISH	❍ HAVE	$27.50	27.50	27.50	27.50	27.50	27

Farm Animals

Item #	Intro	Retired	OSRP	GBTru	↑
5945-5	1989	1991	$15	**$45**	13%

Particulars: Set of 4. New England Village accessory. Chickens, geese, sheep, ewe and lamb.

DATE:_______	$:_______	'91	'92	'93	'94	'95	'9
❍ WISH	❍ HAVE	$15	25	33	36	40	4

Organ Grinder

Item #	Intro	Retired	OSRP	GBTru	NO
5957-9	1989	1991	$21	**$36**	CHAN

Particulars: Set of 3. Christmas In The City accessory. Ma turns handle to produce music for little monkey to dance. Woman and children watch monkey. (Woman and girl missing from photo.)

DATE:_______	$:_______	'91	'92	'93	'94	'95	'9
❍ WISH	❍ HAVE	$21	38	40	40	35	3

Popcorn Vendor

Item #	Intro	Retired	OSRP	GBTru	↑
5958-7	1989	1992	$22	**$38**	19%

Particulars: Set of 3. Christmas In The City accessory. Tru with red and white striped top. Vendor fills red and wh bag. Little girl has a full bag of popcorn.

DATE:_______	$:_______	'91	'92	'93	'94	'95	'9
❍ WISH	❍ HAVE	$22	22	40	35	40	3

RIVER STREET ICE HOUSE CART

ITEM #	INTRO	RETIRED	OSRP	GBTRU	↑
5959-5	1989	1991	$20	**$55**	10%

Particulars: Christmas In The City accessory. Horse pulls a blue and gray ice wagon for ice man.

DATE:_______	$:_______	'91	'92	'93	'94	'95	'96
❍ WISH	❍ HAVE	$20	40	45	45	50	50

ENTRAL PARK CARRIAGE

ITEM #	INTRO	RETIRED	OSRP	GBTRU	NO CHANGE
5979-0	1989	CURRENT	$30	**$30**	

Particulars: Christmas In The City accessory. Gray horse pulls red and black carriage. Driver has mother and child as passengers.

DATE:_______	$:_______	'91	'92	'93	'94	'95	'96
❍ WISH	❍ HAVE	$30	30	30	30	30	30

IV PROMOTIONAL SIGN

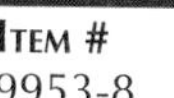

ITEM #	INTRO	RETIRED	OSRP	GBTRU	↑
9953-8	1989	1990	$5	**$28**	12%

Particulars: Vertical sign with arched top and brick base. Gold lettering on white facade. Variation exists of green lettering on green facade. This does not affect secondary market price. Earthenware.

DATE:_______	$:_______	'91	'92	'93	'94	'95	'96
❍ WISH	❍ HAVE	$-	-	-	18	20	25

ILBOX & FIRE HYDRANT

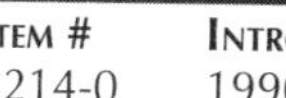

ITEM #	INTRO	RETIRED	OSRP	GBTRU	NO CHANGE
5214-0	1990	CURRENT	$5	**$5**	

Particulars: Set of 2. Christmas In The City accessory. Red & green H.V. mailbox & red fire hydrant. Replaced 1989, #5517-4. Metal.

DATE:_______	$:_______	'91	'92	'93	'94	'95	'96
❍ WISH	❍ HAVE	$5	5	5	5	5	5

Busy Sidewalks

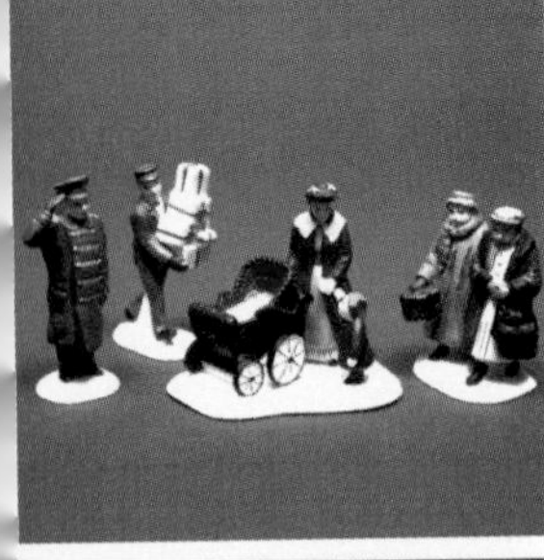

Item #	Intro	Retired	OSRP	GBTru	NO
5535-2	1990	1992	$28	**$45**	CHANGE

Particulars: Set of 4. Christmas In The City accessory. Delivery boy, doorman, two elderly ladies, mother with toddler and baby in carriage.

DATE:_______	$:_______	'91	'92	'93	'94	'95	'96
❍ WISH	❍ HAVE	$28	28	42	42	45	45

'Tis The Season

Item #	Intro	Retired	OSRP	GBTru	NO
5539-5	1990	1994	$12.50	**$20**	CHANGI

Particulars: Christmas In The City accessory. Santa with bel and iron kettle for Season donations. Little girl gives to the needy.

DATE:_______	$:_______	'91	'92	'93	'94	'95	'9(
❍ WISH	❍ HAVE	$12.50	12.50	13	12.95	20	2C

Rest Ye Merry Gentleman

Item #	Intro	Retired	OSRP	GBTru	NO
5540-9	1990	Current	$12.50	**$12.95**	CHANG

Particulars: Christmas In The City accessory. Man sits on bench reading newspaper with purchases all around him. Porcelain and Metal.

DATE:_______	$:_______	'91	'92	'93	'94	'95	'9
❍ WISH	❍ HAVE	$12.50	12.50	12.95	12.95	12.95	12.

Town Crier & Chimney Sweep

Item #	Intro	Retired	OSRP	GBTru	NO
5569-7	1990	Current	$15	**$16**	CHAN

Particulars: Set of 2. Dickens' Village accessory. Crier rin bell and reads out announcements. A Sweep in top hat and tails carries chimney brush.

DATE:_______	$:_______	'91	'92	'93	'94	'95
❍ WISH	❍ HAVE	$15	15	16	16	16

Carolers On The Doorstep

Item #	Intro	Retired	OSRP	GBTru	
5570-0	1990	1993	$25	**$40**	No Change

Particulars: Set of 4. Dickens' Village accessory. Four children sing carols to elderly man and woman, boys carry lanterns, girls have song books.

DATE:_______	$:_______	'91	'92	'93	'94	'95	'96
❍ WISH	❍ HAVE	$25	25	25	36	40	40

Holiday Travelers

Item #	Intro	Retired	OSRP	GBTru	
5571-9	1990	Current	$22.50	**$25**	No Change

Particulars: Set of 3. Dickens' Village accessory. Train conductor, baggage handler, and man and woman passengers.

DATE:_______	$:_______	'91	'92	'93	'94	'95	'96
❍ WISH	❍ HAVE	$22.50	24	25	25	25	25

[Th]e Flying Scot Train

Item #	Intro	Retired	OSRP	GBTru	
5573-5	1990	Current	$48	**$50**	No Change

Particulars: Set of 4. Dickens' Village accessory. Engine and wood supply car and two passenger cars with luggage carriers atop cars.

DATE:_______	$:_______	'91	'92	'93	'94	'95	'96
❍ WISH	❍ HAVE	$48	50	50	50	50	50

[Vi]ctoria Station Train Platform

Item #	Intro	Retired	OSRP	GBTru	
5575-1	1990	Current	$20	**$22**	No Change

Particulars: Dickens' Village accessory. Six-sided ticket booth with windows all around, long metal roof to protect passengers.

DATE:_______	$:_______	'91	'92	'93	'94	'95	'96
❍ WISH	❍ HAVE	$20	20	22	22	22	22

Trimming The North Pole

Item #	Intro	Retired	OSRP	GBTru	↑
5608-1	1990	1993	$10	**$30**	20%

Particulars: North Pole accessory. One elf holds another hang greenery on North Pole sign while blue bird watches.

DATE:_______ $:_______ ❍ WISH ❍ HAVE

'91	'92	'93	'94	'95
$10	10	10	22	22

Santa & Mrs. Claus

Item #	Intro	Retired	OSRP	GBTru	
5609-0	1990	Current	$15	**$15**	No Chan

Particulars: Set of 2. North Pole accessory. Variation exis in title on book: "Good Boys" instead of "Good Kids." No secondary market price has been established for th "Good Boys" variation as very few have ever sold. Mrs Claus and elf wave good-bye to Santa as he does a fin check of delivery book names before leaving North Po

DATE:_______ $:_______ ❍ WISH ❍ HAVE

'91	'92	'93	'94	'95
$15	15	15	15	15

Santa's Little Helpers

Item #	Intro	Retired	OSRP	GBTru	↑
5610-3	1990	1993	$28	**$55**	6%

Particulars: Set of 3. North Pole accessory. Elf stands on presents to hang wreath. Two elves move toy sack. On elf brings two reindeer to sleigh.

DATE:_______ $:_______ ❍ WISH ❍ HAVE

'91	'92	'93	'94	'95
$28	28	28	40	48

Sleigh & Eight Tiny Reindeer

Item #	Intro	Retired	OSRP	GBTru	
5611-1	1990	Current	$40	**$42**	No Chan

Particulars: Set of 5. North Pole accessory. Toys fill sleigh harnessed to Santa's eight reindeer.

DATE:_______ $:_______ ❍ WISH ❍ HAVE

'91	'92	'93	'94	'95
$40	42	42	42	42

THE TOY PEDDLER

ITEM #	INTRO	RETIRED	OSRP	GBTRU	NO
5616-2	1990	CURRENT	$22	**$22**	CHANGE

Particulars: Set of 3. Alpine Village accessory. Toy peddler carries tray with toys. Mother and son look at toy horse. Little girl holds top.

DATE:_______ $:_______

❍ WISH ❍ HAVE

'91	'92	'93	'94	'95	'96
$22	22	22	22	22	22

AMISH FAMILY—"W/MUSTACHE"

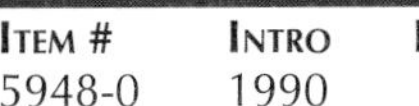

ITEM #	INTRO	RETIRED	OSRP	GBTRU	NO
5948-0	1990	1992	$20	**$55**	CHANGE

Particulars: Set of 3. New England accessory. Two versions produced. In the First Version, the father has a mustache. Realizing that this is against Amish custom, D56 stopped production and redesigned the piece. Early release to Showcase Dealers and the National Association Of Limited Edition Dealers (NALED). Mother w/apples in apron, father stacks boxes, children sort apples.

DATE:_______ $:_______

❍ WISH ❍ HAVE

'92	'93	'94	'95	'96
$40	46	40	50	55

AMISH FAMILY—"NO MUSTACHE"

ITEM #	INTRO	RETIRED	OSRP	GBTRU	↑
5948-0	1990	1992	$20	**$ 40**	14%

Particulars: In this Second Version the father has no mustache as is the Amish custom.

DATE:_______ $:_______

❍ WISH ❍ HAVE

'91	'92	'93	'94	'95	'96
$20	20	32	28	35	35

AMISH BUGGY

ITEM #	INTRO	RETIRED	OSRP	GBTRU	↑
5949-8	1990	1992	$22	**$60**	20%

Particulars: New England Village accessory. Amish man feeds brown horse harnessed to privacy curtained family carriage.

DATE:_______ $:_______

❍ WISH ❍ HAVE

'91	'92	'93	'94	'95	'96
$22	22.50	50	50	50	50

Sleepy Hollow Characters

Item #	Intro	Retired	OSRP	GBTru	↑
5956-0	1990	1992	$27.50	**$45**	7%

Particulars: Set of 3. New England Village accessory. Man carving pumpkin. Squire and Mrs. VanTassel, Ichabod Crane with children.

DATE:________ $:________ ❍ WISH ❍ HAVE

'91	'92	'93	'94	'95	'96
$27.50	27.50	48	45	45	42

Skating Party

Item #	Intro	Retired	OSRP	GBTru	No Chanc
5523-9	1991	Current	$27.50	**$27.50**	

Particulars: Set of 3. New England Village accessory. Skating couple, boy, and girl.

DATE:________ $:________ ❍ WISH ❍ HAVE

'91	'92	'93	'94	'95	'9
$27.50	27.50	27.50	27.50	27.50	27.

All Around The Town

Item #	Intro	Retired	OSRP	GBTru	No Chanc
5545-0	1991	1993	$18	**$28**	

Particulars: Set of 2. Christmas In The City accessory. Mar with "sandwich boards" as a walking ad for "White Christmas." Man with packages stops to get a shoeshin from young boy.

DATE:________ $:________ ❍ WISH ❍ HAVE

'91	'92	'93	'94	'95	'9
$18	18	18	30	30	2

The Fire Brigade

Item #	Intro	Retired	OSRP	GBTru	↑
5546-8	1991	1995	$20	**$32**	33%

Particulars: Set of 2. Christmas In The City accessory. Tw firemen carry ladder and ax. Fireman with pail takes a moment to pet mascot Dalmatian.

DATE:________ $:________ ❍ WISH ❍ HAVE

'91	'92	'93	'94	'95
$20	20	20	20	20

"City Fire Dept." Fire Truck

Item #	Intro	Retired	OSRP	GBTru	↑
5547-6	1991	1995	$18	**$32**	45%

Particulars: Christmas In The City accessory. Ladder attached to side, hose and nozzle assembly on top and rear of red fire truck.

DATE:_______	$:_______	'91	'92	'93	'94	'95	'96
❍ WISH	❍ HAVE	$18	18	18	18	18	22

...roling Thru The City

Item #	Intro	Retired	OSRP	GBTru	NO
5548-4	1991	Current	$27.50	**$27.50**	CHANGE

Particulars: Set of 3. Christmas In The City accessory. Singing man pulls sled with two boys, two women with young girl, man (alone), all with song books.

DATE:_______	$:_______	'91	'92	'93	'94	'95	'96
❍ WISH	❍ HAVE	$27.50	27.50	27.50	27.50	27.50	27.50

...iver Twist Characters

Item #	Intro	Retired	OSRP	GBTru	NO
5554-9	1991	1993	$35	**$45**	CHANGE

Particulars: Set of 3. Dickens' Village accessory. Mr. Brownlow in long coat, stovepipe hat, walks with cane. Oliver in rags next to food cart as another boy reaches to steal food, third boy holds sack.

DATE:_______	$:_______	'91	'92	'93	'94	'95	'96
❍ WISH	❍ HAVE	$35	35	35	58	45	45

Bringing Home The Yule Log

Item #	Intro	Retired	OSRP	GBTru	NO
5558-1	1991	Current	$27.50	**$28**	CHANGE

Particulars: Set of 3. Dickens' Village accessory. Two boys pull on ropes to haul log. One girl holds lantern to light way and another walks alongside.

DATE:_______	$:_______	'91	'92	'93	'94	'95	'96
❍ WISH	❍ HAVE	$27.50	27.50	28	28	28	28

Poultry Market

Item #	Intro	Retired	OSRP	GBTru	↑
5559-0	1991	1995	$30	**$40**	8%

Particulars: Set of 3. Dickens' Village accessory. There is a "proof" version with patches on left hand side of the green drape. No secondary market value has been established for the proof as very few have ever sold. An aproned poulterer holds game bird. Covered stand with display of turkeys and geese. Woman holds purchase as child watches.

DATE:_______	$:_______	'91	'92	'93	'94	'95	'9
❍ WISH	❍ HAVE	$30	30	32	32	32	37

Come Into The Inn

Item #	Intro	Retired	OSRP	GBTru	↑
5560-3	1991	1994	$22	**$30**	11%

Particulars: Set of 3. Dickens' Village accessory. Innkeeper wife pauses to read note as she sweeps snow from the entry. Young boy with lantern lights way for coach driver. Gentleman stands by luggage.

DATE:_______	$:_______	'91	'92	'93	'94	'95	'9
❍ WISH	❍ HAVE	$22	22	22	22	26	27

Holiday Coach

Item #	Intro	Retired	OSRP	GBTru	
5561-1	1991	Current	$68	**$70**	No Change

Particulars: Dickens' Village accessory. Four horses pull coach full of travelers who ride inside and on topside seats. Coachman blows horn on arrival as driver guides horses. The first version had gold chains, the current version has silver chains.

DATE:_______	$:_______	'91	'92	'93	'94	'95	'9
❍ WISH	❍ HAVE	$68	68	70	70	70	70

Toymaker Elves

Item #	Intro	Retired	OSRP	GBTru	↓
5602-2	1991	1995	$27.50	**$40**	5%

Particulars: Set of 3. North Pole accessory. Two elves carr trunk of toys. One elf balances stack of toys. One elf h apron filled with toys.

DATE:_______	$:_______	'91	'92	'93	'94	'95	'9
❍ WISH	❍ HAVE	$27.50	27.50	27.50	27.50	27.50	4

Baker Elves

Item #	Intro	Retired	OSRP	GBTru	⬇
5603-0	1991	1995	$27.50	**$40**	7%

Particulars: Set of 3. North Pole accessory. One elf holds piece of belled harness from sleigh. One elf holds tray of baked goods. One elf takes a cookie from Sweets Cart.

DATE:_______ $:_______

❍ WISH ❍ HAVE

'91	'92	'93	'94	'95	'96
$27.50	27.50	27.50	27.50	27.50	43

Market Day

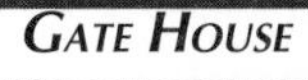

Item #	Intro	Retired	OSRP	GBTru	
5641-3	1991	1993	$35	**$45**	NO CHANGE

Particulars: Set of 3. New England Village accessory. Mother carries baby and basket. Daughter holds bread basket. Merchant tips hat as he pushes sledge with bagged food. Man and boy rest on goat cart while standing boy holds bag.

DATE:_______ $:_______

❍ WISH ❍ HAVE

'91	'92	'93	'94	'95	'96
$35	35	35	48	45	45

Gate House

Item #	Intro	Retired	OSRP	GBTru	⬇
5530-1	1992	1992 Annual	$22.50	**$50**	17%

Particulars: Available at 1992 Village Gatherings and select Showcase Dealer Open Houses. Variations in color between shades of gray or blue do not affect the secondary market value. Walled castle fortified entry is brick and stone archway. Guards check soldiers, carriages, carts and villagers. Narrow, shuttered windows protect against weather and attack.

DATE:_______ $:_______

❍ WISH ❍ HAVE

'92	'93	'94	'95	'96
$22.50	72	65	55	60

Don't Drop The Presents!

Item #	Intro	Retired	OSRP	GBTru	
5532-8	1992	1995	$25	**$36**	NO CHANGE

Particulars: Set of 2. Christmas In The City accessory. Mother cautions father to take care as dog jumps up to sniff presents. Daughter peeks out from mother's skirt as shopping bag rests on snow. Son slips and tumbles in snow.

DATE:_______ $:_______

❍ WISH ❍ HAVE

'92	'93	'94	'95	'96
$25	25	25	25	36

Welcome Home

Item #	Intro	Retired	OSRP	GBTru	↑
5533-6	1992	1995	$27.50	**$37**	9%

Particulars: Set of 3. Christmas In The City accessory. Boy reaches to hug Grandmother visiting for holiday as girl and Grandfather reach out to hug each other. Family pet joins the greeting.

DATE:_______ $:_______
❍ WISH ❍ HAVE

'92	'93	'94	'95	'96
$27.50	27.50	27.50	27.50	34

Churchyard Fence & Gate

Item #	Intro	Retired	OSRP	GBTru	↑
5563-8	1992	Disc 1992	$15	**$55**	22%

Particulars: Set of 3. Wrought iron rails on stone base protect church property. Early release to Gift Creations Concepts (GCC). There were two different sets of *Churchyard Fence & Gate* introduced in 1992:

First Version—*Churchyard Fence & Gate* (1992–1992), Set of 3, Item #5563-8 was a midyear release and a GCC Exclusive. It included one gate, one wall, and one corner. The *Quarterly* pictured it in gray, but it was shipped in brown.

Second Version—*Churchyard Gate & Fence* (1992–Current), Set of 3, Item #5806-8, includes one gate and two corners. In addition, there's *Churchyard Fence Extensions* (1992–Current), Item #5807-6, which is 4 straight wall pieces.

'92	'93	'94	'95	'96
$15	25	40	40	45

Letters For Santa

Item #	Intro	Retired	OSRP	GBTru	↑
5604-9	1992	1994	$30	**$60**	20%

Particulars: Set of 3. North Pole accessory. One elf carries bundles of letters, as another elf tries to lift sack of letter Two additional elves arrive with reindeer cart filled with mailbags of letters for Santa.

DATE:_______ $:_______
❍ WISH ❍ HAVE

'92	'93	'94	'95	'9
$30	30	30	50	5

Testing The Toys

Item #	Intro	Retired	OSRP	GBTru	No
5605-7	1992	Current	$16.50	**$16.50**	Change

Particulars: Set of 2. North Pole accessory. One elf rides downhill on a sled as two others try out a toboggan.

DATE:_______ $:_______
❍ WISH ❍ HAVE

'92	'93	'94	'95	'96
$16.50	16.50	16.50	16.50	16.50

uying Baker's Bread

Item #	Intro	Retired	OSRP	GBTru	↓
5619-7	1992	1995	$20.00	**$30**	6%

Particulars: Set of 2. Alpine Village accessory. Man and woman lift basket together to carry loaves, plus she carries basket on arm. Another man carries basket tray of bread while rest of loaves are carried in his basket backpack.

DATE:_______ $:_______
❍ WISH ❍ HAVE

'92	'93	'94	'95	'96
$20	20	20	20	32

Harvest Seed Cart

Item #	Intro	Retired	OSRP	GBTru	↓
5645-6	1992	1995	$27.50	**$40**	5%

Particulars: Set of 3. Dickens' and New England Village accessory. Boy lifts sack of corn onto wheelbarrow. Man lifts barrow filled with corn sacks as a chicken pecks at sack. Another chicken walks next to him. Girl holds white rooster and has basket on ground by her feet.

DATE:_______ $:_______
❍ WISH ❍ HAVE

'92	'93	'94	'95	'96
$27.50	27.50	27.50	27.50	42

Town Tinker

Item #	Intro	Retired	OSRP	GBTru	↑
5646-4	1992	1995	$24	**$38**	52%

Particulars: Set of 2. Dickens' Village and New England Village accessory. Traveling peddler with cart he pushes, sells pots, pans, trinkets, and all odds and ends. He also repairs household items. He follows countryside roads and paths.

DATE:_______ $:_______
❍ WISH ❍ HAVE

'92	'93	'94	'95	'96
$24	24	24	24	25

The Old Puppeteer

Item #	Intro	Retired	OSRP	GBTru	↑
5802-5	1992	1995	$32	**$40**	11%

Particulars: Set of 3. Dickens' Village accessory. Children watch puppet show. Stage on wheels with man moving the stringed marionettes to tell stories to audiences of al ages.

DATE:________ $:________
❍ WISH ❍ HAVE

'92	'93	'94	'95	'9(
$32	32	32	32	36

The Bird Seller

Item #	Intro	Retired	OSRP	GBTru	↑
5803-3	1992	1995	$25	**$33**	18%

Particulars: Set of 3. Dickens' Village accessory. Woman holds up two bird cages. Delighted child and mother with woman who has made a purchase.

DATE:________ $:________
❍ WISH ❍ HAVE

'92	'93	'94	'95	'9(
$25	25	25	25	28

Village Street Peddlers

Item #	Intro	Retired	OSRP	GBTru	
5804-1	1992	1994	$16	**$25**	NO CHANG

Particulars: Set of 2. Dickens' Village accessory. One man carries pole of fresh dressed rabbits. Second peddler wears wooden tray of spices to be sold in small pinches and ounces.

DATE:________ $:________
❍ WISH ❍ HAVE

'92	'93	'94	'95	'9(
$16	16	16	22	25

English Post Box

Item #	Intro	Retired	OSRP	GBTru	
5805-0	1992	Current	$4.50	**$4.50**	NO CHANG

Particulars: Dickens' Village accessory. Red, six-sided, English-styled post box. Size 2 1/4".

DATE:________ $:________
❍ WISH ❍ HAVE

'92	'93	'94	'95	'9(
$4.50	4.50	4.50	4.50	4.5

Churchyard Gate And Fence

Item #	Intro	Retired	OSRP	GBTru	No
5806-8	1992	Current	$15	**$15**	Change

Particulars: Set of 3. Two different *Churchyard Gate And Fence* sets were produced. This second set includes one gate and two corners. For original set, see Item #5563-8, 1992. Also see *Churchyard Fence Extensions,* Item #5807-6.

DATE:_______ $:_______ ❍ WISH ❍ HAVE

'92	'93	'94	'95	'96
$15	15	15	15	15

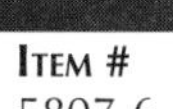

Churchyard Fence Extensions

Item #	Intro	Retired	OSRP	GBTru	No
5807-6	1992	Current	$16	**$16**	Change

Particulars: Set of 4. Stone base with wrought iron posts and connectors to extend fence around church and graveyard.

DATE:_______ $:_______ ❍ WISH ❍ HAVE

'92	'93	'94	'95	'96
$16	16	16	16	16

Lionhead Bridge

Item #	Intro	Retired	OSRP	GBTru	No
5864-5	1992	Current	$22	**$22**	Change

Particulars: Dickens' Village accessory. Massive bridge with two stone lions, each with one raised paw resting on a sphere.

DATE:_______ $:_______ ❍ WISH ❍ HAVE

'92	'93	'94	'95	'96
$22	22	22	22	22

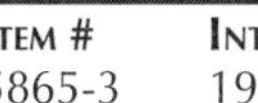

Village Express Van

Item #	Intro	Retired	OSRP	GBTru	↑
5865-3	1992	1996	$25	**$32**	28%

Particulars: Christmas In The City accessory. Green delivery van advertises On Time Service. Rack on van roof holds wrapped packages. License plate is abbreviated address of D56 headquarters, 6436 City West Parkway.

DATE:_______ $:_______ ❍ WISH ❍ HAVE

'92	'93	'94	'95	'96
$25	25	25	25	25

Village Express Van

Item #	Intro	Retired	OSRP	GBTru	⬇
9951-1	1992	Promo 1992	$25	**$135**	27%

Particulars: This van was first given to Department 56 sales representatives as a gift at their National Sales Conference in December 1992. It was later used as a special event piece at Bachman's Village Gathering in 1993.

DATE:________ $:________
❍ WISH ❍ HAVE

'92	'93	'94	'95	'96
$25	-	-	125	185

Village Animated Skating Pond

Item #	Intro	Retired	OSRP	GBTru	No Change
5229-9	1993	Current	$60	**$60**	

Particulars: Set of 15. UL approved. Skaters enjoy frozen pond. Evergreens and bare branch tree edge snow covered pond bank.

DATE:________ $:________
❍ WISH ❍ HAVE

'93	'94	'95	'96
$60	60	60	60

Playing In The Snow

Item #	Intro	Retired	OSRP	GBTru	⬆
5556-5	1993	1996	$25	**$33**	32%

Particulars: Set of 3. Christmas In The City accessory. Children build and dress a snowman.

DATE:________ $:________
❍ WISH ❍ HAVE

'93	'94	'95	'96
$25	25	25	25

Street Musicians

Item #	Intro	Retired	OSRP	GBTru	No Change
5564-6	1993	Current	$25	**$25**	

Particulars: Set of 3. Christmas In The City accessory. Girl gives coin to the street musicians.

DATE:________ $:________
❍ WISH ❍ HAVE

'93	'94	'95	'96
$25	25	25	25

Town Tree

Item #	Intro	Retired	OSRP	GBTru	No
5565-4	1993	Current	$45	**$45**	Change

Particulars: Set of 5. Lighted. Christmas In The City accessory. Decorated town tree and stone sections to encircle tree.

DATE:_______ $:_______
❍ WISH ❍ HAVE

'93	'94	'95	'96
$45	45	45	45

own Tree Trimmers

Item #	Intro	Retired	OSRP	GBTru	No
5566-2	1993	Current	$32.50	**$32.50**	Change

Particulars: Set of 4. Christmas In The City accessory. Ladder and three helpers to decorate town tree.

DATE:_______ $:_______
❍ WISH ❍ HAVE

'93	'94	'95	'96
$32.50	32.50	32.50	32.50

mb Every Mountain

Item #	Intro	Retired	OSRP	GBTru	No
5613-8	1993	Current	$27.50	**$27.50**	Change

Particulars: Set of 4. Alpine Village accessory. Three climbers and companion St. Bernard dog roped together for safety.

DATE:_______ $:_______
❍ WISH ❍ HAVE

'93	'94	'95	'96
$27.50	27.50	27.50	27.50

Woodsmen Elves

Item #	Intro	Retired	OSRP	GBTru	↑
5630-8	1993	1995	$30	**$55**	17%

Particulars: Set of 3. North Pole Village accessory. Elves cut tree and wood to warm North Pole buildings.

DATE:_______ $:_______
❍ WISH ❍ HAVE

'93	'94	'95	'96
$30	30	30	47

Sing A Song For Santa

Item #	Intro	Retired	OSRP	GBTru	NO
5631-6	1993	Current	$28	**$28**	CHAN

Particulars: Set of 3. North Pole Village accessory. Carolir North Pole elves.

DATE:_______ $:_______
❍ WISH ❍ HAVE

'93	'94	'95	'9
$28	28	28	2

North Pole Gate

Item #	Intro	Retired	OSRP	GBTru	NO
5632-4	1993	Current	$32.50	**$32.50**	CHAN

Particulars: North Pole Village accessory. Entry gate to North Pole Village.

DATE:_______ $:_______
❍ WISH ❍ HAVE

'93	'94	'95	'9
$32.50	32.50	32.50	32

Knife Grinder

Item #	Intro	Retired	OSRP	GBTru	↑
5649-9	1993	1996	$22.50	**$28**	24%

Particulars: Set of 2. New England Village accessory. Mar pedal-powered grinding wheel keeps sharp edges on knives and tools.

DATE:_______ $:_______
❍ WISH ❍ HAVE

'93	'94	'95	'9
$22.50	22.50	22.50	22

Blue Star Ice Harvesters

Item #	Intro	Retired	OSRP	GBTru	NO
5650-2	1993	Current	$27.50	**$27.50**	CHAN

Particulars: Set of 2. New England Village accessory. Mer cut up pond, lake, and river ice to stack in icehouse fo food storage and cooling. Early storage was dug into th ground which helped to insulate. Later wood and ston buildings were built to storehouse ice. Sawdust and str were used to keep ice blocks from sticking together.

DATE:_______ $:_______
❍ WISH ❍ HAVE

'93	'94	'95	'9
$27.50	27.50	27.50	27

HELSEA MARKET FRUIT MONGER & CART

ITEM #	INTRO	RETIRED	OSRP	GBTRU	NO
5813-0	1993	CURRENT	$25	**$25**	CHANGE

Particulars: Set of 2. Dickens' Village accessory. Pushcart vendor of fresh fruit and vegetables.

DATE:_______ $:_______
❍ WISH ❍ HAVE

'93	'94	'95	'96
$25	25	25	25

HELSEA MARKET FISH MONGER & CART

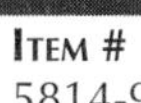

ITEM #	INTRO	RETIRED	OSRP	GBTRU	NO
5814-9	1993	CURRENT	$25	**$25**	CHANGE

Particulars: Set of 2. Dickens' Village accessory. Pushcart vendor of fresh fish.

DATE:_______ $:_______
❍ WISH ❍ HAVE

'93	'94	'95	'96
$25	25	25	25

ELSEA MARKET FLOWER MONGER & CART

ITEM #	INTRO	RETIRED	OSRP	GBTRU	NO
5815-7	1993	CURRENT	$27.50	**$27.50**	CHANGE

Particulars: Set of 2. Dickens' Village accessory. Pushcart vendor of fresh cut flowers and nosegays.

DATE:_______ $:_______
❍ WISH ❍ HAVE

'93	'94	'95	'96
$27.50	27.50	27.50	27.50

IELSEA LANE SHOPPERS

ITEM #	INTRO	RETIRED	OSRP	GBTRU	NO
5816-5	1993	CURRENT	$30	**$30**	CHANGE

Particulars: Set of 4. Dickens' Village accessory. Woman and girl, each with flowers. Couple walking with package and basket. Gentleman with walking stick.

DATE:_______ $:_______
❍ WISH ❍ HAVE

'93	'94	'95	'96
$30	30	30	30

Visions Of A Christmas Past

Item #	Intro	Retired	OSRP	GBTru	↑
5817-3	1993	1996	$27.50	**$35**	27%

Particulars: Set of 3. Dickens' Village accessory. Innkeeper with coach dogs, traveling merchant, 2 young travelers.

DATE:_______ $:_______
❍ WISH ❍ HAVE

'93	'94	'95	'96
$27.50	27.50	27.50	27.5

C. Bradford, Wheelwright & Son

Item #	Intro	Retired	OSRP	GBTru	↑
5818-1	1993	1996	$24	**$30**	25%

Particulars: Set of 2. Dickens' Village accessory. Father and son wagon wheel makers and repairers.

DATE:_______ $:_______
❍ WISH ❍ HAVE

'93	'94	'95	'96
$24	24	24	24

Bringing Fleeces To The Mill

Item #	Intro	Retired	OSRP	GBTru	No
5819-0	1993	Current	$35	**$35**	Chang

Particulars: Set of 2. Dickens' Village accessory. Shepherd takes wagon load of fleeces to market. Child stands wit sheep.

DATE:_______ $:_______
❍ WISH ❍ HAVE

'93	'94	'95	'9
$35	35	35	3

Dashing Through The Snow

Item #	Intro	Retired	OSRP	GBTru	No
5820-3	1993	Current	$32.50	**$32.50**	Chan

Particulars: Dickens' Village accessory. Horse drawn slei takes couple for ride across snowy roads.

DATE:_______ $:_______
❍ WISH ❍ HAVE

'93	'94	'95	
$32.50	32.50	32.50	3

...istmas At The Park

Item #	Intro	Retired	OSRP	GBTru	No Change
5866-1	1993	Current	$27.50	**$27.50**	

Particulars: Set of 3. Christmas In The City accessory. Seated father, mother and child. Seated boy and girl with dog.

DATE:_______ $:_______
❍ WISH ❍ HAVE

'93	'94	'95	'96
$27.50	27.50	27.50	27.50

...age Express Van—Gold

Item #	Intro	Retired	OSRP	GBTru	⬇
9977-5	1993	Promo	$25	**$825**	13%

Particulars: Gold "Road Show" Edition of the Village Express Van. Packed in a special gold box. Presented to potential investors before initial public offering.

DATE:_______ $:_______
❍ WISH ❍ HAVE

'95	'96
$1200	945

...age Express Van For Gatherings

Item #	Intro	Retired	OSRP	GBTru
Various	1994	Promo	$25	See Below

Particulars: Black van for store delivery service. Right side is D56 logo and left side features specific D56 dealer name logo. 14 Vans were produced—13 for dealer D56 sponsored Village Gatherings where the Van was sold. The Lemon Tree received the other Van to be sold to members of the store's Collector's Club:

Bachman's .... #729-3 .... $75
Bronner's Christmas Wonderland .... #737-4 .... $60
European Imports .... #739-0 .... $60
Fortunoff .... #735-8 .. $125
Lemon Tree .... #721-8 .... $50
Lock, Stock & Barrel .... #731-5 .. $135
North Pole City .... #736-6 .... $60
Robert's Christmas Wonderland ...... #734-0 .... $60
Stats .... #741-2 .... $60
The Christmas Dove .... #730-7 .... $60
The Incredible Christmas Place .... #732-3 .... $80
The Limited Edition .... #733-1 .. $125
The Windsor Shoppe .... #740-4 .... $60
William Glen .... #738-2 .... $60

Village Streetcar

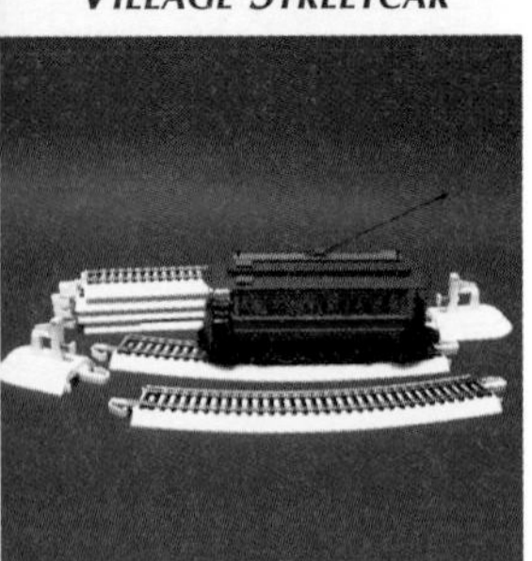

Item #	Intro	Retired	OSRP	GBTru	NO
5240-0	1994	Current	$65	**$65**	CHAN

Particulars: Set of 10. Midyear release. Track setup for inn city traveling. Car lights up. Passenger's silhouettes on windows. Appropriate for Snow Village as well.

DATE:_______ $:_______
❍ WISH ❍ HAVE

'94	'95	'9
$65	65	6

Village Animated All Around The Park

Item #	Intro	Retired	OSRP	GBTru	NO
5247-7	1994	1996	$95	**$95**	CHAN

Particulars: Set of 18. People stroll through park on path that circles tree. Stone wall edges park and archway marks entrance. UL Approved. Size is 19" x 15" x 16". Appropriate for Snow Village as well.

DATE:_______ $:_______
❍ WISH ❍ HAVE

'94	'95	'9
$95	95	9

Mickey & Minnie

Item #	Intro	Retired	OSRP	GBTru	↑
5353-8	1994	1996	$22.50	**$35**	56%

Particulars: Set of 2. Disney Parks Village accessory. Mic and Minnie characters welcome guests to the Disney Theme Parks.

DATE:_______ $:_______
❍ WISH ❍ HAVE

'94	'95	'9
$22.50	22.50	22

Disney Parks Family

Item #	Intro	Retired	OSRP	GBTru	↑
5354-6	1994	1996	$32.50	**$35**	8%

Particulars: Set of 3. Family of seven enjoys a day at a Disney Park. Mom photographs kids in Mouse ears, as two others eat ice cream cones, and one tot is seated o Dad's shoulders for best view.

DATE:_______ $:_______
❍ WISH ❍ HAVE

'94	'95	'9
$32.50	32.50	32

Olde World Antiques Gate

Item #	Intro	Retired	OSRP	GBTru	↑
5355-4	1994	1996	$15	**$18**	20%

Particulars: Disney Parks Village accessory. Entry gate with wooden door. Brick frames door and is base for wrought iron fencing.

DATE:_______ $:_______
❍ WISH ❍ HAVE

'94	'95	'96
$15	15	15

Polka Fest

Item #	Intro	Retired	OSRP	GBTru	
5607-3	1994	Current	$30	**$30**	No Change

Particulars: Set of 3. Alpine Village accessory. Musicians play polka as a couple dances. Boy sings and yodels to the music.

DATE:_______ $:_______
❍ WISH ❍ HAVE

'94	'95	'96
$30	30	30

...st Minute Delivery

Item #	Intro	Retired	OSRP	GBTru	
5636-7	1994	Current	$35	**$35**	No Change

Particulars: Set of 3. North Pole Village accessory. Elves hand-power a rail car pulling doll car and teddy car as another elf hangs onto rear bumper. Shipping delayed until 1996 due to production problems.

DATE:_______ $:_______
❍ WISH ❍ HAVE

'94	'95	'96
$35	35	35

Snow Cone Elves

Item #	Intro	Retired	OSRP	GBTru	
5637-5	1994	Current	$30	**$30**	No Change

Particulars: Set of 4. North Pole Village accessory. Elves taste test new batch of snow cones. Cart holds more flavors. Icicles form on snow cone sign.

DATE:_______ $:_______
❍ WISH ❍ HAVE

'94	'95	'96
$30	30	30

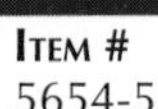

Over The River And Through The Woods

Item #	Intro	Retired	OSRP	GBTru	NO
5654-5	1994	Current	$35	**$35**	CHANG

Particulars: New England Village accessory. After cutting tree for home, father and kids use horse-drawn sleigh to bring it in. Their dog runs along side.

DATE:_______ $:_______
❍ WISH ❍ HAVE

'94	'95	'96
$35	35	35

The Old Man And The Sea

Item #	Intro	Retired	OSRP	GBTru	NO
5655-3	1994	Current	$25	**$25**	CHANC

Particulars: Set of 3. New England Village accessory. Two children listen closely as the man tells stories of the sea Boy holds telescope.

DATE:_______ $:_______
❍ WISH ❍ HAVE

'94	'95	'9
$25	25	2

Two Rivers Bridge

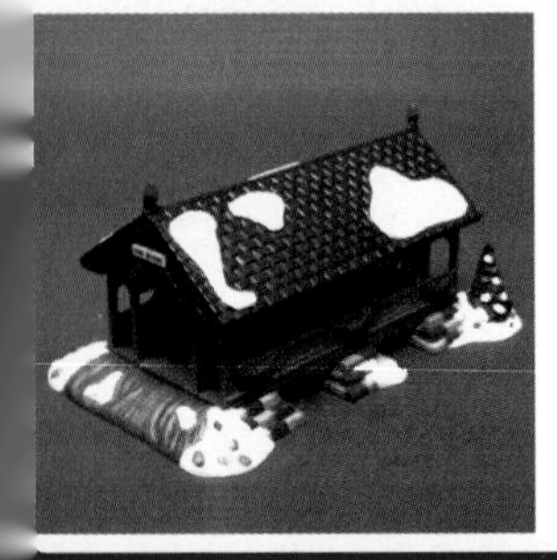

Item #	Intro	Retired	OSRP	GBTru	NO
5656-1	1994	Current	$35	**$35**	CHANC

Particulars: New England Village accessory. Wooden bric on 3 sets of pilings spans 2 rivers. Horses, carriages an carts use center. Walkers use side passages. Porcelain and Resin. Size: 8 1/2" x 4 1/2" x 4".

DATE:_______ $:_______
❍ WISH ❍ HAVE

'94	'95
$35	35

Winter Sleighride

Item #	Intro	Retired	OSRP	GBTru	NC
5825-4	1994	Current	$18	**$18**	CHAN

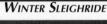

Particulars: Dickens' Village accessory. Ice-skating boys give a sleigh ride to a friend.

DATE:_______ $:_______
❍ WISH ❍ HAVE

'94	'95
$18	18

...elsea Market Mistle-...oe Monger & Cart

Item #	Intro	Retired	OSRP	GBTru	
5826-2	1994	Current	$25	**$25**	No Change

Particulars: Set of 2. Dickens' Village accessory. Vendor sells greens from basket as wife sells from cart.

DATE:_______ $:_______
❍ WISH ❍ HAVE

'94	'95	'96
$25	25	25

...lsea Market Curiosi-...es Monger & Cart

Item #	Intro	Retired	OSRP	GBTru	
5827-0	1994	Current	$27.50	**$27.50**	No Change

Particulars: Set of 2. Dickens' Village accessory. Vendor stands next to cart playing concertina. He sells everything from toys to clocks to quilts.

DATE:_______ $:_______
❍ WISH ❍ HAVE

'94	'95	'96
$27.50	27.50	27.50

...Portobello Road Peddlers

Item #	Intro	Retired	OSRP	GBTru	
5828-9	1994	Current	$27.50	**$27.50**	No Change

Particulars: Set of 3. Dickens' Village accessory. Peddlers sell toys and carol song sheets to passing villagers.

DATE:_______ $:_______
❍ WISH ❍ HAVE

'94	'95	'96
$27.50	27.50	27.50

Thatchers

Item #	Intro	Retired	OSRP	GBTru	
5829-7	1994	Current	$35	**$35**	No Change

Particulars: Set of 3. Dickens' Village accessory. Workers gather up and place thatch bundles on cart.

DATE:_______ $:_______
❍ WISH ❍ HAVE

'94	'95	'96
$35	35	35

A Peaceful Glow On Christmas Eve

Item #	Intro	Retired	OSRP	GBTru	N
5830-0	1994	Current	$30	**$30**	CHA

Particulars: Set of 3. Dickens' Village accessory. Clergyr watches children sell candles for church service.

DATE:_______ $:_______
❍ WISH ❍ HAVE

'94	'95
$30	30

Christmas Carol Holi-day Trimming Set

Item #	Intro	Retired	OSRP	GBTru	N
5831-9	1994	Current	$65	**$65**	CHA

Particulars: Set of 21. Dickens' Village accessory. Holid trimming set with gate, fence, lamppost, trees, garlan wreaths, and 3 figurine groupings.

DATE:_______ $:_______
❍ WISH ❍ HAVE

'94	'95
$65	65

Chamber Orchestra

Item #	Intro	Retired	OSRP	GBTru	N
5884-0	1994	Current	$37.50	**$37.50**	CHA

Particulars: Set of 4. Christmas In The City accessory. Conductor and four musicians play outdoor holiday music concert.

DATE:_______ $:_______
❍ WISH ❍ HAVE

'94	'95
$37.50	37.50

Holiday Field Trip

Item #	Intro	Retired	OSRP	GBTru	N
5885-8	1994	Current	$27.50	**$27.50**	CHA

Particulars: Set of 3. Christmas In The City accessory. Fi students walk with their teacher as they visit the City sights.

DATE:_______ $:_______
❍ WISH ❍ HAVE

'94	'95
$27.50	27.50

Hot Dog Vendor

Item #	Intro	Retired	OSRP	GBTru	No Change
5886-6	1994	Current	$27.50	**$27.50**	

Particulars: Set of 3. Christmas In The City accessory. Mother buys hot dog for son from a street vendor.

DATE:________ $:________
❍ WISH ❍ HAVE

'94	'95	'96
$27.50	27.50	27.50

Postern

Item #	Intro	Retired	OSRP	GBTru	↑
9871-0	1994	1994 Annual	$17.50	**$27**	8%

Particulars: Dickens' Village Ten Year Anniversary Piece. Cornerstone with dates. Special commemorative imprint on bottom. Arched, timbered entry connected to gatehouse. Flag flies at top of arch; village sign hangs below it. Posterns were entrances to important places or village gathering areas.

DATE:________ $:________
❍ WISH ❍ HAVE

'94	'95	'96
$17.50	25	25

Dedlock Arms Ornament

Item #	Intro	Retired	OSRP	GBTru	↑
9872-8	1994	1994 Annual	$12.50	**$20**	11%

Particulars: Miniature version of 1994 Signature Collection lit piece. Special Keepsake box.

DATE:________ $:________
❍ WISH ❍ HAVE

'94	'95	'96
$12.50	16	18

Squash Cart

Item #	Intro	Retired	OSRP	GBTru	No Change
0753-6	1995	Promo	$50	**$95**	

Particulars: New England Village accessory. Commemorates 110th Anniversary of Bachman's. Special bottomstamp. Introduced at the Bachman's Village Gathering, 1995. Green squash are taken to market in horse drawn burgundy wagon by Bachman's workers. See 1995, *Harvest Pumpkin Wagon,* Item #56591, for the Heritage Dealers piece with the orange pumpkins in place of green squash.

DATE:________ $:________
❍ WISH ❍ HAVE

'95	'96
$50	95

Village Express Van For Gatherings

Item #	Intro	Retired	OSRP	GBTru
Various	1995	Promo	*	*

Particulars: *See Particulars. The Black Village Express Promotional Van design introduced in 1994 was continued in 1995 adding the following special pieces:

1) *St. Nick's Van,* #7560, was produced for St. Nick's in Littleton, CO. This van does not say D56 on the passenger door. Both doors read "1995." **GBTru$: $70**

2) *Parkwest Van,* #7522, was produced for the NALED affiliated Parkwest Catalog Group to commemorate their 10th Anniversary. The group has 350 dealers. The panel of the van featured the symbol of a running deer, "Parkwest, 10th Anniversary" was printed below. **GBTru$: $525**

3) *Canadian Van,* #21637, was produced for Canadian dealers and distributed by Millard Lister Sales Ltd. The 1 Canadian Provinces were listed on the van's top rail. One side panel says "On-Time Delivery Since 1976: Th Village Express." The other panel has a Red Maple Leaf, Canadian Event 1995. Doors have 1995. SRP was $40.00. **GBTru$: $60**

Balloon Seller

Item #	Intro	Retired	OSRP	GBTru	↑
53539	1995	1996	$25	**$55**	120%

Particulars: Set of 2. Disney Parks Village accessory. Girl buys her brother a helium balloon from park vendor.

DATE:________ $:________
❍ WISH ❍ HAVE

'95	'9
$25	2

"Silent Night" Music Box

Item #	Intro	Retired	OSRP	GBTru	No
56180	1995	Current	$32.50	**$32.50**	Chan

Particulars: Music Box which commemorates Christmas song "Silent Night," debuted at Bronner's Christmas Wonderland, Frankenmuth, MI, a Gold Key Dealer. It based on Silent Night Memorial Chapel in Oberndorf, Austria. A replica of the Chapel is at Bronner's. Music box was available to all Heritage Dealers as of 6/1/96.

DATE:________ $:________
❍ WISH ❍ HAVE

'95	'
$32.50	32

"Alpen Horn Player" Alpine Village Sign

Item #	Intro	Retired	OSRP	GBTru	No
56182	1995	Current	$20	**$20**	Change

Particulars: Alpen horn player in tyrolean outfit plays long mountain horn.

DATE:_______ $:_______
❍ WISH ❍ HAVE

'95	'96
$20	20

Charting Santa's Course

Item #	Intro	Retired	OSRP	GBTru	No
56364	1995	Current	$25	**$25**	Change

Particulars: Set of 2. North Pole Village accessory. Elves plan Santa's sleighride. One checks skies with telescope as other checks constellation maps with globe of earth.

DATE:_______ $:_______
❍ WISH ❍ HAVE

'95	'96
$25	25

I'll Need More Toys

Item #	Intro	Retired	OSRP	GBTru	No
56365	1995	Current	$25	**$25**	Change

Particulars: Set of 2. North Pole Village accessory. Santa tells elf that more toys are needed from the workshop.

DATE:_______ $:_______
❍ WISH ❍ HAVE

'95	'96
$25	25

"A Busy Elf" North Pole Sign

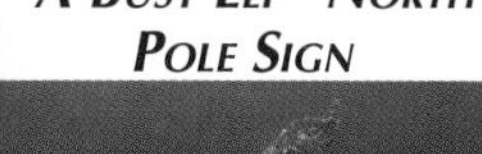

Item #	Intro	Retired	OSRP	GBTru	No
56366	1995	Current	$20	**$20**	Change

Particulars: Red bird watches carver elf create village sign. Porcelain and acrylic.

DATE:_______ $:_______
❍ WISH ❍ HAVE

'95	'96
$20	20

Farm Animals

Item #	Intro	Retired	OSRP	GBTru	NO
56588	1995	Current	$32.50	**$32.50**	CHANGE

Particulars: Set of 8 with 8 hay bales. New England Village accessory. Cows, horses, sheep, pig, goat, hen and rooster.

DATE:_______ $:_______
❍ WISH ❍ HAVE

'95	'96
$32.50	32.50

Lobster Trappers

Item #	Intro	Retired	OSRP	GBTru	NO
56589	1995	Current	$35	**$35**	CHANGE

Particulars: Set of 4. New England Village accessory. Boat a dock with lobster filled traps. Boy checks traps and lobsterman holds up a three pounder.

DATE:_______ $:_______
❍ WISH ❍ HAVE

'95	'96
$35	35

Lumberjacks

Item #	Intro	Retired	OSRP	GBTru	NO
56590	1995	Current	$30	**$30**	CHANGE

Particulars: Set of 2. New England Village accessory. One man chops tree with ax as second worker saws trunk int logs. Porcelain and Wood.

DATE:_______ $:_______
❍ WISH ❍ HAVE

'95	'96
$30	30

Harvest Pumpkin Wagon

Item #	Intro	Retired	OSRP	GBTru	NO
56591	1995	Current	$45	**$45**	CHANG

Particulars: New England Village accessory. Farm workers gather pumpkins which are loaded onto green wagon. Driver and helper with horse drawn wagon. Though there are slight color modifications, this piece is based o the Bachman's 110th Anniversary Squash Cart sold at th Bachman's Village Gathering in 1995, #753-6.

DATE:_______ $:_______
❍ WISH ❍ HAVE

'95	'9
$45	4

"Fresh Paint" New England Village Sign

Item #	Intro	Retired	OSRP	GBTru	
56592	1995	Current	$20	**$20**	No Change

Particulars: Sign maker completes lettering of village sign.

DATE:________ $:________
❍ WISH ❍ HAVE

'95	'96
$20	20

A Partridge In A Pear Tree—#I

Item #	Intro	Retired	OSRP	GBTru	
5835-1	1995	Current	$35	**$35**	No Change

Particulars: Dickens' Village accessory. The 12 Days Of Dickens' Village. Three children dance around tree as a partridge sits on top.

DATE:________ $:________
❍ WISH ❍ HAVE

'95	'96
$35	35

wo Turtle Doves—#II

Item #	Intro	Retired	OSRP	GBTru	
5836-0	1995	Current	$32.50	**$32.50**	No Change

Particulars: Set of 4. Dickens' Village accessory. The 12 Days Of Dickens' Village. Woman carries two turtle doves and boy carries cage. Another woman and daughter watch.

DATE:________ $:________
❍ WISH ❍ HAVE

'95	'96
$32.50	32.50

hree French Hens—#III

Item #	Intro	Retired	OSRP	GBTru	
58378	1995	Current	$32.50	**$32.50**	No Change

Particulars: Set of 3. Dickens' Village accessory. The 12 Days Of Dickens' Village. Farmyard with water pump, farm worker collecting eggs, farm worker scattering grain feed for hen and rooster.

DATE:________ $:________
❍ WISH ❍ HAVE

'95	'96
$32.50	32.50

Four Calling Birds—#IV

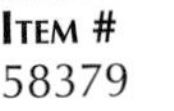

Item #	Intro	Retired	OSRP	GBTru	NO
58379	1995	Current	$32.50	**$32.50**	CHANGE

Particulars: Set of 2. Dickens' Village accessory. The 12 Days Of Dickens' Village. Street musicians play violin and bass as birds atop clock respond with song.

DATE:______ $:______
❍ WISH ❍ HAVE

'95	'96
$32.50	32.5(

Five Golden Rings–#V

Item #	Intro	Retired	OSRP	GBTru	NO
58381	1995	Current	$27.50	**$27.50**	CHANGE

Particulars: Set of 2. Dickens' Village accessory. The 12 Days Of Dickens' Village. Townsfolk watch as juggler balances five rings.

DATE:______ $:______
❍ WISH ❍ HAVE

'95	'96
$27.50	27.5

Six Geese A-Laying—#VI

Item #	Intro	Retired	OSRP	GBTru	NO
58382	1995	Current	$30	**$30**	CHANG

Particulars: Set of 2. Dickens' Village accessory. The 12 Days Of Dickens' Village. Six geese follow boy and girl.

DATE:______ $:______
❍ WISH ❍ HAVE

'95	'9
$30	3(

Brixton Road Watchman

Item #	Intro	Retired	OSRP	GBTru	NO
58390	1995	Current	$25	**$25**	CHANC

Particulars: Set of 2. Dickens' Village accessory. Early method of protection and enforcement of village rules and regulations. Watchman gave warnings, assistance and monitored activities. Guard house used for rest anc foul weather.

DATE:______ $:______
❍ WISH ❍ HAVE

'95	'9
$25	2

"Tally Ho!"

Item #	Intro	Retired	OSRP	GBTru	
58391	1995	Current	$50	**$50**	No Change

Particulars: Set of 5. Dickens' Village accessory. Country aristocracy ride Hunters for the sport of following scent hounds as they pick up the trail of a fox. Jumping fences and hedges, they ride the countryside, guided by the Whipper-in who sounds the tally-ho.

DATE:_______ $:_______
❍ WISH ❍ HAVE

'95	'96
$50	50

…helsea Market Hat Monger & Cart

Item #	Intro	Retired	OSRP	GBTru	
58392	1995	Current	$27.50	**$27.50**	No Change

Particulars: Set of 2. Dickens' Village accessory. Hat maker seated on trunk holds up hats for sale for every occasion. Apprentice sits on hand cart with cat on lap.

DATE:_______ $:_______
❍ WISH ❍ HAVE

'95	'96
$27.50	27.50

…Olde Lamplighter" …ckens' Village Sign

Item #	Intro	Retired	OSRP	GBTru	
58393	1995	Current	$20	**$20**	No Change

Particulars: Lamplighter reaches up to light lamp wick in lantern on village sign.

DATE:_______ $:_______
❍ WISH ❍ HAVE

'95	'96
$20	20

…obbler & Clock Peddler

Item #	Intro	Retired	OSRP	GBTru	
58394	1995	Current	$25	**$25**	No Change

Particulars: Set of 2. Dickens' Village accessory. Clock peddler sells and repairs clocks and timepieces while cobbler makes and repairs shoes.

DATE:_______ $:_______
❍ WISH ❍ HAVE

'95	'96
$25	25

"Yes, Virginia..."

Item #	Intro	Retired	OSRP	GBTru	N
58890	1995	Current	$12.50	**$12.50**	CHA

Particulars: Set of 2. Christmas In The City accessory. Yo girl speaks to gentleman with close resemblance to S Claus. Famous letter to the editor once written by Virginia is remembered every holiday.

DATE:_______ $:_______
❍ WISH ❍ HAVE

'95
$12.50

One-Man Band & The Dancing Dog

Item #	Intro	Retired	OSRP	GBTru	N
58891	1995	Current	$17.50	**$17.50**	CHA

Particulars: Set of 2. Christmas In The City accessory. M wears contraption to allow playing of 5 instruments a costumed dog dances to the music.

DATE:_______ $:_______
❍ WISH ❍ HAVE

'95
$17.50

Choir Boys All-In-A-Row

Item #	Intro	Retired	OSRP	GBTru	N
58892	1995	Current	$20	**$20**	CHA

Particulars: Christmas In The City accessory. Choir boys red, white and gold robes sing Christmas service.

DATE:_______ $:_______
❍ WISH ❍ HAVE

'95
$20

"A Key To The City" Christmas In The City Sign

Item #	Intro	Retired	OSRP	GBTru	N
58893	1995	Current	$20	**$20**	CHA

Particulars: Mayor stands at city gate to welcome dignit and give the key to the city. Porcelain and metal.

DATE:_______ $:_______
❍ WISH ❍ HAVE

'95
$20

Sir John Falstaff Inn Ornament

Item #	Intro	Retired	OSRP	GBTru	
9870-1	1995	1995 Annual	$15	**$18**	No Change

Particulars: Miniature version of Signature Collection lit piece. Special Keepsake box.

DATE:_______ $:_______
❍ WISH ❍ HAVE

'95	'96
$15	18

Elves On Ice

Item #	Intro	Retired	OSRP	GBTru	
52298	1996	Current	$7.50	**$7.50**	No Change

Particulars: Set of 4. North Pole Village accessory. Midyear release. Four skating elves can be used on Village Animated Skating Pond. One skates as he rings bells. One pushes another on skates. One speeds on ice with stocking hat blown by wind. One hatless elf glides along ice. Resin.

DATE:_______ $:_______
❍ WISH ❍ HAVE

'96
$7.50

Nutcracker Vendor & Cart

Item #	Intro	Retired	OSRP	GBTru
56193	1996	Current	$20	**$20**

Particulars: Alpine Village accessory. Track compatible. Movable metal wheels allow vendor to sell his nutcrackers throughout the village. A metal arch above cart advertises the finely crafted pieces.

DATE:_______ $:_______
❍ WISH ❍ HAVE

North Pole Express

Item #	Intro	Retired	OSRP	GBTru
56368	1996	Current	$37.50	**$37.50**

Particulars: Set of 3. North Pole accessory. Train brings vacationing elves and polar bear home to North Pole. Wood fire box engine, open freight car and passenger car topped with a gift carrier arrive at depot.

DATE:_______ $:_______
❍ WISH ❍ HAVE

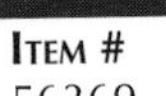

Early Rising Elves

Item #	Intro	Retired	OSRP	GBTru
56369	1996	Current	$32.50	**$32.50**

Particulars: Set of 5. North Pole accessory. Elves dressed in traditional costumes make early bakery deliveries.

DATE:________ $:________
❍ WISH ❍ HAVE

End Of The Line

Item #	Intro	Retired	OSRP	GBTru
56370	1996	Current	$28	**$28**

Particulars: Set of 2. North Pole accessory. Elf in ticket booth welcomes home vacationers from Miami. Crate oranges will fill many stockings with treats.

DATE:________ $:________
❍ WISH ❍ HAVE

Holiday Deliveries

Item #	Intro	Retired	OSRP	GBTru
56371	1996	Current	$16.50	**$16.50**

Particulars: North Pole accessory. Track compatible. Elf pedals three-wheeled velocipede with rear basket filled with gifts to deliver.

DATE:________ $:________
❍ WISH ❍ HAVE

New Potbellied Stove For Christmas

Item #	Intro	Retired	OSRP	GBTru
56593	1996	Current	$35	**$35**

Particulars: Set of 2. New England Village Accessory. Track compatible.

DATE:________ $:________
❍ WISH ❍ HAVE

Christmas Bazaar: Handmade Quilts

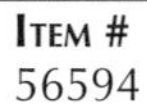

Item #	Intro	Retired	OSRP	GBTru
56594	1996	Current	$25	**$25**

Particulars: Set of 2. New England Village accessory. Woman holds up a quilt while child admires assortment piled on display table and shelves.

DATE:_______ $:_______
❍ WISH ❍ HAVE

Christmas Bazaar: Woolens & Preserves

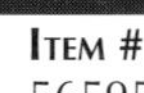

Item #	Intro	Retired	OSRP	GBTru
56595	1996	Current	$25	**$25**

Particulars: Set of 2. New England Village accessory. Young boy at street stall sells preserves and pies while a woman and child sell knitted woolen items.

DATE:_______ $:_______
❍ WISH ❍ HAVE

Seven Swans-A-Swimming—#VII

Item #	Intro	Retired	OSRP	GBTru
58383	1996	Current	$27.50	**$27.50**

Particulars: Set of 4. Dickens' Village accessory. The 12 Days Of Dickens' Village. Dickensian couple watch swimming swans.

DATE:_______ $:_______
❍ WISH ❍ HAVE

Eight Maids-A-Milking—#VIII

Item #	Intro	Retired	OSRP	GBTru
58384	1996	Current	$25	**$25**

Particulars: Set of 2. Dickens' Village accessory. The 12 Days Of Dickens' Village. Maid carries milk pails on shoulder yoke after milking the cow.

DATE:_______ $:_______
❍ WISH ❍ HAVE

Tending The New Calves

Item #	Intro	Retired	OSRP	GBTru	NO CHANGE
58395	1996	Current	$30	**$30**	

Particulars: Set of 3. Dickens' Village accessory. Midyear release. Boy leads calf. Girl churns butter from fresh milk. Small building to house young calves.

DATE:_______ $:_______ '96
❍ WISH ❍ HAVE $30

Caroling With The Cratchit Family (Revisited)

Item #	Intro	Retired	OSRP	GBTru	NO CHANGE
58396	1996	Current	$37.50	**$37.50**	

Particulars: Set of 3. Dickens' Village accessory. Midyear release. Bob Cratchit pushes sleigh of family carolers as two sons lead the way, one with lantern and the other with songbook.

DATE:_______ $:_______ '96
❍ WISH ❍ HAVE $37.5

Yeomen Of The Guard

Item #	Intro	Retired	OSRP	GBTru	NO CHANG
58397	1996	Current	$30	**$30**	

Particulars: Set of 5. Dickens' Village accessory. Midyear release. Head Warder and Guards that protect royal buildings and residences. Can be used with the The Tower of London set.

DATE:_______ $:_______ '9
❍ WISH ❍ HAVE $3

The Fezziwig Delivery Wagon (Revisited)

Item #	Intro	Retired	OSRP	GBTru
58400	1996	Current	$32.50	**$32.50**

Particulars: Dickens' Village accessory. Track compatible. Piece comes with a miniature storybook created and written by designers which sets scene for piece. Metal wheels turn on horse-drawn delivery wagon driven by Mr. Fezziwig.

DATE:_______ $:_______
❍ WISH ❍ HAVE

Red Christmas Sulky

Item #	Intro	Retired	OSRP	GBTru
58401	1996	Current	$30	**$30**

Particulars: Dickens' Village accessory. Track compatible. Horse-drawn two metal wheels movable carriage carries driver and one passenger.

DATE:_______ $:_______
❍ WISH ❍ HAVE

Gingerbread Vendor

Item #	Intro	Retired	OSRP	GBTru
58402	1996	Current	$22.50	**$22.50**

Particulars: Set of 2. Dickens' Village accessory. Track compatible. Vendor sells large baked gingerbread cakes from a sleigh. Boy and girl hold their purchase as they nibble pieces.

DATE:_______ $:_______
❍ WISH ❍ HAVE

A Christmas Carol" Reading By Charles Dickens

Item #	Intro	Retired	OSRP	GBTru
58403	1996	Current	$45	**$45**

Particulars: Set of 4. Dickens' Village accessory. Fewer piece set is non-limited and non-numbered. Color palette changes for all pieces except Dickens. D56 logo on bottomstamp. Dickens reads his *A Christmas Carol* story to spectators in park setting. This is an addition to the *Christmas Carol Revisited Series.*

DATE:_______ $:_______
❍ WISH ❍ HAVE

A Christmas Carol" Reading By Charles Dickens

Item #	Intro	Retired	OSRP	GBTru
58404	1996	Ltd Ed 42,500	$75	**$75**

Particulars: Set of 7. Dickens' Village accessory. This limited edition set is based on the 4 piece set by the same name. Additional characters and ornaments make up the difference. The edition number is on the base of platform piece with Crest and Lion Badge of the Charles Dickens Heritage Ltd. Foundation. 6 pieces will have Lion decal. This is an addition to the *Christmas Carol Revisited Series.*

DATE:_______ $:_______
❍ WISH ❍ HAVE

City Taxi

Item #	Intro	Retired	OSRP	GBTru
58894	1996	Current	$12.50	**$12.50**

Particulars: Christmas In The City accessory. Track compat ible. Green fender trim on brown cab with metal wheel Roof rack holds packages and holiday tree.

DATE:_______ $:_______
❍ WISH ❍ HAVE

The Family Tree

Item #	Intro	Retired	OSRP	GBTru
58895	1996	Current	$18	**$18**

Particulars: Christmas In The City accessory. Track compa ible. Father pulls sled with evergreen tree as son, daughter and family pet help bring it home to trim.

DATE:_______ $:_______
❍ WISH ❍ HAVE

Going Home For The Holidays

Item #	Intro	Retired	OSRP	GBTru
58896	1996	Current	$27.50	**$27.50**

Particulars: Set of 3. Christmas In The City accessory. Mother, father and two children carry gifts, family pet, and gifts. Train porter with other luggage whistles for taxi.

DATE:_______ $:_______
❍ WISH ❍ HAVE

Christmas Bells

Item #	Intro	Retired	OSRP	GBTru	↑
98711	1996	1996 Annual	$35	**$50**	43

Particulars: This is the Homes For The Holidays, Novem 1996 Event Piece. Gazebo with boy ringing town bell one child holds ears and another watches.

DATE:_______ $:_______
❍ WISH ❍ HAVE

The Grapes Inn Ornament

Item #	Intro	Retired	OSRP	GBTru	↑
98729	1996	1996 Annual	$15	**$17**	13%

Particulars: Midyear release. Miniature version of the Signature Collection lit piece. Special Keepsake box.

DATE:_______ $:_______
❍ WISH ❍ HAVE

'96
$15

Crown & Cricket Inn Ornament

Item #	Intro	Retired	OSRP	GBTru	↑
98730	1996	1996 Annual	$15	**$17**	13%

Particulars: Midyear release. Miniature version of the Signature Collection lit piece. Special Keepsake box.

DATE:_______ $:_______
❍ WISH ❍ HAVE

'96
$15

The Pied Bull Inn Ornament

Item #	Intro	Retired	OSRP	GBTru	↑
98731	1996	1996 Annual	$15	**$17**	13%

Particulars: Midyear release. Miniature version of the Signature Collection lit piece. Special Keepsake box.

DATE:_______ $:_______
❍ WISH ❍ HAVE

'96
$15

;achman's Wilcox Truck

Item #	Intro	Retired	OSRP	GBTru
8803	1997	1997 Annual	$29.95	**$29.95**

Particulars: 2nd Issue in Bachman's Exclusive Accessories. Replica of a Wilcox truck modeled after a 1919 Wilcox restored by the Bachman family.

DATE:_______ $:_______
❍ WISH ❍ HAVE

The Holly & The Ivy

Item #	Intro	Retired	OSRP	GBTru
56100	1997	1997 Annual	$17.50	**$17.50**

Particulars: Set of 2. This is the Homes For The Holidays, November 1997 Event piece.

DATE:_______ $:_______
❍ WISH ❍ HAVE

A New Batch Of Christmas Friends

Item #	Intro	Retired	OSRP	GBTru
56175	1997	Current	$27.50	**$27.50**

Particulars: Set of 3. Midyear release. Alpine Village accessory. St. Bernard pup plays with little girl. Lederhosen dressed boy pulls pups on a sled.

DATE:_______ $:_______
❍ WISH ❍ HAVE

Delivering Coal For The Hearth

Item #	Intro	Retired	OSRP	GBTru
58326	1997	Current	$32.50	**$32.50**

Particulars: Set of 2. Midyear release. Dickens' Village accessory. Horse-drawn coal cart comes with a small package of coal. Hanging from the rear is a coal scuttl Coal merchant with broom and another scuttle completes set.

DATE:_______ $:_______
❍ WISH ❍ HAVE

Steppin' Out On The Town

Item #	Intro	Retired	OSRP	GBTru
58885	1997	Current	$35	**$35**

Particulars: Set of 5. Midyear release. Christmas In The C accessory. Track compatible limo. Doorman stands by limo that transports a couple in evening clothes ready an evening on the town. Musicians hurry to the nightc to take their places on the bandstand.

DATE:_______ $:_______
❍ WISH ❍ HAVE

ɢAD'S HILL PLACE ORNAMENT

ITEM #	INTRO	RETIRED	OSRP	GBTRU
98732	1997	1997 ANNUAL	$15	**$15**

Particulars: Midyear release. Dickens' Village accessory. Miniature version of the 1997 Signature Collection lit piece. Special Keepsake box.

DATE:_______ $:_______
❍ WISH ❍ HAVE

ENS' "VILLAGE MILL" ORNAMENT

ITEM #	INTRO	RETIRED	OSRP	GBTRU
98733	1997	CURRENT	$15	**$15**

Particulars: 1st Edition Classic Ornament Series. Midyear release. Each series edition will be in a special package created for that ornament. Ornament miniature of the *Village Mill.*

DATE:_______ $:_______
❍ WISH ❍ HAVE

RTH POLE "SANTA'S VORKSHOP" ORN

ITEM #	INTRO	RETIRED	OSRP	GBTRU
98734	1997	CURRENT	$16.50	**$16.50**

Particulars: 2nd Edition Classic Ornament Series. Midyear introduction. Each series edition will be in a special package created for that ornament. Ornament miniature of *Santa's Workshop.*

DATE:_______ $:_______
❍ WISH ❍ HAVE

TES: ______________________________

5175-6

Frosted Norway Pines

Set of 3.
Sizes: 7", 9" & 11".

$12.95/set

5200-0

Village Frosted Topiary Cone Trees, Large

2 pieces per package.
Size: 11 1/2".

$12.50/pkg

5201-9

Village Frosted Topiary Cone Trees, Medium

Set of 4.
Sizes: 2 @ 7 1/2" &
2 @ 6".

$10/set

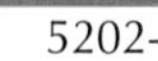

5202-7

Village Frosted Topiary Trees, Large

Set of 8.
Sizes: 4 cones &
4 oblong, 4" each.

$12.50/set

5203-5

Village Frosted Topiary Trees, Sm

Set of 8.
Sizes: 4 @ 2" roun
4 @ 3" high.

$7.50/set

5205-1

Village Evergreen Trees

Set of 3.
Sizes: 3 1/4", 4 1/4"
& 6 1/2".
Cold cast porcelai

$12.95/set

5218-3

Village Porcelain Pine, Large

Size: 8 1/2".

$12.50/ea

5219-1

Village Porcelain Pine Tree, Small

Size: 7".

$10/ea

5243-4

Village Bare Branch Tree, With 25 Lights

This item is Battery Operated or can be used with Adapter, Item #5225-6.
Size: 9".

$17.50/ea

52590

Village Landscape

Set of 14.

$16.50/set

5246-9

Village Pencil Pines

Set of 3.
Sizes: 12", 8" & 5".

$15/set

52596

Village Flexible Sisal Hedge

3 pieces per package. Each piece is 12" long.

$7.50/pkg

5251-5

Porcelain Pine Tree

Set of 2.
Sizes: 4 3/4" & 3 3/4".

$15/set

52600

Village Hybrid Landscape

Set of 22.

$35/set

5254-0

Village Autumn Maple Tree

Size: 11".

$15/ea

52603

Lighted Snowcapped Revolving Tree

Lighted. Battery Operated or can be used with Adapter, Item #5225-6.
Size: 8". Resin.

$35/ea

52604

Lighted Snowcapped Trees

Set of 2.
Lighted.
Sizes: 10" & 8".
Resin.

$45/set

52605

Village Frosted Fir Trees

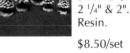

Set of 4.
Sizes: 15", 12", 9" & 6 1/4".

$15/set

52606

Village Cedar Pine Forest

Set of 3.
Sizes: 12", 10" & 8".

$15/set

52607

Village Ponderosa Pines

Set of 3.
Sizes: 12", 10" & 9".

$13/set

52608

Village Arctic Pin

Set of 3.
Sizes: 10", 8" & 6".

$12/set

52610

Village Fallen Leaves

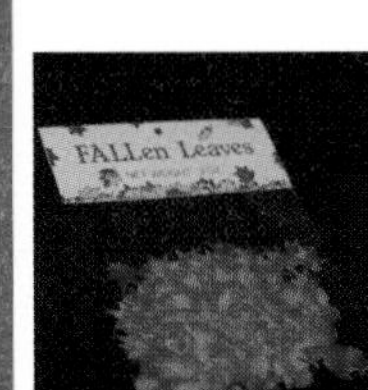

Size: 3 oz. bag.
Fabric.

$5/bag

52612

Village Snowy Evergreen Trees, Small

Set of 6.
Sizes: 3 1/2", 3", 2 1/4" & 2".
Resin.

$8.50/set

52613

Village Snowy Evergreen Trees, Medium

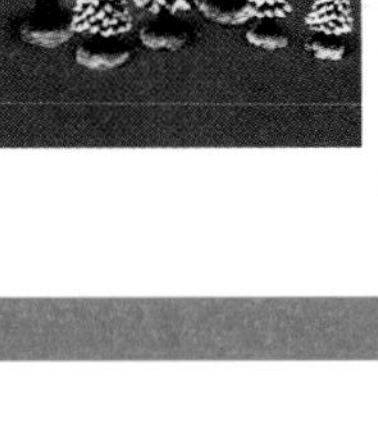

Set of 6.
Sizes: 7 1/4", 5 1/2", 5 1/4", 5" & 4 1/4".
Resin.

$25/set

52614

VILLAGE SNOWY EVERGREEN TREES, LARGE

Set of 5.
Sizes: 9 1/4", 9", 7 1/4" & 7".
Resin.

$32.50/set

52615

VILLAGE SNOWY SCOTCH PINES

Set of 3.
Sizes: 7", 5 1/4" & 5".
Resin.

$15/set

52616

VILLAGE AUTUMN TREES

Set of 3.
Sizes: 7 3/4", 6" & 4 3/4".
Resin.

$13.50/set

52617

VILLAGE WAGON WHEEL PINE GROVE

Size:
6 3/4" x 6 1/4" x 6 1/2".
Resin.

$22.50

52618

VILLAGE PINE POINT POND

Size:
9 1/4" x 8" x 5 3/4".
Resin.

$37.50

52619

VILLAGE DOUBLE PINE TREES

Size:
5 1/4" x 5 1/2" x 6".
Resin.

$13.50

52622

JACK PINES

Set of 3.

$18/set

52623

VILLAGE BARE BRANCH TREES

Set of 6.

$22.50/set

52630
Holly Tree

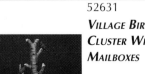

$10.00/ea

52631
Village Birch Tree Cluster With 2 Mailboxes

$20

52632
Towering Pines

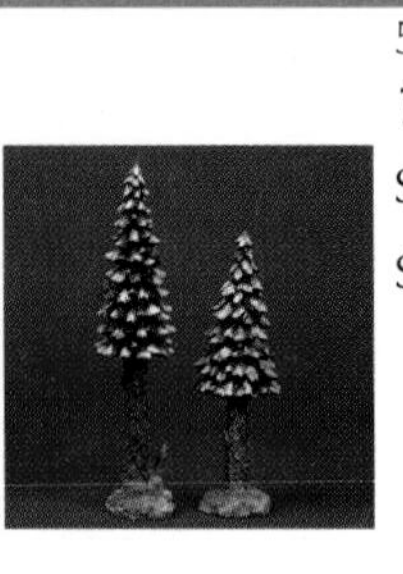

Set of 2.

$13.50/set

52636
Winter Birch

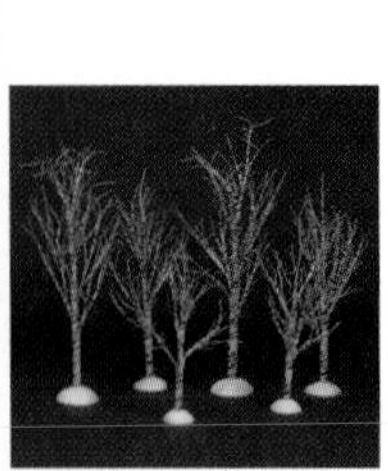

Set of 6.

$22.50/set

52637
Frosted Spruce

Set of 2.

$25/set

52638
Frosted Hemlock Trees

Set of 2.

$32.50/set

52639
Town Tree With 50 Lights

$37.50

5419-4
Sisal Wreaths

6 pieces per packa
Size: 1" diameter.

$4/pkg

5527-1

VILLAGE POLE PINE FOREST

Set of 5.
4 trees in a snow base.
Size: 10" x 5" x 12".

$48/set

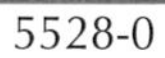

5528-0

POLE PINE TREE, SMALL

Size: 8".

$10/ea

5529-8

POLE PINE TREE, LARGE

Size: 10 ½".

$12.50/ea

NOTES:

ther GREENBOOK Guides In Development:

GREENBOOK Guide to HARBOUR LIGHTS

GREENBOOK Guide to DREAMSICLES

GREENBOOK Guide to THOMAS KINKADE

GREENBOOK Guide to BOYDS BEARS

GREENBOOK Guide to SWAROVSKI

5110-1

Town Clock

2 assorted—green or black.
Size: 3 1/2" tall.

$3/ea

5208-6

Village Mylar Skating Pond

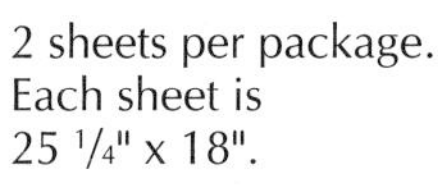

2 sheets per package.
Each sheet is 25 1/4" x 18".

$6/pkg

5210-8

Village Brick Road

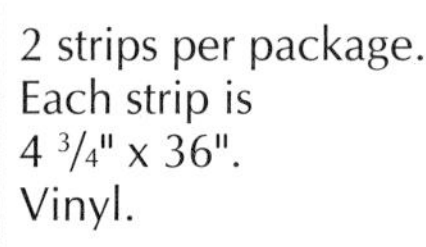

2 strips per package.
Each strip is 4 3/4" x 36".
Vinyl.

$10/pkg

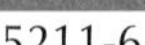

5211-6

Village Acrylic Icicles

4 pieces per package.
Each piece is 18" long.

$4.50/pkg

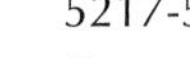

5217-5

Tacky Wax

Size: 1″ diameter x 1″ deep tub.

$2/tub

5230-2

Wrought Iron P
Bench

Size: 2 1/4".
Metal.

$5/ea

5233-7

Village Sled & S

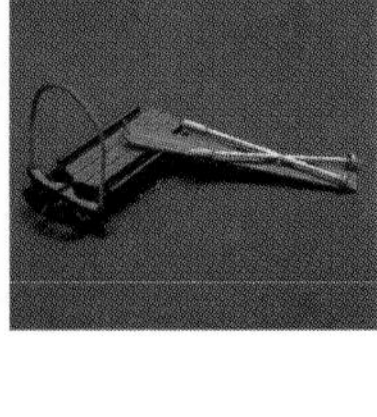

Set of 2.
Sizes: 2" & 2 1/4".

$6/set

52594

Village Let It Sn
Snowman Sign

Size: 6".
Resin.

$12.50

52595

Village Pink Flamingos

4 pieces per package. Size: 1 3/4".

$7.50/pkg

52620

Village Magic Smoke

6 oz. bottle.

$2.50

52599

Village Election Yard Signs

Set of 6, assorted. Size: 2 1/4".

$10/set

52633

Village Mill Creek Straight Section With Trees

Straight section of creek bed with evergreens.

$12.50

52601

Village Brick Town Square

Size: 23 1/2" square. Vinyl.

$15

52634

Village Mill Creek Curved Section With Trees

Curved section of creek bed with evergreens.

$12.50

52602

Village Cobblestone Town Square

Size: 23 1/2" square. Vinyl.

$15

52635

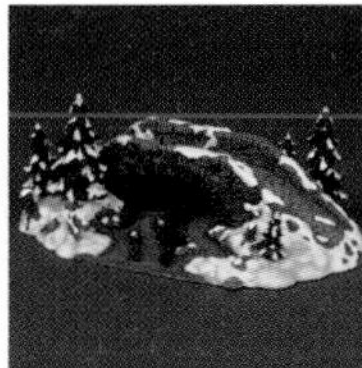

Village Mill Creek Bridge

Stone bridge over section of creek.

$35

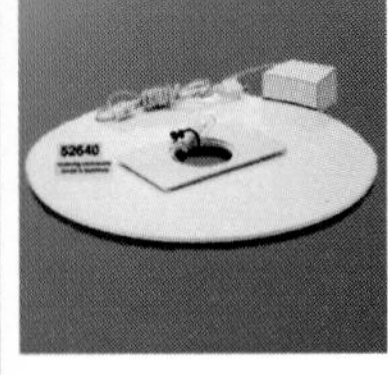

52640

Revolving Display Stand

$50

5511-5

'Christmas Eave' Trim

Non-electric bulb garland.
24" long.

$3.50/ea

52644

Village Waterfall

Water cascades down hilly terrain to form small lake before entering creek.

$65

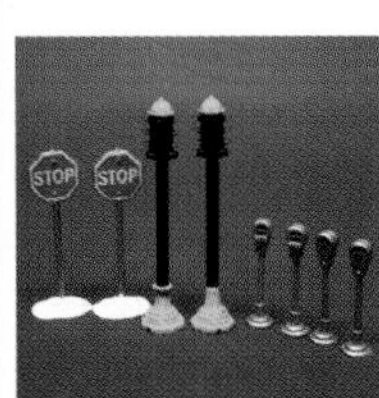

5512-3

Heritage Village Utility Accessor

Set of 8.
2 stop signs,
4 parking meters,
2 traffic lights.
Sizes: $1\frac{3}{4}$", 2" &

$12.50/set

5417-8

"It's A Grand Old Flag"

2 pieces per package.
Size: $2\frac{1}{4}$".
Metal.

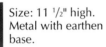

$4/pkg

5984-6

Village Cobblest Road

2 strips per packa
Each strip is
$4\frac{3}{4}$" x 36".

$10/pkg

5456-9

Windmill

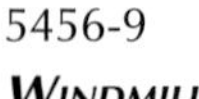

Size: $11\frac{1}{2}$" high.
Metal with earthen base.

$20

98841

"The Building C Village Traditio Video, With Instruction Boc

35 Minutes.

$19.95

4995-6

Village "Blanket Of New Fallen Snow"

Size: 2' x 5' 1".

$7.50

49979

Village Fresh Fallen Snow

7 oz. bag.

$4/bag

49980

Fresh Fallen Snow

2 lb. box.

$12/box

4998-1

Real Plastic Snow

7 oz. bag.

$3/bag

4999-9

Real Plastic Snow

2 lb. box.

$10/box

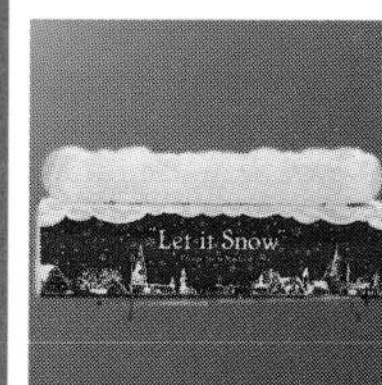

52592

Village Let It Snow Machine, With 1 lb. Bag Village Fresh Fallen Snow

Size:
38 1/2" x 9" x 5 1/2".

$85

Notes: ____________________

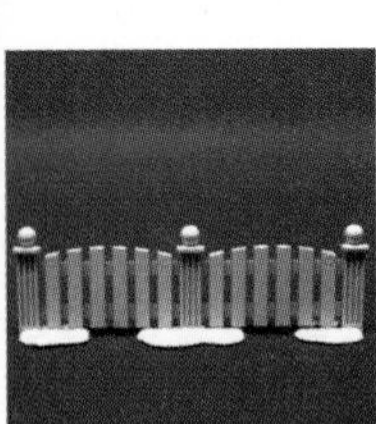

5100-4

WHITE PICKET FENCE

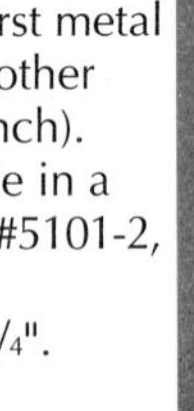

One of the first metal accessories (other was Park Bench). Also available in a Set of 4, Item #5101-2, @ $12.00.
Size: 6" x 1 3/4".
Cast Iron.

$3/ea

5212-4

TREE-LINED COURTYARD FENCE

1 1/2" high x 4" lon
Metal with resin.

$4/ea

5101-2

WHITE PICKET FENCE

Set of 4.
Each piece is 6" x 1 3/4".
Cast Iron.

$12/set

5220-5

COURTYARD FENCE WITH STEPS

1 1/4" high x 4 1/4" long.
Metal with resin.

$4/ea

5204-3

VILLAGE SNOW FENCE, FLEXIBLE WOOD & WIRE

2" high x 36" long.

$7/ea

5234-5

CHAIN LINK FENCE WITH GATE

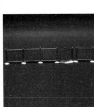

Set of 3.
2" high.

$12/set

5207-8

FROSTY TREE-LINED PICKET FENCE

3 posts & 3 attached trees.
5 3/4" x 2 1/2".
Metal with resin.

$6.50/ea

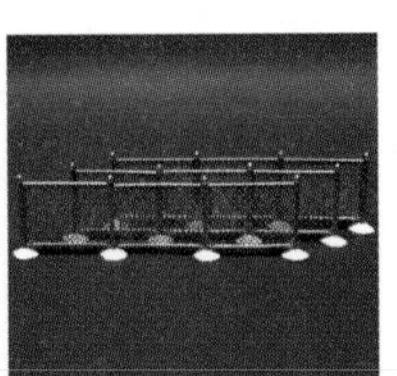

5235-3

CHAIN LINK FENCE EXTENSIONS

Set of 4.
Each piece is 4 1/
long.

$15/set

5252-3

Victorian Wrought Iron Fence and Gate

Set of 5.
Size: $5\,^{1}/_{2}$" x 3".
Metal.

$15/set

52624

Village White Picket Fence With Gate

Set of 5.

$10/set

5253-1

Victorian Wrought Iron Fence Extension

Size: 3". Metal.

$2.50/ea

52625

Village White Picket Fence Extensions

Set of 6.

$10/set

52597

Village Split Rail Fence, With Mailbox

Set of 4.
Hand-hewn wood.

$12.50/set

52629

Village Stone Wall

Set of 2.

$2.50/set

52598

Village Twig Snow Fence, Wood

$2\,^{3}/_{4}$" x 4' roll.

$6

5514-0

Village Wrought Iron Gate And Fence

Set of 9.
Gate & 4 fence pieces with 4 posts.
Size: $9\,^{1}/_{4}$" x 3".
Metal.

$15/set

5515-8

Village Wrought Iron Fence Extensions

Set of 9.
4 fence pieces &
5 posts.
Size: 9 1/4" x 3".
Metal.

$12.50/set

5541-7

City Subway Entrance

Size:
4 1/2" x 2 3/4" x 4 1/2".
Metal.

$15/ea

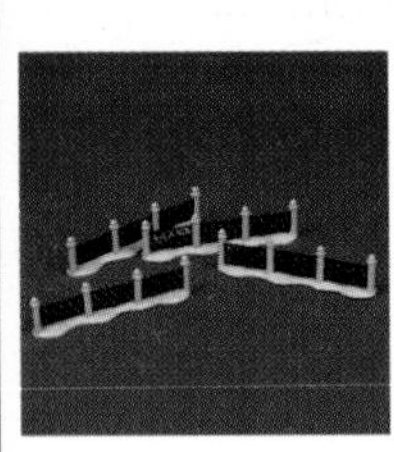

5998-6

Wrought Iron Fence

White & black or
white & green.
Each piece is 4" long.

$2.50/ea

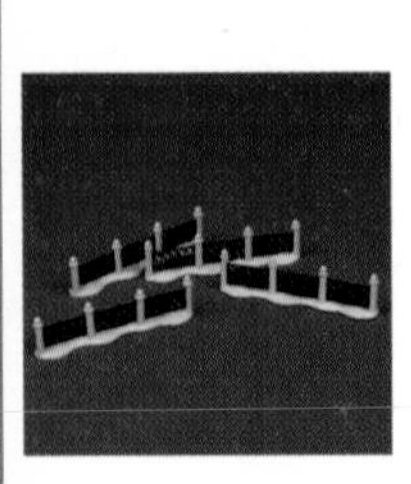

5999-4

Wrought Iron Fence

4 pieces per package.
White & black.
Size: 4" long.

$10/pkg

Notes: ______________________

5226-4

VILLAGE MOUNTAIN WITH FROSTED SISAL TREES, SMALL

Set of 5.
With 4 trees.
Size:
12" x 10 ½" x 8".
Foam and sisal.

$32.50/set

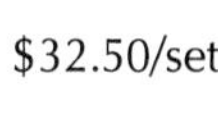

5227-2

VILLAGE MOUNTAIN WITH FROSTED SISAL TREES, MEDIUM

Set of 8.
With 7 trees and 1 niche to display Village piece.
Size: 22" x 12" x 10 ½".

$65/set

5228-0

VILLAGE MOUNTAINS WITH FROSTED SISAL TREES, LARGE

Set of 14. With 13 trees. Can accommodate 3 lighted pieces.
Size: 35" x 13" x 15 ½".
Foam and sisal.

$150/set

5257-4

VILLAGE MOUNTAIN BACKDROP

Set of 2.
Without trees.
Sizes: 27" x 11" & 22" x 9 ½".
Foam.

$65/set

52582

VILLAGE MOUNTAIN TUNNEL

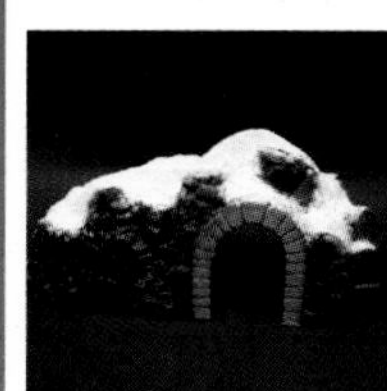

Size:
19 ½" x 9 ½" x 5 ½".

$37.50

52641

ANIMATED SKI MOUNTAIN

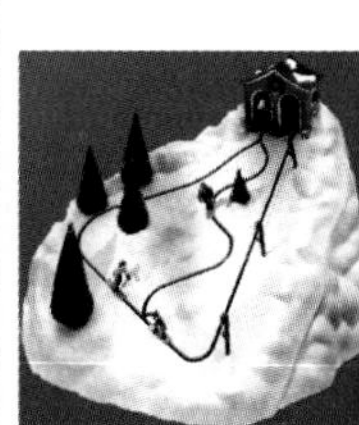

(Will not be available until 1998.)

$75

52643

MOUNTAIN CENTERPIECE

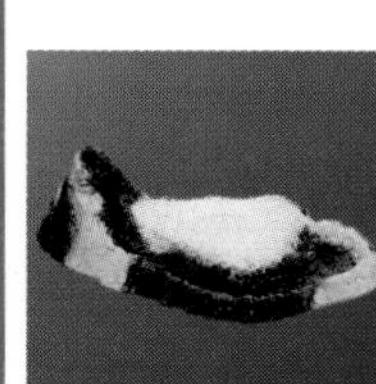

$45

NOTES: ______________________

____

____

____

____

____

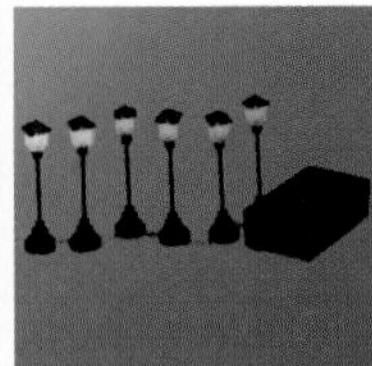

3636-6

Street Lamps

6 pieces per package. Battery Operated (2 "AA" Batteries) or can be used with Adapter, Item #5502-6. Cord 60" long, lamps 2 1/4" tall.

$10/pkg

52626

Mini Lights

20 light strand.

$10

5215-9

Village Mini Lights

14 bulbs.
Battery Operated or can be used with Adapter, Item #5502-6.
27" long cord.

$12.50

52627

Village Boulevar
Lampposts

4 pieces per pack

$15/pkg

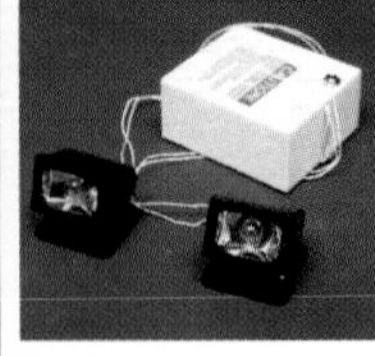

52611

Village Spotlight

Battery Operated or can be used with Adapter, Item #5225-6.

$7/ea

52628

Village Country
Road Lampposts

2 pieces per pack

$12/pkg

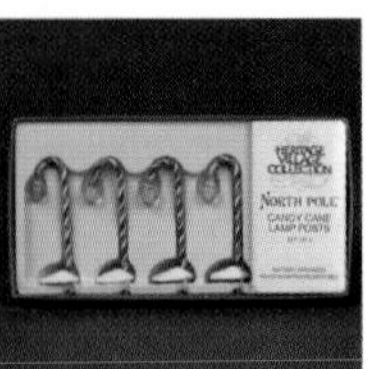

52621

Candy Cane
Lampposts

4 pieces per package.

$13/pkg

5500-0

Traffic Light

2 lights per packa
Battery Operated
"C" Batteries) or c
be used with Adapt
Item #5502-6.
4 1/4" tall.

$11/pkg

5501-8

RAILROAD CROSSING SIGN

2 signs per package. Battery Operated or can be used with Adapter, Item #5502-6. 4 1/4" tall.

$12.50/pkg

5504-2

TURN OF THE CENTURY LAMPPOST

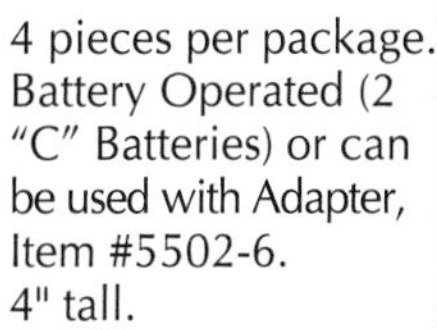

4 pieces per package. Battery Operated (2 "C" Batteries) or can be used with Adapter, Item #5502-6. 4" tall.

$16/pkg

5996-0

DOUBLE STREET LAMPS

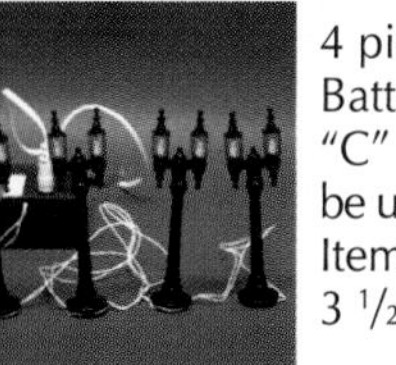

4 pieces per package. Battery Operated (2 "C" Batteries) or can be used with Adapter, Item #5502-6. 3 1/2" tall.

$13/pkg

NOTES:

OTES:

All Brite Lites are Battery Operated or they can be used with Adapter, Item #5225-6.

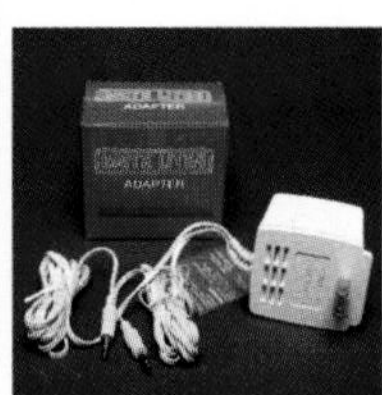

5225-6

VILLAGE BRITE LIT
ADAPTER

For use with 2 "B
Lites" only.

$10/ea

5222-1

VILLAGE BRITE LITES 'I LOVE MY VILLAGE', ANIMATED

Size: 6 1/2".

$15/ea

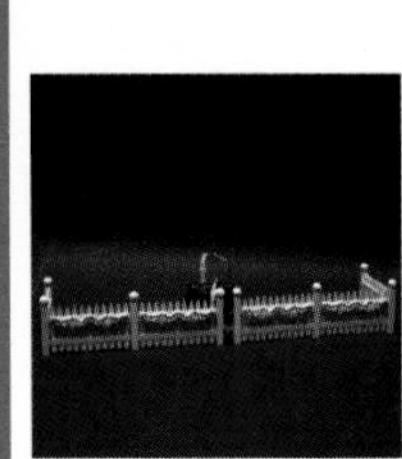

5236-1

VILLAGE BRITE LIT
FENCE, ANIMATED

Set of 4.
Size: 11".

$25/set

5223-0

VILLAGE BRITE LITES 'MERRY CHRISTMAS', ANIMATED

Size: 7 1/2".

$15/ea

5237-0

VILLAGE BRITE LIT
SNOWMAN, ANIM

Size: 3 3/4".

$20/ea

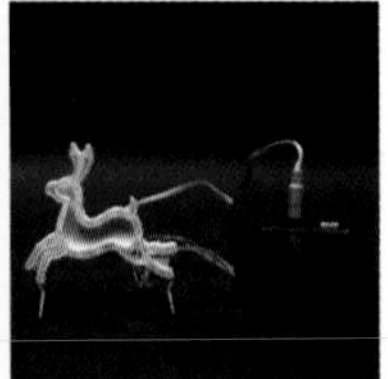

5224-8

VILLAGE BRITE LITES REINDEER, ANIMATED

Size: 3 1/4".

$13.50/ea

5238-8

VILLAGE BRITE LIT
TREE, ANIMATED

Size: 3 1/2".

$13.50/ea

5239-6

Village Brite Lites Santa, Animated

Size: 3 1/2".

$20/ea

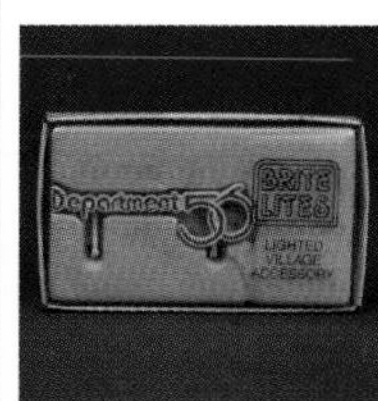

9846-9

Village Brite Lites 'Department 56', Animated

Size: 5".

$10/ea

5244-2

Village Brite Lites Waving Flag, Animated

Size: 5".

$12.50/ea

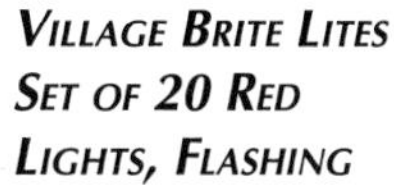

5245-0

Village Brite Lites Set of 20 Red Lights, Flashing

$9/ea

5482-8

Coca–Cola® brand Neon Sign

Size: 4 1/2" x 2".

$22.50/ea

Notes: ______________________

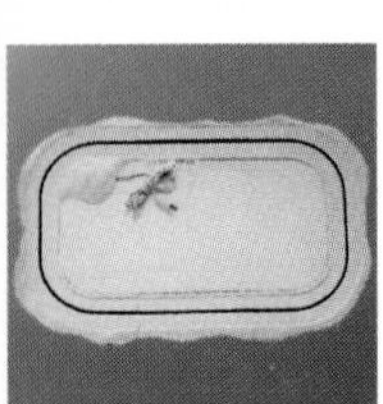

52642

Animated Mechanical Track For All Villages

Accepts all Track Compatible pieces by fitting included adapter to base.
38" x 24".

$65

99247

LED Light Bulb

$6.50/ea

5502-6

AC/DC Adapter, For Battery Operated Accessories

Not for use with Brites Lites.

$14/ea

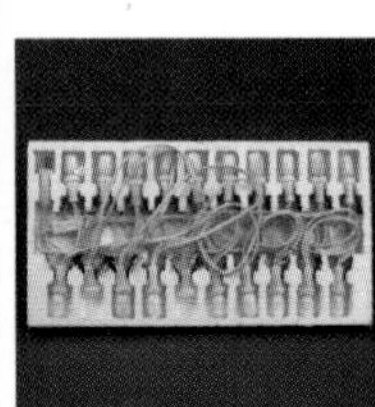

99278

20 Socket Light With Bulbs

$25/set

9902-8

Single Cord Set, With Switched Cord And Bulb

$3.50/set

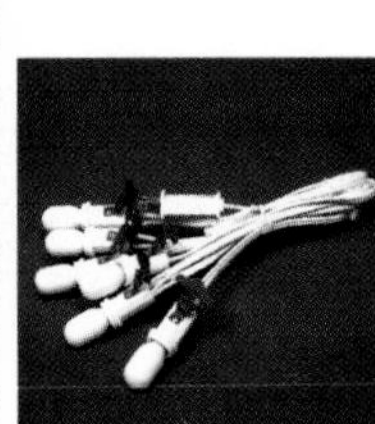

9927-9

Village 6 Socket Lite Set With Bu White Switched Cord

Size: 12'.

$12.50/set

9924-4

Village Replacement Light Bulbs

3 pieces per package.
6 Watt, 12 Volt.

$2/pkg

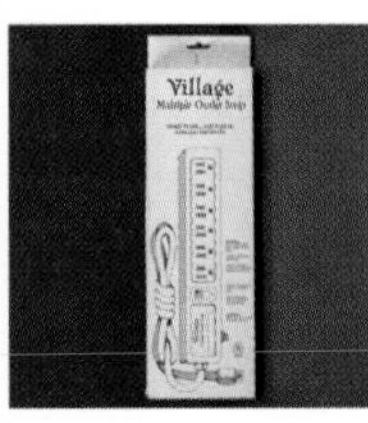

9933-3

Village Multi-Outlet Plug Str 6 Outlets

UL Approved.
Size:
12" x 2" x 1 1/2".

$10/ea

948-2

Heritage Village Collection Promotional Logo Banner

Giveaway at 1992 events.

5112-8

SV Garland Trim

3 pieces per package. Each piece is 24" long.

4996-4

"Let It Snow" Crystals, Plastic Snow

photo not available

Size: 8 oz. box.

5115-2

Frosted Topiary Village Garden

photo not available

Set of 8. 4 cones & 4 ovals.

5109-8

Village Park Bench

Size: 2 $^{1}/_{2}$".

5181-0

Bare Branch Winter Oak, Small

Size: 4 $^{1}/_{4}$".

5111-0

Christmas Wreaths

8 pieces per package. Sizes: 1" & $^{3}/_{4}$".

5182-9

Bare Branch Winter Oak, Large

Size: 7 $^{3}/_{4}$".

photo not available

5183-7

Sisal Tree Set

Set of 7.
4 cones & 3 ovals.

photo not available

5184-5

Winter Oak Tree With 2 Red Birds

photo not available

5185-3

Topiary Garden Sisal

36 pieces assorted.
Sizes:
2 1/2", 4", 6", 8" & 12".

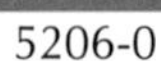

5206-0

Candles By The Doorstep

4 pieces per package.
2 "AA" Batteries.
Size: 2 1/4".

5213-2

"Lights Out" Remote Contro

Turns lights on/o
up to 60 houses
once.

5216-7

Village Winter Birch Tree

Size: 11 1/2".

5221-3

Pine Cone Trees

Set of 2.
Sizes: 8 3/4" & 7

5231-0

Village Frosted Spruce Tree

Size: 15".

5232-9

Village Frosted Spruce Tree

Size: 22".

5241-8

Village Frosted Bare Branch Tree, Small

Size: 9 1/2".

5242-6

Village Frosted Bare Branch Tree, Large

Size: 13".

5248-5

Spruce Tree Forest

Set of 4.
Size: 16" x 14".

5249-3

Village Frosted Zig–Zag Tree, White

Set of 3.
Sizes: 9", 7" & 4 1/2".

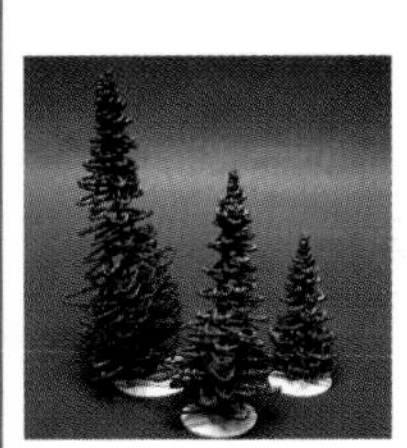

5250-7

Village Frosted Zig–Zag Tree, Green

Set of 3.
Sizes: 9", 7" & 4 1/2".

5255-8

Snowy White Pine Tree, Small

Size: 18".

5256-6

Snowy White Pine Tree, Large

Size: 24".

52593

Village Up, Up & Away, Animated Sleigh

UL Approved.
Size: 17" tall.

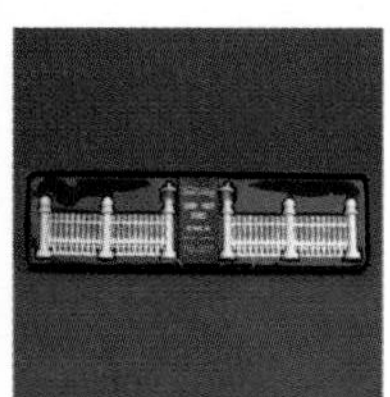

5506-9

Lamp Post Fence

Set of 10.
2 lamps,
4 posts,
4 fence pieces.

5416-0

Yard Lights (2 Santas, 2 Snowmen)

Set of 4.
Size: 1 $^{3}/_{4}$".

5508-5

Lamp Post Fence Extension

Set of 12.
6 posts &
6 fence pieces.

5503-4

Old World Streetlamp

4 pieces per package.
2 "C" Batteries.
Size: 4".

5524-7

"Village Sounds Tape With Speak

23 minute tape.

5505-0

Turn of the Century Lamppost

6 pieces per package.
2 "C" Batteries.
Size: 4".

5525-5

"Village Sounds Tape

23 minutes,
continuous play.

5526-3

HERITAGE BANNERS

Set of 4, 2 each of 2.
Size: 1 1/4".

59803

"VILLAGE EXPRESS" HO SCALE TRAIN SET

Set of 22 with transformer.

5993-5

STREETLAMP WRAPPED IN GARLAND

2 pieces per package.
Size: 4".

6582-0

FROSTED EVERGREEN TREES

Set of 3.
Sizes:
8 1/2", 6 1/2" & 4 1/2".

photo not available

6595-1

SPRUCE TREE WITH WOODEN BASE, SMALL

Size: 6".

photo not available

6597-8

SPRUCE TREE WITH WOODEN BASE, MEDIUM

Size: 9".

photo not available

6598-6

SPRUCE TREE WITH WOODEN BASE, LARGE

Size: 12".

9926-0

BATTERY OPERATED LIGHT

6 watts, 12 volts.

see below

This short-lived series was produced for Bachman's In
of Minneapolis, MN, the original parent company of
Department 56. Three buildings were manufactured a
distributed, but a planned fourth building, a bookstore
never made it past the drawing board.

Hometown Boarding House

Item #	Intro	Retired	OSRP	GBTru	N(
670-0	1987	1988	$34	$300	CHA

Particulars: Inspired by the Sprague House in Red Wing, MN. Three story brick building with rented rooms ab the main floor parlor and dining room.

DATE:_______ $:_______

		$	'92	'93	'94	'95
❍ WISH	❍ HAVE		275	330	330	325

Hometown Church

Item #	Intro	Retired	OSRP	GBTru	N(
671-8	1987	1988	$40	$305	CHA

Particulars: Designed after a St. Paul, MN church. Buildi has cross-shaped floor plan with a spire rising from o side of the transept. A simple entry door at the base o the spire is in contrast to the large arched windows th fill the end walls.

DATE:_______ $:_______

		$	'92	'93	'94	'95
❍ WISH	❍ HAVE		300	300	300	325

Hometown Drugstore

Item #	Intro	Retired	OSRP	GBTru	↑
672-6	1988	1989	$40	$595	5

Particulars: Same mold as the Christmas In The City *Var Store,* #5972-2. Inspired by a store in Stillwater, MN. Drugstore is corner store in a two attached buildings structure. Taller three story building houses barber sh on main level and eye glass shop above. Garlands decorate the awnings over display windows.

DATE:_______ $:_______

		$	'92	'93	'94	'95
❍ WISH	❍ HAVE		675	675	675	625

#7826
GBTru $75

This building was manufactured by Department 56 for the H.J. Heinz Company for them to use in promotions. Heinz gave it as a gift to its vendors and suppliers in late 1996 and sold it to their stockholders by a direct mail campaign in early 1997. It is packed in a white, flap-top box with red lettering.

DATE:_______ $:_______
❍ WISH ❍ HAVE

Notes: ____

D

U

V

W

Y